KAREN OLIVETO

PRENTICE-HALL
FOUNDATIONS OF MODERN SOCIOLOGY SERIES

D0921879

PRENTICE-HALL
FOUNDATIONS OF MODERN SOCIOLOGY SERIES

Alex Inkeles, Editor

THE SCIENTIST'S ROLE IN SOCIETY
Joseph Ben-David

DEVIANCE AND CONTROL
Albert K. Cohen

MODERN ORGANIZATIONS
Amitai Etzioni

SOCIAL PROBLEMS
Amitai Etzioni

LAW AND SOCIETY: An Introduction
Lawrence M. Friedman

THE FAMILY
William J. Goode

SOCIETY AND POPULATION, Second Edition
David M. Heer

WHAT IS SOCIOLOGY? An Introduction to the Discipline and Profession
Alex Inkeles

THE SOCIOLOGY OF SMALL GROUPS
Theodore M. Mills

SOCIAL CHANGE, Second Edition
Wilbert E. Moore

THE SOCIOLOGY OF RELIGION
Thomas F. O'Dea

THE EVOLUTION OF SOCIETIES
Talcott Parsons

RURAL SOCIETY
Irwin T. Sanders

THE AMERICAN SCHOOL: A Sociological Analysis
Patricia C. Sexton

THE SOCIOLOGY OF ECONOMIC LIFE, Second Edition
Neil J. Smelser

FOUNDATIONS OF MODERN SOCIOLOGY
Metta Spencer

SOCIAL STRATIFICATION: The Forms and Functions of Inequality
Melvin M. Tumin

THE EVOLUTION OF SOCIETIES

THE
EVOLUTION
OF
SOCIETIES

TALCOTT PARSONS
Harvard University

edited and with an introduction
by
JACKSON TOBY
Rutgers University

Prentice-Hall, Englewood Cliffs, New Jersey 07632

Library of Congress Cataloging in Publication Data

Parsons, Talcott, (date)
    The evolution of societies.

    Combined and edited version of the author's
Societies (1966) and The system of modern
societies (1971).
    Bibliography: p. 253
    Includes index.
    1. Social evolution. 2. Social history.
3. Social systems. I. Toby, Jackson.
II. Parsons, Talcott Societies.
III. Parsons, Talcott The system of
modern societies. IV. Title.
HM106.P24   301   76-56196
ISBN 0-13-293647-X
ISBN 0-13-293639-9 pbk.

© 1977 by Prentice-Hall, Inc., Englewood Cliffs, N.J. 07632

Most of this book was previously published in two volumes
entitled *Societies: Evolutionary and Comparative Perspectives* and
The System of Modern Societies.

Printed in the United States of America

10 9 8 7 6 5 4

Prentice-Hall International, Inc., London

Prentice-Hall of Australia Pty. Ltd., Sydney

Prentice-Hall of Canada, Ltd., Toronto

Prentice-Hall of India Private Limited, New Delhi

Prentice-Hall of Japan, Inc., Tokyo

Prentice-Hall' of Southeast Asia Pte. Ltd., Singapore

Whitehall Books Limited, Wellington, New Zealand

CONTENTS

CHAPTER 3

ARCHAIC SOCIETIES:
Legitimation by a Literate Priesthood,   50

CHAPTER 4

THE HISTORIC EMPIRES:
Further Differentiation of the Society
from Its Legitimate Cultural System,   71

CHAPTER 5

CULTURAL LEGACIES FOR LATER SOCIETIES:
The Hebrew and Greek Concepts of a Moral Order,   99

CHAPTER 6

THE RELIGIOUS LEGITIMATION OF SECULAR SOCIETY,   115

PREFACE

This book consists of the republication in one volume of two previously published books by Talcott Parsons on the subject of societal evolution. I hope it is also something more: a clearer guide to Parsons' thinking about societal evolution than was available in either book. In order to achieve this goal of clarity, I have tampered with the original texts in three ways:

1. By eliminating both of the purely theoretical chapters in the original volumes and scattering the theoretical material throughout the text, as needed, I sought to integrate more completely Parsons' *theory* with the detailed accounts of particular societies. After all, Parsons was less interested in Egypt or in medieval Europe in themselves than as illustrations of societal differentiation. But this was drastic surgery. This editorial decision makes it difficult for the reader to examine his theory separately from the empirical materials. There may also be places that are unclear because all of the theoretical distinctions Parsons uses did not find their way into the revised text—although a glossary of Parsonian definitions, newly prepared for this edition, ought to address this problem. I hope that, for most readers, the advantage of integrating theoretical discussions with empirical data will outweigh the disadvantages.

2. By combining what were two separate volumes published five years apart, I sought to emphasize Parsons' conception of the sweep of the evolutionary process from prehistory, through historic epochs, and into the contemporary world. I also wrote a new Chapter One to serve as a guide not only to Parsons' theory of societal evolution but also to

some of the broader issues of sociological theory with which Parsons has been concerned.

3. By careful editing of the text, sentence by sentence, I sought to clarify Parsons' meaning by simplifying his prose style. Occasionally I deleted sentences that seemed to carry the reader toward a peripheral rather than a central point. More usually I deleted adjectives, adverbs, or entire phrases that Parsons had intended to qualify an overgeneral statement but which might confuse the reader. Thus, there are places where Parsons would prefer to state his argument more tentatively than he does in this edited version of his theory of societal evolution.

Although not an easy task, editing a masterpiece brings its own reward: the satisfaction of contributing to the accessibility of a work that will be studied by sociologists still unborn.

JACKSON TOBY
Rutgers University

THE EVOLUTION OF SOCIETIES

CHAPTER 1
PARSONS' THEORY OF SOCIETAL EVOLUTION

by JACKSON TOBY

Parsons' interest in societal evolution may have surprised some sociologists because it seems on first thought unrelated to his previous intellectual preoccupations. Actually it represents a return in a more sophisticated form to a problem that engaged him as a young man. Recall that his earliest publications were concerned with the development of capitalism (1928; 1929; 1930). In particular, he was impressed with Max Weber's interpretation of the role of religious values in the emergence of capitalism in the Christian West rather than in China or in India. His analysis of societal evolution in this book revises and extends the Weber thesis so as to make it relevant not merely to the emergence of capitalism but to the development of modern societies from the earliest beginnings of social organization. Parsons approaches this monumental task with a three-fold strategy:

1. He goes much further back in time than Weber. Since the historical record is only about five thousand years old, he relies on archeological evidence to place some societies in his scheme. For very primitive societies, he shifts to contemporary anthropological evidence—on the reasonable assumption that the simple social structure of the Murngin of Australia and the Shilluk of the Sudan tell us what human societies were like at early stages of social evolution.

2. He uses as his pivotal concept, not religious values, as Weber did, but shared symbolic systems (culture) of which religious values are only one subtype (constitutive symbols). Cognitive symbols, moral-evaluative

I am grateful to Victor Lidz and Frank Pearson for suggestions clarifying passages that would otherwise have been misleading.

symbols, and expressive-appreciative symbols are the other subtypes.

3. He formulates a theory of social change *logically* more compelling than Weber's. It provides a cybernetic model for the cultural direction of change; the model emphasizes four processes (differentiation, adaptive upgrading, inclusion, and value generalization) that clarify the ambiguous relationship between religious ideas and modernization in Weber (1964).

THE THEORY OF ACTION

Shared symbolic systems (culture) is the pivotal idea in Parsons' analysis not only of societal evolution but of human behavior generally. As early as *The Structure of Social Action* (1937) he explained what he meant by "action" and the implications of this orienting concept for understanding human behavior. By action, Parsons means the attempt of human beings to realize their symbolically defined intentions in symbolically defined environments. The definition does not sound revolutionary. In fact, it sounds as though Parsons is a symbolic interactionist in the Cooley-Mead-Thomas-Blumer tradition. It ought to; there is no important intellectual distinction between the action frame of reference and that provided by symbolic interaction. Both perspectives insist that the meaning of behavior to the participants, a meaning provided by their common interpretation of shared symbols, is essential for sociological understanding (Turner, 1974). The reason Parsons is not ordinarily thought of as a symbolic interactionist is that he has built a complex theoretical edifice on the symbolic-interactionist starting point, and it is not generally appreciated that the theory is inseparable from its point of departure.

Consider what Parsons accomplished in *The Structure of Social Action*. He demonstrated the intellectual inadequacy of two perspectives on human behavior, the positivistic perspective that denied the independent role of *values* and the idealistic perspective that denied the importance of environmental *conditions*. Parsons was reacting against purported explanations of human behavior that he considered unsucessful, such as John Watson's behaviorist psychology (1925), an example of positivism, and Ruth Benedict's cultural determination (1934), an example of idealism. Despite Parsons, neither positivistic nor idealistic models of human behavior have disappeared, so it might be useful to point to more current illustrations of the intellectual errors that Parsons was trying to prevent. In Kinsey's surveys of American sexual behavior (1948; 1953), the basic strategy was to count the number of orgasms that a human individual produced during his or her life cycle. True, Kinsey classified orgasms in terms of the circumstances in which they occurred, e.g., whether with a member of the same sex, with the opposite sex, with a lower animal, or through self-stimulation, but he was basically uninterested in the *meaning* of the orgasm for the persons involved. As a biologist whose original specialty was the taxonomy of the gall wasp, he assumed that the *biology* of human sexuality *explained* human sexuality. But a sociologist coming to the study of sexuality within the action frame of reference would insist that the *values* and *beliefs* of the participants in a sexual act (their definitions of the situation) must be known in order to understand their behavior adequately. Thus, heterosexual intercourse may mean to the male participant an affirmation of his masculinity, an expression of affection for his partner, an act of aggression, or a combination of these meanings. For Parsons such meanings are crucial; for Kinsey they were theoretically unimportant. Kinsey's research illustrates the positivistic error against which Parsons warned. The idealistic error can be illustrated by the attempt to explain the delinquent behavior of members of adolescent gangs entirely in terms of the cultural values of the neighborhoods in which they live (Miller, 1958). Miller, an anthropologist by training, discussed the "focal concerns" of lower-class culture—"trouble," "toughness," "smartness," "excitement," "fate," and "autonomy"—and ignored circumstantial conditions American males face in their life situations, e.g., adapting to school and later to occupational requirements.

According to Parsons, action, organized in systems and subsystems, takes place in environments. These environments include other action systems—that is, other human beings and their symbolically meaningful behavior—but also include *nonaction* environments, of which there are two. One is the physical-organic world including subhuman species and the nonsymbolic aspect of human anatomy and physiology. This is what Parsons called the *conditions* of action in *The Structure of Social Action*. These conditions must be controlled or adapted to, and, as we will see, Parsons regards the incentive to improve adaptation as the major factor in social evolution. The other nonaction environment Parsons calls "ultimate reality," a term with a metaphysical flavor. He is not referring to the supernatural so much as to the univeral tendency for societies to address symbolically the uncertainties, concerns, and tragedies of human existence that challenge the meaningfulness of social organization. In an effort to resolve enduring problems of good and evil in society, of justice and injustice, of chance and fate, men formulate the fundamental premises of their cultures; these implicit assumptions constitute the normative patterns of social action. Most theorists would not insist on referring constitutive values to a nonempirical realm, but Parsons does so because of logical considerations. Here is how he put it:

> As humans, we know the physical world *only* through the organism. Our minds have no direct experience of an external physical object unless we perceive it through physical processes and the brain processes information about it. Only in their psychologically known sense are physical objects aspects of action.

Similar considerations apply to the environment above action—the "ultimate reality" with which we are concerned in grappling with the problems of meaning—e.g., evil and suffering and the temporal limitations of human life. Ideas in this area, as cultural objects, are symbolic representations (e.g., gods, totems, the supernatural) of the ultimate realities, but are not themselves such realities. [Parsons, 1966:8, slightly edited]

THE DIFFERENTIATION OF ACTION SYSTEMS

The concept of action is Parsons' criterion of relevance; it explains why he is interested in some human behavior and not in other behavior. In point of fact, Parsons interprets action so as to include nearly all behavior that social scientists study. Thus, the only human behavior excluded from "action" is unmotivated behavior, i.e., the circulation of the blood or the blinking of the eye. Even physiological behaviors like belching, crying, or eating are action in Parsons' sense if they are used to communicate meanings, as they usually are. And if a sex researcher like Kinsey insisted that he wished to count orgasms because for many human beings sexual intercourse does not communicate meanings any more than it does for terriers, Parsons would reply that human behavior is inescapably meaningful and that the same order of difference exists between human sexuality and terrier sexuality as between linguistic communication and barking.

So far, Parsons' theory of action does not depart from symbolic interaction theory. Where it begins to depart is in Parsons' conception of the *differentiation* of action systems. What does he mean by the differentiation of action systems? On what he calls the level of the "general theory of action," he means that behavior tends to have four distinct, symbolically organized emphases: (1) a search for psychic satisfactions, (2) an interest in decoding symbolic meanings, (3) a need to adapt to the physical-organic environment, and (4) an attempt to relate to other members of the human species. These four tendencies may not seem controversial in the form I have stated them, but when Parsons gives them the descriptive label he does—personality systems, cultural systems, behavioral organisms, and social systems—some sociologists become uneasy. They fear that Parsons may be reifying these analytical constructs. They cannot see how a cultural system can exist without personality systems or social systems, not to mention behavioral organisms.

Parsons would agree; he denies explicitly that one of these four action systems can exist without the others. They are simply the four directions in which meaningful human behavior tends to go. But as Figure 1 tries to suggest, Parsons does not believe that these tendencies are present to the same extent in all societies. One aspect of his theory of social evolution—or "action evolution," as he has recently termed it—is that

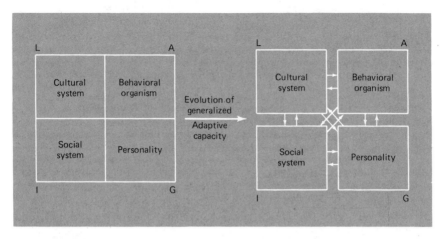

Figure 1. The differentiation of the general action system

differentiating tendencies are relatively undeveloped in primitive social organization, while in modern societies they have evolved much further. Take cultural systems as an example. Parsons would hold that all societies from the most primitive to the most advanced face the problem of interpreting the world, the people in it, and their activities, e.g., birth, death, dancing, and worship. In modern societies, however, cultures and subcultures have developed so much further and in so many specialized directions that they appear to be self-contained. Ogburn (1922) based his theory of social change on the seemingly uncontrollable proliferation of technological innovations. Actually, technological innovations grow at a compound rate in modern societies, not because inventions breed inventions by automatic reproduction but because people are more likely to think of new technological relationships when the scientific and technological base is large than when it is small. In the same way, *sociology* as a cultural system—a system of ideas about the structures of and the processes in social systems—now has a momentum of its own. Sociology could not continue as a functioning cultural system without a host society containing personalities and their associated behavioral organisms. Nevertheless, in modern society, sociology is sufficiently differentiated as to have much greater autonomy than do cultural systems among the Murngin.

Consider one implication of the differentiation of the general action system: Cultures and personalities can be critical of their host societies in a way that is literally unimaginable with less differentiation. In modern societies, personality systems function *relatively* autonomously vis-à-vis social, cultural, and even organistic systems; this is Parsons' way of describing the individualism of Western societies. Modern individualism is purchased at a price: a more problematic relationship between the personality system and the cultural system and between the social system and the cultural system. In modern societies there is less likelihood, as contrasted with more primitive social organization, that inputs of meaning from the cultural system will give personalities a sense of identity and direction and give legitimation to social systems. To put the same point another way, the differentiation of the general action system requires complex integrative processes. Identity crises and anomie are symptoms of malintegration between these differentiated action systems.

As Figure 1 makes clear, Parsons regards social evolution on the general action level as consisting of the increasing differentiation of personality systems, cultural systems, social systems, and the behavioral organisms *from one another.* But this is only part of his theory of action evolution, indeed a part only incidentally discussed in this book. His main interest is in the differentiating process *within societies*—societies being the most nearly self-sufficient type of social system vis-à-vis their environments. The differentiating process *within* societies consists of increasing specialized functioning parallel to that which characterizes the general action system. Parallel to the increased autonomy of the cultural system is the more clearly differentiated pattern-maintenance system (one aspect of which is the separation of the family as a socializing agency from the economic and political participations of individual members). Parallel to the increased autonomy of the personality is the more distinct polity. Parallel to the increased autonomy of the behavioral organism is the more distinct economy. Parallel to the increased autonomy of social systems generally and societies in particular is the greater specialization of an integrative subsystem—what Parsons calls the societal community—with responsibility for maintaining the solidarity of society. Figure 2 attempts to represent this differentiation of societal subsystems.

WHAT IS A SOCIETY?

At this point it is useful to explain more fully Parsons' conception of a society. Recall that he regards a social system as one of four analytically distinct aspects of human behavior—specifically the one concerned with the coordination of mutually responding actors with one another. Most social systems—local communities, schools, firms, families—are not societies but *subsystems* of a society. He defines a society as a special type of social system, one characterized by the highest level of *self-sufficiency in relation to its environments,* including environing social systems. Self-sufficiency in relationship to environments means that, although the society is dependent on its environments, it is *less* at the mercy of its environments than are most social systems. That is to say, a society can

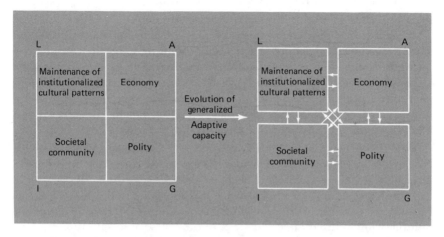

Figure 2. The differentiation of society

control interchanges with its environments fairly successfully so as to promote societal functioning—and thereby societal survival. Consider this relative autonomy in relation to each of the various environments of a society in turn.

1. *The physical-organic environment,* being the source of the resources which the society can utilize to satisfy the needs of its members, must be controlled or adapted to. Self-sufficiency with respect to the physical-organic environment implies sufficient control over the economic-technological complex so that, for example, food and shelter can be obtained. A family is less self-sufficient with respect to the food and shelter supply than is American society as a whole.

2. The *personalities* of members of the society are also part of its environment in the sense that the society must be able to count on its members to contribute to societal functioning. Just as the society must maintain some control over the physical-organic environment through technology, so it must maintain some control over the personalities of its members so that most personalities can assume roles in the society without undue strain. The society could not be considered self-sufficient with respect to environing personalities if the majority of its personalities were radically alienated. All societies guarantee a favorable personality environment by shaping personalities (largely in the family) through the socialization process. As a result of socialization, personalities learn adequate motivation for participating in socially valued patterns of action, and these internalized norms help to solve the problem of social order. Parsons assumes that American society is more self-sufficient with respect to its

constituent personalities than are smaller social systems like schools or business firms.

3. The *symbolic environment of a society* (cultural systems) includes empirical knowledge, expressive symbol systems, religious ideas and practices that define the society's collective identity, and conceptions of the desirable (values). Self-sufficiency with regard to the symbolic environment means that the institutions of the society are legitimated by the cultural system. Enough members of the society have made commitments to the values and other symbols of the culture so that a sociological observer could infer a sufficient level of consensus on the legitimacy of institutions. Of course, no social system is self-legitimating; all social systems must appeal for legitimation of their norms to the larger culture. But a *society* is in a stronger position to obtain legitimation than more limited social systems because the cultural elements embodied in its institutions are routinely internalized in personalities in the course of socialization.

4. The *social environment* of society includes all the environing social systems with which it must deal. Other societies are obviously part of the social environment, but the social environment of a society is far more inclusive. Some social systems cut across societies (such as the organization known as the Roman Catholic Church), and other social systems, though fully included within a society, must be adapted to, for example, the millions of individual families, schools, governmental organizations, and voluntary associations of American society. Self-sufficiency with regard to the social environment means (1) that clear boundaries exist defining who is a member of the society and who is not and (2) that greater solidarity exists among members than between members and nonmembers. These criteria, while not so difficult for a small social system to fulfill, are extremely difficult to fulfill on a large scale. That is why problems in the "societal community"—Parsons' term for the fulfillment of these two conditions—are often the most serious problems faced by a society.

THE CYBERNETIC HIERARCHY

In a weak moment Parsons called himself a cultural determinist (1966: 113). By this he does not mean that cultural developments are the only or even the main source of social change. Rather he means that the conditions of action set limits but do not thereby give *direction* to change; direction is given by cultural values. The concept of the cybernetic hierarchy represents Parsons' return to the relationship between values and conditions. He grappled with this intellectual problem in *The Structure of Social Action,* but this time he achieves a more elegant solution. As Figure 3 shows diagramatically, he conceives of a hierarchy of value guidance leading down from the cultural system into the society by way of the pattern-maintenance subsystem, then into the societal community, the polity, the economy, then out of the society into the personality system, and finally into the behavioral organism. Thus, the adaptive needs of the behavorial organism vis-à-vis the physical-organic environment must be solved; food and clothing are necessary. But the personality system and the values incorporated in it control the behavioral organism in the sense that the learned predispositions of the personality direct the organism to steak or to rattlesnake meat. Higher than the personality system in the cybernetic hierarchy is the social system (society) where the search of a multiplicity of personalities for gratifications must be coordinated. Within society, the economy directs personalities by allocating resources for gratifying some desires but not others. The polity is superordinate to the economy in the cybernetic hierarchy because collective goals must take precedence in a society over individual goals. The societal community is in turn superordinate to the polity because the preservation of solidarity is a paramount collective goal. Superordinate to the societal community is what Parsons has recently begun to call the fiduciary subsytem, the subsystem of society concerned with the maintenance of institutionalized cultural patterns. In this subsystem are processes of socializing motivation for role playing through teaching the norms and values of the society. Finally, since the values institutionalized in the role structure are not self-legitimizing, the cultural system stands higher in the cybernetic hierarchy than the fiduciary subsystem of the society.

The theory of the cybernetic hierarchy is not without its intellectual problems; some of the assumptions as to what controls what are arguable. But the theory of cybernetic control is not a theory of cultural determinism in the same sense as Ruth Benedict's theory of cultural patterning. The difference lies in the role of conditioning factors in Parsons' thinking. As he shows in his detailed examination of societies, Parsons does not treat social evolution as inevitable. In order for differentiation to occur, crucial problems must be solved, and these problems emerge at every level, even the sub-action level, e.g., an epidemic or an Ice Age. An adequate solution to a problem posing an obstacle to further evolution is not necessarily discovered. If it is not found, the society does not evolve further; it may disintegrate as Greece and ancient Israel did. If, however, a solution is discovered, the direction in which the solution proceeds is provided by controlling factors on higher levels of the cybernetic hierarchy. Thus Parsons explains the ultimate failure of the Roman Empire in terms of its inability "to develop a dynamic religious system which could legitimate and strengthen the enormously expanded societal community" (1966:92). Detailed knowledge of the societies about which Parsons writes is necessary to assess the extent to which his theoretical framework illuminates the responses of societies to challenging problems.

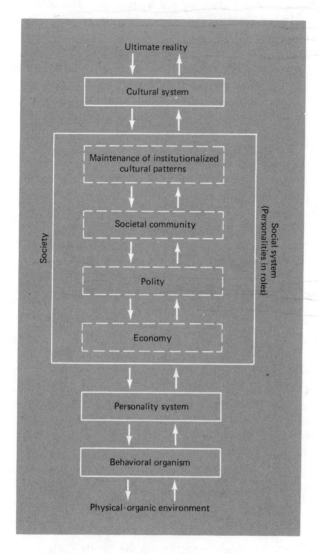

Ultimate reality

Cultural system

Maintenance of institutionalized
cultural patterns

Societal community

Polity

Economy

Society

Social system
(Personalities in roles)

Personality system

Behavioral organism

Physical-organic environment

Figure 3. The cybernetic hierarchy

EVOLUTIONARY BREAKTHROUGHS

Although a society has, by definition, greater control over its environments than other social systems, some societies are more effectively in control of their environments than others. Growth in ability to control their environments is, for Parsons, the explanation of societal evolution. When Parsons talks about increased "generalized adaptive capacity," he means increased societal control over their environments. However, Parsons does more than *define* the principle governing societal evolution. He attempts to identify the major evolutionay spurts. Each spurt forward constituted a solution to an environmental problem of some kind. Or, to put it another way, each solution marked an evolutionary breakthrough. Parsons identifies the breakthroughs partly on the basis of theoretical analysis of functional requirements of societies and partly through an examination of archeological, anthropological, and historical evidence (Parsons, 1964).

One of the first breakthroughs, according to Parsons, is the emergence of a system of social stratification. Stratification? Why should the division of society into more privileged and less privileged strata increase its "generalized adaptive capacity"? Parsons' answer to this question is mainly theoretical. A society organized in terms of a seamless web of kinship but not integrated in hierarchical terms has certain limitations in utilizing environmental resources. No member has sufficient prestige, including prestige based on universalistically assessed abilities (merit), to claim leadership in dealing with a military threat or a national disaster. And even if a charismatic member with superior ability attempted to provide leadership, he could not command the resources needed to carry out the new initiatives. In short, in a society where kinship is the paramount organizational principle, kinship considerations intrude into every allocation of resources.

Parsons is calling attention to an aspect of stratification that is usually forgotten—even by experts in the field of stratification—namely, that stratification increases mobility of human and nonhuman resources over the level of mobility possible in a system of kinship ascription. For those egalitarians who might object that resource mobility is purchased at too high a price, Parsons would answer that he is not talking about social "progress," which must be judged in terms of the values of the observer, but of social evolution, which is a matter of whether generalized adaptive capacity has increased or not. Thus, in the course of explicating an early breakthrough, Parsons begins to differentiate *his* theory of societal evolution from the nineteenth-century theories that failed to distinguish between scientific and valuational questions.

As soon as social stratification emerges, that is, as soon as social status is based on considerations that go beyond biological relatedness (kinship), the centralization of responsibility for economic, religious, or political activities becomes posible. But before such centralization actually occurs, a secondary evolutionary breakthrough is necessary: *explicit cultural legitimation*. "Explicit cultural legitimation" means sufficient differentiation of the cultural system from the society so that the cultural system can justify societal asymmetries of authority and prestige. This may not seem like much of a breakthrough because we are so familiar with differentiated cultural and social systems. But Parsons argues that in primitive societies the social and cultural aspects of action are closely linked. Until that link is broken by legitimizing myths that account for differential wealth, prestige, and power, evolutional development must mark time. Note that Parsons does not consider this cultural breakthrough inevitable. But if evolution is to proceed futher, explicit cultural legitimation must occur. When it *does* occur, Parsons argues that it occurs in conjunction with the development of a written language. At this point Parsons begins to speak of "intermediate societies" instead of "primitive societies":

> *Written language,* the focus of the development out of primitiveness, increases differentiation between the social and cultural systems and extends the control of the latter. The symbolic contents of a culture can, with writing, be embodied in forms independent of concrete interaction contexts. This makes possible wider cultural diffusion, both in space (e.g., relative to populations) and in time. It initiates the phenomenon of broadcasting—i.e., the orientation of messages to undefined audiences, to whoever is literate in the language and comes across the document. There is no inherent time limitation on the relevance of a message. Only literate cultures can have a *history* in the sense of an awareness, based on documentary evidence, of past events beyond the memories of living persons and the vague hearsay of oral traditions. . . .
>
> Written language and the availability of documents act to stablize many social relations. For example, the terms of a contractual agreement need not depend on the fallible memories of the parties or witnesses but can be written and made available for verification as need arises. Such stability is a condition for increasing the extent of many components of social organization. At the same time, writing is a source of flexibility and an opportunity for innovation. However frequently classical documents have provided the basis for a rigid traditionalism, the availability of officially correct documents makes possible critical analysis of relevant cultural issues. If the document is normative for some sphere of action, it poses the problem of how, in practical situations, its injunctions may actually be fulfilled. Written documents form a basis for a *cumulative* cultural development; they permit the *differences* introduced by an innovation to be defined more precisely than by oral tradition alone. In short, written language furthers the *independence* of the cultural system from the more conditional exigencies of the society. [Parsons, 1966: 26–27, slighty edited]

Parsons considers a variety of societies "intermediate": ancient Egypt, Mesopotamia, China, India, the Islamic empires, Rome. Like Weber, he wants to know why these societies were, despite undeniable development on the evolutionary scale, qualitatively different from modern societies. What crucial breakthroughs did they fail to make? Although he describes several necessary breakthroughs—the institutionalization of the authority of office, the use of market mechanisms for mobilizing resources, a generalized legal order, and the democratic association (Parsons, 1964)—he seems to consider the development of a generalized legal order as the special hallmark of modernity:

> Law furthers the independence of the normative components of the societal structure from the exigencies of political and economic interests and from the personal, organic, and physical-environmental factors operating through them. It is the *kind* of law, the institutionalization of which marks the transition from intermediate to modern societies, that poses the theoretical problem. Its organization must be *generalized* according to universalistic principles. This requirement precludes such imposing systems as the Talmudic law or that of tradtional Islam from being classed as modern law. They lack the generality which Weber called *formal rationality*. Modern legal systems must also emphasize the factor of *procedure*, as distinguished from substantive precepts and standards. Only on the basis of procedural primacy can the system cope with a variety of changing circumstances and cases without prior commitment to specific solutions. [Parsons, 1966:27, slighty edited]

Ancient Greece and ancient Israel were the twin sources of a generalized legal order—even though both failed to capitalize on their invention because historical circumstances put them out of business as functioning societies. They provided a cultural legacy that was necessary if modern societies were to evolve—Parsons calls them "seed-bed" societies —but the legacy was not incorporated into an institutional structure of a going society until more than a thousand years later. Thus Parsons once again calls attention to the interplay between conditioning circumstances and cultural direction; he does not regard the evolutionay process as inexorable. What was the cultural seed that Greece and Israel planted? It was the idea of a *moral order*. In the Israelite case the moral order was thought of as a divine mandate; the Greek conception was more secular; the order existed in nature. But both enunciated universalistic principles that transcended vested interests, including political interests, and particularisms, including the kinship and ethnic particularisms, that interfere with the emergence of a principled normative order. According to Parsons, the English common law seized upon this universalistic idea and thereby opened up the possibility of modernity.

> A generalized legal system is an integrated system of universalistic norms, applicable to the society as a whole rather than to a few functional or segmental sections, highly generalized in terms of principles and standards, and relatively independent of both the religious agencies that legitimize the normative order of the society and vested interests in the operative sector, particularly in government. [Parsons, 1964:351]

Consider where Parsons has taken us so far. His account of the emergence of social stratification, of explicit cultural legitimation, and of a generalized legal system is simultaneously an account of the subordination of ascription and particularism as organizing principles of society to achievement and universalism. His examination of the other evolutionary breakthroughs proceeds in the same general direction. Take his discussion of money and the market system. Every society must mobilize human and nonhuman resources to deal with its responsibilities. There are only three ways to do this. One is political coercion: a military draft or the requisition of property by the state. The second is appeal to particularistic loyalties—help to one's family, one's neighbors, one's countrymen. The third is to go into the marketplace with a generalized inducement (money) and bid for whatever resources are needed. The disadvantage of nonmarket techniques for mobilizing resources is that they tend to produce cleavages in the society. Coercion is resented—by some persons at any rate. Appeals to particularistic loyalties force a choice between solidarities, all of which may be important; the other side of the loyalty coin is possible disloyalty to other groups. The market, on the other hand, emancipates resources from ascriptive and particularistic roots; resources can be mobilized for instrumental purposes without pulling apart the fabric of community. Thus, Parsons argues that, other things being equal, a society with a monetary system for mobilizing resources through markets has greater generalized adaptive capacity than a society having only non-market methods of mobilizing resources.

He uses similar reasoning to explain why the institutionalization of the authority of *office* is another breakthrough in the direction of modernity. "Office implies the differentiation of the role of the incumbent from a person's other role involvements, above all from his kinship roles" (Parsons, 1964:347). Every society allocates rights to make decisions on behalf of collectivities or on behalf of the ultimate collectivity, society itself. These rights to make binding decisions on behalf of collectivities is what is mean by "authority." But in pre-modern societies authority is more often *ascribed* on the basis of biological or relational factors irrelevant to the use of that authority in the interest of effective attainment of societal goals. A king is king because his father was king. The concept of office frees authority from this ascriptive limitation. Parsons, like Weber before him, swims against the ideological current that decries bureaucratic *in*efficiency. Parsons maintains that administrative bureaucracies, institutionalizing as they do the authority of office, are potentially *more* effective than pre-modern types of authority.

When capacity to carry out large-scale organized operations is important, e.g., military operations with mass forces, water control, tax administration, policing of large and heterogeneous poulations, and productive enterprises requiring large capital investment and much manpower, the unit that commands effective bureaucratic organization is inherently superior to one that does not. . . . it is built on further specializations ensuing from the broad emancipation that stratification and specialized legitimation make possible. [Parsons, 1964:349]

The development of authority of office is an evolutionay break-through because it makes possible a more flexible use of power. Flexibility in the mobilization of power doesn't *necessarily* imply greater adaptive capacity for the society, but other things being equal, it tends to produce this result by opening political opportunities up to a larger number of potential leaders. Another way of making this same point is to say that institutionalization of the authority of office created fluid symbolic power systems, which had not existed before. Parsons puts it this way to emphasize the analogy between power and money (as symbolic media of interchange among role players in modern societies). Unfortunately, though, this creates some confusion among readers not aware of the special definitions that Parsons gives to power and authority 1963a; 1963b). Authority is an aspect of a status; it is the *right to* use power. Power itself circulates in modern societies; it is dynamic, as contrasted with authority, which is static. The process of voting involves a transfer of power; the *right* to vote as a method of selecting leadership is part of the definition of political authority.

These definitions are rather different from traditional treatments of power and authority in the sociological literature. But, taken together with the other elements in his approach, they help to explain why Parsons regards the *democratic polity* as an evolutionary breakthrough also. First, Parsons emphasizes the *collective* aspects of power, the opportunity power gives to accomplish something important on behalf of society, rather than the *distributive* aspect of power, the opportunity power gives individual A to oppress individual B. Obviously, the theorist who discusses power in the benign terms of effective attainment of societal goals will talk past the theorist worried about the possibility that, to use the modern idiom, "the strong will screw the weak." Related to *this* point is a second; Parsons refuses to treat power as *either* coercive *or* consensual; he inisists that it is *both*. This insistence is related to a problem Parsons wrestled with in *The Structure of Social Action* (1937:460–470), namely, the Durkheimian characterization of a social fact as "exterior" and "constraining" despite the voluntary aspect of it on the aggregative level. A trivial example will make this point clear. If I ask a male undergraduate why he wears trousers instead of a kilt or a dress, he will tell me that he has no effective choice, that the social disapproval that he would evoke if he wore a kilt or a dress would make that an unbearable alternative. If I ask him further whether he felt *oppressed* when he put on his pants that morning, he will say that he never thought about it; his own inclinations and the social rules happen to coincide. But they didn't just *happen* to coincide, Parsons tells us. What on the *collective* level is a *voluntary* commitment to certain norms, e.g., wearing trousers, for some individuals may be coerced consent. Whether it is coercive or not depends on the degree to which they share a normative consensus prescribing trousers for males. Several years ago Swedish society illustrated the reationship between these levels by changing at one moment of one day from driving on the left hand of the street to driving on the right. The collective commitment to make this change took a long time to make. Sweden is a democratic country, and the change not only ran counter to existing habits; it cost a great deal of taxpayers' money to put into effect. Nevertheless, once the political process produced this collective decision, the individual who continued to drive on the left would thereafter be coerced by the police—just as right-lane drivers had been coerced before.

This distinction between the individual and the collective levels explains why power is simultaneously consensual and coercive. On the individual level it is sometimes coercive. By definition, power wielders have the right (and the obligation) to impose negative sanctions in order to enforce binding decisions. If American society has collectively agreed on a 55-mile-per-hour speed limit and I exceed it for idiosyncratic reasons, I may legitimately be coerced. Furthermore, however much I dislike receiving a ticket for speeding from a policeman, on one level I may even agree that I deserve it. What does all this have to do with Parsons' contention that the democratic polity is another evolutionary breakthrough? Parsons contends that the larger and more complex a society, the more necessary it is to legitimate its universalistic legal order. Furthermore, the democratic polity, through its elective leadership and its fully enfranchised membership, links the consensual and coercive aspects of power more closely together than is likely in other types of political structure. If Parsons is correct, the democratic polity potentially has greater generalized adaptive capacity because its four structural features make possible the achievement of a broadly-based consensus. These four features are as follows:

1. *Electing leaders by popular vote.* Abiding by the verdict of the electorate means dispersing power widely in the society. An election is an institutionalized mechanism for collecting the power that has been dispersed. Those skeptical about the dispersal of power in democratic polities argue that elections are meaningless because a single vote counts so little. To this, Parsons responds that a little power is power just as a little money is money. But the real issue is whether or not leaders are actually *chosen* by an electoral process. Clearly, they are not chosen in this way in the Soviet Union despite public rituals that resemble democratic elections. Equally clearly, high officials *are* selected for office in countries like the United States, Great Britain, Sweden, Holland, France, Japan.

2. *Institutionalizing an opportunity for the participation of a large proportion of the adult population in collective decision making.* The

significance of the franchise, according to Parsons, is that it encourages participation not only in the choice of leaders but even in the selection of specific policies. From this point of view, higher voter turnout is an expression of involvement in the decision-making process and failure to participate in a particular election may mean dissatisfaction with all the candidates. However, it may also mean that the nonvoter was reasonably satisfied with the candidate and policy options offered and therefore did not take the trouble to vote. The democratic election offers an *opportunity* to participate; it is the opportunity that is important for a sense of involvement, not necessarily the actual vote.

3. *Institutionalizing procedural rules for the voting process, for determining its outcome, and for campaigning for votes by candidates for election.*   Such procedural rules protect the integrity of the voting process, thereby giving voters confidence that the competition for support is conducted fairly.

4. *Institutionalizing an approximation to voluntary participation in the polity.*   Actually, even in democratic polities, citizenship is ascribed and therefore not as fully voluntary as it is in voluntary associations of persons linked *only* by their common interests, e.g., a tennis club or a religious sect. But unlike the situation in totalitarian societies, where voting is a civic ritual in which the citizen is obliged to participate, the individual is permitted to participate or not participate in the democratic political process, as he wishes. Parsons considers the invention of the democratic polity—he calls this invention the "democratic revolution"—another evolutionary breakthrough. Although undemocratic political forms can organize and legitimate authority and power, the democratic polity is potentially more effective at mediating the consensual aspect of power. Certainly those who have been socialized in a democratic polity are tempted to think so. Is Parsons merely rationalizing his preferences for a democratic society by arguing that democratic polities have greater generalized adaptive capacity? Given the political alienation that seems to afflict democratic societies, the distrust of politicians, the loss of a sense of national mission, why is Parsons optimistic about the superior adaptive capacity of the democratic polity? Basically, his answer is (1) that he has made a plausible theoretical argument for its greater adaptive capacity and (2) that he can account for temporary fluctuations in trust and distrust in other ways. He is willing to put his theories to the empirical test, but he is aware that a war or an economic crisis can cause temporary fluctuations in political morale. His theories are long-run theories, and they require long-run empirical tests. He discusses some of the current tensions in American society not as evidence of declining adaptive capacity but as due to transitional strains. He denies that he has an ethnocentric value preference for American society; he believes that American society has simply proceeded further along the evolutionary path than even its

European counterparts. To assess the validity of this line of reasoning, let us consider in some detail Parsons' analysis of the inclusion problem of modern societies.

THE INCLUSIVE SOCIETAL COMMUNITY
OF MODERN SOCIETIES

Parsons points out that one consequence of the democratic and industrial revolutions was to weaken the ascriptive framework of early modern societies. Monarchy moved toward constitutionalism. Aristocracy lost its political power. National citizenship and representative government spread. A universalistic legal system became further rationalized. Residential communities grew more associational and less ascriptive. The factory broke the ascriptive link between the family and the occupational system. Religion lost the protection of establishment in state churches; denominations moved toward the status of voluntary associations.

At the same time that the ascriptive framework was weakening, the evolutionary process was differentiating one societal subsystem from another. Thus, the industrial revolution differentiated the economy from the polity, and the democratic revolution differentiated the polity from the societal community. He gives this last point special emphasis. The societal community, "the patterned normative order through which the life of a population is collectively organized" (1966:10) does not necessarily coincide with the society's human population. Every society contains within it persons not fully included at all levels of citizenship. Migrant laborers and inner-city slum dwellers are second-class citizens within the American societal community (Toby, 1971:223–230). But Parsons' evolutionary analysis reveals that premodern societies had a much smaller proportion of their populations fully included in the societal community than modern societies. To put it another way, premodern societies had difficulty developing a large citizen base, and one important reason for this difficulty was the ascriptive barriers that relegated so many people to undifferentiated inferiority. When the industrial and democratic revolutions undermined ascriptive limitations while at the same time differentiating the societal community from its previous economic and political involvements, a breathtaking possibility began to emerge. Why not include *everybody?*

Parsons argues that, partly because of American ethnic and religious diversity, the logic of this possibility in the United States was more attractive than in other modernizing societies. Consequently the inclusion process has been proceeding rapidly as Irish, Italians, Jews, and (most recently) nonwhite minorities move toward full participation. If Parsons is right and that is what is happening, why are so many intellectuals so sour about the United States? Why the complaints about poverty, the erosion of community, the power élite, immorality, bureaucracy, student unrest? Parsons' answer is a twofold one. First, he examines the three subsystems of society other than the societal community and does not find a worsening capacity to adapt. In the fiduciary subsystem, he does not observe moral deterioration but rather a more flexible application of value commitments legitimated by the cultural system. In the economy, he does not find increasing polarization between the rich and the poor, the owners and the proletariat, but instead growth of professional and white-collar groups that cannot easily be categorized in terms of the rhetoric of traditional Marxism. In the polity, he does not find power more centralized but rather more dispersed to electorates and more subject to veto groups.

Second, he concludes that the objectively incorrect charges concerning the polity, the economy, and the fiduciary subsystem stem from *residual problems of exclusion from the societal community.* Exclusion is minimal and growing less, but what remains is more painful because of a relative deprivation effect. The destruction of the ascriptive framework makes anything less than equality of *outcome* difficult to justify. Yet achievement leads to new forms of inequality (Parsons, 1970). The pain of partial exclusion may be subjectively experienced as political, economic, or moral dissatisfaction, but the real source of the malaise is the pressure of egalitarian ideals on an achievement-oriented societal community. Egalitarian pressure is expressed in calls for a greater sense of community, for participatory democracy, and for the elimination of race prejudice and poverty. But difficult problems must be faced in trying to reconcile the ideal of equality of results with the hierarchical role structure necessary for an efficient economy, for an effective polity, and even for competent scientific research. The educational revolution (through which the modern world is now passing) may help with this reconciliation by legitimating hierarchical distinctions based on technical competence. The educational revolution is closely associated with the rise of the professions, which bring influential ideas from university centers to the occupational and political systems. Since the power of the expert seems less arbitrary than the power of ascription, the educational revolution may help to integrate society by legitimating a new kind of stratification. Stratification by achievement requires radical equality of opportunity (if it is to seem—and be—fair) as well as greater accountability on the part of those accorded superior status in the economic, cultural, and political systems. (Accountability in the polity can be illustrated by officials seeking reelection on the basis of their performance in office.)

CONCLUSION

Societal evolution can hardly be called an idea whose time has come. Many sociologists would say it came in the nineteenth century—and went, along with Herbert Spencer. Parsons is attempting to breathe new life into the theory despite a contemporary preference for explanations of the immediate present over explanations of long-run trends. Thus, many sociologists—and not just radical sociologists—cannot muster enthusiasm for a theory of social change so detached from current anxieties that it disregards the latest war and the next presidential election. His focus on the long view makes Parsons seem complacent about the present. As Keynes put it, in the long run we are all dead. But Parsons' theory of societal evolution is not a retooled version of the romantic faith in the inevitability of progress—despite the congratulatory tone that creeps into his analysis when cultural or social innovations solve conditional problems at lower cybernetic levels. He sounds this way because he is aware of the inability of many societies to meet such challenges. Parsons' theory faces another obstacle to popularity; it claims to account mainly for the sequence of stages rather than for detailed processes by which one societal stage evolves into the next. Failure to deal with process is perceived as a serious drawback by those with social psychological interests.

On the other hand, Parsons is not the only contemporary social scientist interested in societal evolution. The distinguished psychologist, Donald Campbell, in his presidential address to the American Psychological Association (1975) chose to focus on sociobiology in relation to moral development in human societies. Campbell argued that evolutionary genetics and his own field, experimental psychology, were insufficient to account for the "socially useful, individually self-sacrificial altruism" (1975:1123) necessary for social order; he considered the possibility of a religious and ethical tradition for societal survival. In short, there is growing interest in the basic *intellectual* problem that Parsons has addressed. There ought to be interest also in the application of evolutionary theory to the *practical* problem of modernization; without economic and social development some considerable proportion of the four billion persons on the planet have a bleak future. Parsonian theory may turn out to be surprisingly "relevant."

ADDENDUM TO CHAPTER 1

Talcott Parsons has supplied Figures 4 and 5 to make even more explicit the theoretical basis of his evolutional scheme.

Figure 4 presents the relations between the social system and its total system of environments in terms of the functional scheme I have used. Column I lists the functional categories, interpreted here at the general action level. Column II singles out the social system from the others according to its integrative functions within the action system. Column III, corresponding to column IV of Figure 5, lists the other three subsystems of action as immediate (i.e., as intra-action) environments of the social

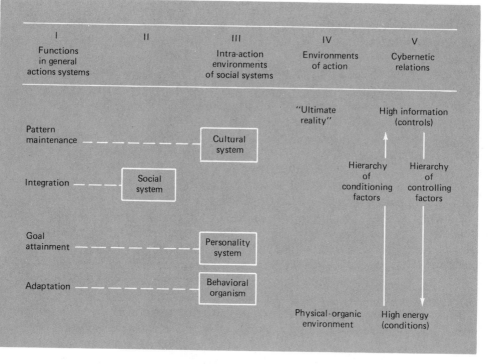

Figure 4. Subsystems of action

system. Column IV presents the two environments within which action systems function—namely, the physical-organic environment, relations with which are mediated through the behavioral organism and the environment called "ultimate reality," relations with which are mediated through the constitutive symbol systems (i.e., religious components) of the cultural system. Finally, column V indicates the two directions in which factors exert their effect on these systems. The upward-pointed arrow indicates the hierarchy of conditions, which at any given cumulative level in the upward series is necessary but not sufficient. The downward-pointed arrow designates the hierarchy of controlling factors in the cybernetic sense. As we move downward, control of more and more necessary conditions makes the implementation of patterns, plans, or programs possible. Systems higher in the order are relatively high in information while those lower down are relatively high in energy.

Figure 5 presents schematically the set of relationships concerning the structure of the society as a system, centering on the place of the societal community. Column I lists the four functional categories according to their place in the cybernetic hierarchy of control. In relation to col-

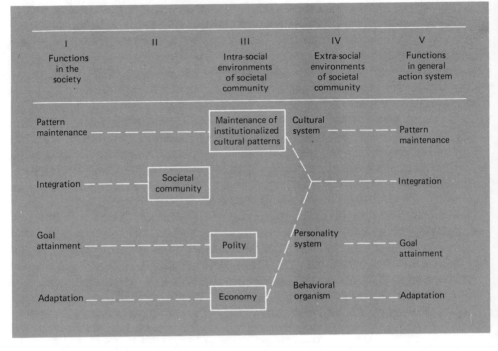

Figure 5.   The societal community and its environments

umn I, column II identifies the societal community as the integrative subsystem of the society—i.e., that *analytically* defined subsystem characterized by the primacy of integrative function in the larger system. Column III designates the other three primary analytical subsystems (the functions of which are also given in relation to column I) as constituting environment of the society community which are *internal* to the society as a social system. It carries on processes of input-output interchange and shares zones of interpenetration with them. Column IV details in the cognate order the primary subsystems of action other than the society itself, showing them as constituting environments for the society, presuming the same order of interchange and interpenetration, but with different specific content. The slanting dashed lines indicate that the *entire* societal system, not each of its subsystems, is involved in these interchanges with the action environments. Finally, column V lists the functional categories in terms of which action systems are differentiated, this time in the context of the general action system rather than of the social system. Note that the functions in the general action system and in the social system are identical.

REFERENCES

BENEDICT, RUTH
　　1934　*Patterns of Culture.* Boston: Houghton Mifflin.
CAMPBELL, DONALD T.
　　1975　"On the conflicts between biological and social evolution and between psychology and moral tradition." *American Psychologist* 30:1103–1126.
KINSEY, ALFRED C., WARDELL B. POMEROY, and CLYDE E. MARTIN
　　1948　*Sexual Behavior in the Human Male.* Philadelphia: Saunders.
KINSEY, ALFRED C., WARDELL B. POMEROY, CLYDE E. MARTIN, and PAUL H. GEBHARD
　　1953　*Sexual Behavior in the Human Female.* Philadelphia: Saunders.
MILLER, WALTER B.
　　1958　"Lower class culture as a generating milieu of gang delinquency." Journal of Social Issues 14 (no. 3):5–19.
OGBURN, WILLIAM F.
　　1922　*Social Change.* New York: Huebsch.
PARSONS, TALCOTT
　　1928　" 'Capitalism' in recent German literature: Sombart and Weber, I." *Journal of Political Economy* 36:641–661.
　　1929　" 'Capitalism' in recent German literature: Sombart and Weber, II." *Journal of Political Economy* 37:31–51.
　　1930　Translation of Max Weber, *The Protestant Ethic and the Spirit of Capitalism.* London: Allen and Unwin; New York: Scribners.
　　1937　*The Structure of Social Action.* New York: McGraw-Hill.
　　1951　*The Social System.* Glencoe, Ill.: Free Press.
　　1964　"Evolutional universals in society." *American Sociological Review* 29 (June):339–357.
　　1966　*Societies: Evolutionary and Comparative Perspectives.* Foundations of Modern Sociology Series, Alex Inkeles (ed.), Englewood Cliffs, N.J.: Prentice-Hall.
　　1970　"Equality and inequality, or social stratification revisited." *Sociological Inquiry* 40 (Spring): 1–71.
　　1971　*The System of Modern Societies.* Foundations of Modern Sociology Series, Alex Inkeles (ed.), Englewood Cliffs, N.J.: Prentice-Hall.
TOBY, JACKSON
　　1971　*Contemporary Society,* rev. ed. New York: Wiley.
TURNER, JONATHAN
　　1974　"Parsons as a symbolic interactionist: a comparison of action and interaction theory." *Sociology Inquiry* 44:283–294.
WATSON, JOHN B.
　　1925　*Behaviorism.* Chicago: University of Chicago Press.
WEBER, MAX
　　1964　*The Sociology of Religion.* Boston: Beacon.

CHAPTER 2
PRIMITIVE
SOCIETIES
THE EMERGENCE OF
SOCIAL STRATIFICATION

Socio-cultural evolution, like organic evolution, has proceeded by differentiation from simple to progressively more complex forms. Contrary to early conceptions in the field, it has not proceeded in a single definable line, but at every level has included a variety of different forms and types.[1] Nevertheless, longer perspectives make it evident that forms apparently equally viable in given stages have not been equal in terms of their potentialities for contributing to further evolutionary developments. Still, the variability of human patterns of action is one of the facts about the human condition.

In this light, there are four interdependent aspects of the theoretical problems facing us. First, we must use the general conceptual scheme of the social system which underlies all sociological analysis, whatever the size and functional importance of the system of reference to other systems. Second, we must consider the problems of the society that arise from its being a type of social system more inclusive of controls over action than all others. Third, we must be concerned with the evolutionary development of societies as wholes and in their principal structural parts. (We are concerned with the sequences of changing structural patterns which characterize societies as social systems in the course of their evolution and with the processes by which the transitions have occurred. We hope to delineate coherent patterns of order in these respects.) Finally, we must consider variability as a prob-

1. In biological theory, variation is conceived as a factor in evolution operating at every level of development. In overlooking its importance, the early social evolutionists fell short of developing a truly evolutionary perspective.

lem distinct from that of evolutionary stage and sequence. That the cultural, physical, biological, psychological, and social environments of societies, as of other social systems, are variable is reason enough to expect that the societies, being interdependent with these environmental factors as well as autonomous, will also vary. Some attempts to specify the variations found at different stages of evolution, the reasons for them, and the potentialities for their further development are necessary.

I divide the evolution of societies (so far) into three stages: primitive, intermediate, and modern. Our neighboring discipline, social anthropology, has studied primitive societies intensively, and many anthropological studies approach primitive societies in comparative and evolutionay terms. I shall lean on these studies in an effort to show (1) what primitive societies are like and (2) how primitive societies begin to evolve into a more advanced social organization. My hypothesis is that social stratification developed in what was previously a mosaic of kinship groups of equivalent prestige, economic resources, authority, and access to the gods. I shall discuss two main types of stratification, one emphasizing religious differentiation, the other political differentiation. Bear in mind that even at this early evolutionary stage, development is not inevitable. Instead of becoming stratified, a primitive society may remain primitive or it may break up into separate segments. *Stratification* rather than *segmentation* can occur only if the solidarity of members of the society is sufficient to overcome the centrifugal forces of social differentiation. Somehow the emergence of hierarchy must be legitimated by the culture. And this means that the collective identity of the society had to grow strong enough to withstand the divisive tendencies toward fission that superordination and subordination involve.

ORGANIC EVOLUTION

The qualitative gap between man and the other species, though redefined since Darwin, remains. Man is the only *cultural* animal and his culture, being interdependent with his society, makes his social organization different from that of other species; e.g., the social insects or even other primates. A process of organic evolution crossed this gap at least once. Its final stages so enhanced adaptation that species intermediate between the higher primates and man could not stabilize viable niches in the organic world and were eliminated by natural selection. Hence, laborious reconstruction—still incomplete—has been necessary to conceptualize them.

Distinctively human organic developments are the basis of the capacities which underlie cultural-social life and organization; they are capacities for learning and for organizing learned materials and patterns.

They comprise conditions for organizing behavior in terms of symbolic systems, which constitutes *action* in our terminology. In the realm of action, the gene has been replaced by the symbol as the basic structural element.[2] The oldest of these organic developments was the emergence of arms and hands as manipulative organs.[3] Having two hands, each located at the end of a movable jointed arm and each with four fingers and an opposable thumb, man has a general purpose tool immensely superior to any mouth-and-paw combination. It entails erect posture and hence a sacrifice in effective locomotion. Human runners do not match a horse in speed over short distances. But the hands are the basis of human skills.

Skills constitute the manipulative techniques of human goal attainment and control in relation to the physical world insofar as artifacts or machines designed as tools do not yet supplement them. Human skills are guided by codified *knowledge* of the things to be manipulated and the human capacities used to manipulate them. Such knowledge is an aspect of cultural-level symbolic processes and requires the capacities of the human central nervous system, particularly the brain. This organic system is essential to symbolic processes; the human brain is superior to the brain of any other species.[4] The most general aspect of the symbolic process is language, the organic implementation of which is speech. Speech involves secondary utilization of the oral organs, some of which originally evolved in relation to food intake and respiration. The hollow throat chamber (its air flow controlled by breathing and by opening and closing the mouth and its shape controlled by movements of the lips, cheeks, and tongue) combined with the vocal chords (which provide reverberations) can produce varied and controlled sounds. Since human manual skills permit the mouth to specialize in receiving and masticating food, instead of having also to grasp and tear it, the oral organs presumably specialized around such flexibility. A brain which can control this apparatus and an aural system with which the brain can decode the sound-speech information transmitted to the organism make linguistic symbolic communication possible.

Another organic complex significant for learning is the prolonged dependence of offspring characteristic of advanced species. Humans follow the mammalian pattern of gestating in the maternal body and depending on maternal feeding, but also exhibit the trait—present in lower primates

2. Alfred Emerson, "Homeostasis and Comparison of Systems," in Roy R. Grinker (ed.), *Toward A Unified Theory of Behavior* (New York: Basic Books, 1956).

3. Ernst Mayr, *Animal Species and Evolution* (Cambridge, Mass.: Harvard University Press, 1963), chap. 20.

4. Ralph W. Gerard, "Brains and Behavior," in J. N. Spuhler (ed.), *The Evolution of Man's Capacity for Culture* (Detroit: Wayne State University Press, 1957).

but accentuated in man—of *psychological* dependence on an older, nuturing organism.[5] In this context, as well as that of physiological reproduction, the family is foreshadowed at pre-human levels, but the human emphasis on the *continuing* care of young offspring is unique not only organically through feeding and protection, but in psychological terms.[6]

The *erotic complex* plays a role in the control of learning processes. Its organic mechanism is the capacity to be motivated by erotic pleasure. In learning early disciplines, the human infant finds that contacts with the mother are pleasurable and that in his relationship with her, they reward his learning. These disciplines include feeding skills, sleeping and waking routines, toilet-training, and even language-learning. The internalization and organization at the symbolic level of the erotic significance of social objects underlies the learning of more complicated disciplines and eventually the erotic complex of adulthood. In the psychological-motivational contexts, the erotic complex is the bridge between the organic and action system levels.

These classes of organic capacity are essential to a human individual's acquisition and use of culture, to his interaction with others, and to the formation of his own personality. They exhibit in common the basic property called *plasticity*. They are all *genetically* determined—*any* normal human organism will develop them in adequate degree under normal conditions. They are, however, simply *capacities*. Their organic foundations do not determine the actual *content* of the behavorial patternings which their utilization makes possible. Having hands and arms and good coordination are necessary for acquiring manual skills, but they do not determine *what skills* will be acquired. Having a properly functioning brain is essential to intellectual achievement, but does not determine whether the learning will involve philosophy, mathematics, or biology, or Christian, Buddist, or Confucian beliefs. An adequate vocal apparatus is necesary to speak a language but has nothing to do with what language is learned. Erotic capacities are essential for psycho-sexual development, but the different patternings of Australian aboriginal pschosexual development and modern European psycho-sexual development are not related to the genetic differences between the respective races.

Thus, the *organization* of action systems is learned, but is based on a set of *generalized* organic facilities, the availability of which is the distinctive genetic heritage of human beings. The ways in which they are used—and are built into cultures, social systems, and personalities at the human action level—are independent of *any* genetic particularities of the organic stock. This is the view of the organic bases of human behavior

---

5. Harry F. Harlow, "Basic Social Capacity of Primates," in Spuhler (ed.), *op. cit.*

6. Mayr, *op. cit.*

which modern biological and social science has substituted for the instinct theories that held sway during the early part of this century.[7]

THE COMPONENTS OF PRIMITIVE SOCIETY

All these organic components are involved in *all* types of human socio-cultural behavior, though in differing patterns of combination. Hence, no one-to-one correspondence exists between these components and the institutional complexes of even the most primitive human societies. However, there are patterns of special relevance—e.g., manual skills are important in technological adaptation and the organization of erotic relations is important to contexts of kinship and the socialization of children.

The organic components all exhibit plasticity; and the socio-cultural components of behavior are all *organized* on symbolic bases. For example, even in the areas of action which contemporary ideologies often reduce to the operation of organic factors, I deny that *any* patterned human behavior can be understood as purely organic rather than as controlled by socio-cultural mechanisms. Food-getting and eating are subject to the nutritional imperatives of organic life and are motivated by the hunger drive, but, beyond their *conditional* relevance, these factors cannot account for human *ways* of securing and eating food. Similarly, though sexual intercourse is essential for human reproduction and there is an organic factor in sexual desire, the patternings of erotic relations in human societies are *never* understandable as functions of this organic need alone.

Insofar as an action system is primitive in the evolutionary sense, it is *undifferentiated* at the social, cultural, and personality levels. Its societal system will be simple by standards of differentiation. There will be little differentiation between the societal and the other components of the action system. "Society" and 'cultural system" do not have generalized bases for keeping independent of each other; "society" and "personality" have characteristic modes by which their structures fuse at more generalized levels. It may even be difficult to distinguish adjacent societies from one another; some primitive societies are not clearly bounded either in territory or in membership, as more advanced societies are.

I suggest two criteria of societal primitiveness. One is the importance in all spheres of action of religious (and magical) orientations to the

---

7. It is unfortunate that Freud's term *trieb*, which was neutral between these different views, has been translated into English as *instinct*. As Freud made clear, the erotic complex is a *generalized* capacity to mobilize the organic components of motivation to action, not a propensity to specific modes of behavior.

world. The other is the prominence of kinship relations; kinship structures are a factor in practically all social organization in primitive systems.[8] Attention has also been given to other complexes: technology and the symbolic nature of social communication. We can reformulate these four complexes (religion, kinship, technology, and symbolic communication) as analytically defined components of a primitive societal system, relating them to the exigencies of functioning in primitive societies and later to developmental trends toward more complex societies.

Religion

A system of *constitutive symbolism* gives members of the society their own self-definition or collective identity so that the conception, "We, the . . ." is meaningful. This is an answer to the two questions of who and what *we* are.[9]

Kinship

This constitutive system of symbolism is connected with the kinship system. Often the connection is grounded in an ancestral reference to those from whom *we* are descended and a conception of a transition from human ancestors to those conceived as being supernatural. The latter are regarded as the original founders of the society, and the normative order is believed to have been established by their actions and/or decrees. For example, it is a common belief among primitive societies that the founders had incestuous relations but decreed that their human descendants should be forbidden them. The framework of the kinship system is often explained by such foundation myths.

In such cases, the humanness of the founding ancestors is equivocal in two directions. In the supernatural direction they are regarded as immortal and as possessing various other supernatural powers. In the opposite direction, the ancestors tend to become sub-humanized and are portrayed as or associated with animals, plants, or physical objects. Totemism is a common phenomenon, but there may also be superanimals, such as the serpent *Yu* (*Yurlunggur* or *Wollunqua*) of Murngin myth.[10] These are symbols that operate in a variety of contexts. Finally, there is always a territorial reference, including the country in which the people live,

---

8. Claude Lévi-Strauss, *Totemism* (Boston: Beacon Paperbacks, 1962), especially chap. II.

9. Emile Durkheim and Marcel Mauss, *Primitive Classification* (Chicago: University of Chicago Press, 1963).

10. W. Lloyd Warner, *A Black Civilization*, 2nd ed. (New York: Harper, 1958), chaps. IX and X.

sometimes complicated by tales of migration. It includes conceptions of their hunting, gathering, and residence areas, and of special locations that have a sacred significance, such as the water holes from which ancestors are thought to have emerged in Australia. Thus, the constitutive symbolism gives meaning to the components of the human condition in their salience to the group in question. It includes symbolism of organic life, as limited by birth and death; of the physical environment and the exigencies of living, including territory; of the social statuses of men and their involvements with reproduction and biological descent; and of the modes of social communication, especially through language. It is the original boundary structure between the cultural and social systems in primitive societies.

Symbolic Communication

Constitutive symbolism becomes engaged in social processes through its inclusion in a more comprehensive system of communicative codes, at once normative and operative. This system contains rules regulating the interactions of people in such situations as marriages, intergenerational relations, subsistence technology, and relations to sacred entities, in terms of the symbolic meanings of their social statuses. Language is crucial to this communication complex; it enables symbolically formulated information to be conveyed among persons. Along with the common meanings embodied in the constitutive symbolism, what brings a people together as a society is a common system of operative codes which regulate their communications with one another. Like the system of constitutive symbolism, such codes articulate with all the principal contexts of the human condition, technological, social, moral, religious, and so on. Within the societal system, there must be a code system which regulates the processes of communicating and acting on information specifically in terms of the *social statuses* of the actors involved. For example, within a given type of social situation people of a certain social status are to be believed or obeyed more than people of other statuses. Regulations of this type, when organized into ramified systems, allocate generalized properties of influence to the statuses—especially the high ones—within the society. In advanced societies, there is provision for the fulfillment of commitments, the exercise of power, and the expenditure of money under regulations that assure the structural independence of these processes from the use of influence. The system of regulations must be differentiated in these cases in order to link the various modes of social communication with the appropriate statuses and situations. In primitive societies, the generalized standards by which the codes are organized tend to be undifferentiated. The modes of communication are intertwined, can be exercised only in stereotyped fashion, and are controlled by exigencies of social solidarity. The code system is the law of a society, even the most primitive.[11] Among the components of primitive societies, it has reference to the internal maintenance of societal solidarity and is the farthest removed from the boundaries with the non-social subsystems of action.

Constitutive symbol systems and their associated codes order relations among the individuals and social groups that comprise a population. In the first instance, however, the population is established in terms of its kinship organization. At the mammalian level, the complex of biological reproduction, hence of filiation, socialization, and selection of those who will join in reproduction, constitutes the conditional focus of the *genesis* of solidary groups within the population of a species. But, to quote Durkheim, a *society* (especially a primitive one) constitutes "a moral community called a church"; the basis of *societal* solidarity is not primordial in the sense of inhering either *in* discrete kinship units or in biological principles of their organization. Only on a basis which morally integrates an extended, complex set of kinship units can a population take the step from primordial solidarity to societal solidarity.[12] In speaking of a kinship *system,* we use a concept with an essentially societal reference. However, in its general functioning, kinship is the boundary structure between the social and personality systems by virtue of its primordial involvements.

Technology

Physical skills, related to a cultural technology and the population's control of its physical environment, constitute the fourth basic component of primitive action systems, as they are institutionalized in a division of labor and patterns of cooperation and allocation of resources. In the economic situations within which they are most salient, skills structure the boundary between the society and the behavioral organism.

THE PRIMITIVE SOCIETY
OF ABORIGINAL AUSTRALIA

The societies of aboriginal Australia provide a good example of primitive societal organization, for they are among the most primitive societies known and have been studied by both field observers and theorists.

The social organization of the Australians can be described in terms

11. Cf. Marcel Mauss, *The Gift* (London: Cohen and West, 1954). Noam Chomsky, *Syntactic Structures* (The Hague: Moulton, 1953).

12. Emile Durkheim, *The Elementary Forms of the Religious Life* (London: Allen and Unwin, 1915); Cf. Rodney Needham, *Structure and Sentiment* (Chicago: University of Chicago Press, 1960.)

of the kinship system and its articulations with the totemic cults, the circulating rights and obligations of solidary relationships, and ways of controlling the environment.[13] The economy rests on hunting and the gathering of berries, roots, and certain edible insects. It requires that the bands (generally composed of patrilineal kin) range over considerable territory. The normative order has territorial references; within traditionally established areas, kin groups are conventionally entitled to hunt and gather food. However, considerable numbers of such independent bands get together for special ceremonial occasions. Not only is kinship central to the social organization, but there is little differentiation among kinship units;[14] no set of clans occupies a generally superior status, with special political authority, religious preferment, or access to wealth. Furthermore, kinship statuses are components of practically all social roles.

Given the incest taboo, kinship systems are organized on the double basis of descent and affinity (relationship established by marriage). The child is located in the society by his parentage—as is the case in all societies, with only a few exceptions. In primitive societies, such location is diffuse; practically all of an individual's privileges and obligations tend to be *prescribed* in terms of his kinship status, especially his affiliation with his kinship group. The major problem for such prescriptive systems arises from the fact that marriage, because of the incest taboo, involves relations with units outside the primary descent group. Nevertheless, marriage choice may be prescribed in terms of kinship categories; the descent group to which a person belongs may have institutionalized relations with other descent groups which prescribe the groups into which he (or she) may and may not marry.[15] The situation contrasts with modern societies in which all opposite-sex members are eligible for marriage except limited categories of close relatives.

In such primitive systems, the *whole society* constitutes a single *affinal collectivity* composed of descent groups allied through the marriages of their members. Descent and marriage are so linked that those who belong in specific descent groups not only can but *must* marry persons belonging to specific other descent groups. Hence the society consists of an intricate network of groupings composed by variations on the themes of descent, sex, and age-grouping. These groupings are interrelated by the principle of cross-cousin marriage. This defines the marriage obligation in a way which makes eligible the closest same generation relative outside the nuclear family and descent group of birth. The prescriptive

13. Levi-Strauss, *op. cit.*

14. Warner, *op. cit.*, chap. I.

15. Claude Levi-Strauss, *Les Structures Elèmentaires de La Parentè* (Paris: Presses Universitaires 1949); Needham, *op. cit.*

rules, operating along generation lines, establish the categorical equivalence of same-sex generation-mates of a descent group. In terms of the
structure of the kinship system, it seems not to matter which person is
chosen as a marriage partner so long as he or she falls in the proper
kinship category—a category which equally includes all the collaterals
from the proper type of first cousin outward to more distant relatives,
even though anthropologists commonly call it by the type of first cousin
involved.[16] These systems involve a complex geometry of marriage and
descent groups, the analysis of which has generated controversy among
anthropologists.[17] The underlying principle is prescription of marriage
by kinship category. Though specific systems may vary with differing
conditions, the general *kind* of system is a direct outcome of this
principle.[18]

Certain societies exhibit an interesting consequence of such categorization of marriage precription. While the inside limit of eligibility is
defined by the prohibition on brother-sister marriage, the outside boundary may be left undefined. Although the whole society constitutes an
affinal collectivity, there is sometimes no precise way of defining who are
members of the societal community on the outer fringes of the kinship
network. For example, all fellow-Murngin are relatives, but from any
band-centered perspective, the boundary between Murngin and non-
Murngin is unclear. Furthermore, this kinship unboundedness seems to
apply to religion and the communicative code system. There are bases,
especially territorial and religious, on which the seamless web of particularistic kinship and totemic ties becomes so attenuated that relationships
are no longer effective. However, the aborigines have foregone clarity of
societal boundedness as a feature of their adaptation to the Australian
environment and their situation of being surrounded by groups quite
similar in cultural and social characteristics. Such unboundedness is not
characteristic of all primitive societies—all have scant capacity to ensure
their boundaries (e.g., against invasion), but only some of them seem to
institutionalize positive unboundedness. Yet no society could attain the

---

16. *Ibid.*

17. *Ibid.* Cf. Edmund Leach, "The Structural Implications of Matrilateral Cross-
Cousin Marriage," in his *Rethinking Anthropology* (London: Athlone Press, 1961).

18. The structural intricacy of Australian kinship systems seems to conflict with the
assertion that Australian society is undifferentiated. However, our proposition relates
to the differentiation of other functional categories of social structure *from* the
kinship nexus—e.g., political, economic, legal, religious. This is a different problem
from that of the internal differentiation of any one of these sub-systems of a society.
The pattern of the isolated nuclear family in modern societies reduces the complexity
of the kinship system relative to primitive cases. However, this increases the differentiation from the kinship system of the other sectors of the society and makes
possible their integration in terms of a more generalized societal code and underlying cultural system.

advanced primitive level of societal evolution without developing bound-edness. Thus, a lack of boundedness is a mark of a society's primitiveness. The rigidity of prescription so striking in Australian kinship involves the brittleness of the institutional safeguards against reversion to sub-human levels of motivational organization. Such reversion would affect the maintenance of a solidary societal community. The focus is the problem of incest and these societies' elaboration of precautions against incestuous marriages.[19]

Aboriginal Australian economic organization is simple, consisting of hunting and food gathering in a difficult environment. It is ascribed to the kinship system; one performs specific technological-economic functions by virtue of one's kinship status, including sex. Along with technological measures, such as control of fire and the production and use of simple tools, the distinctively human character of these societies, as compared to primate groups, includes the *flexible social organization* of technological-economic function: institutionalization of division of labor (notably be-tween the sexes), cooperative organization of activities (as in hunting), and allocation of resources among specified kin groups.[20] Perhaps closer analogies with sub-human groups exist in the technological-economic sphere than in the others, but technological-economic integration with kinship, religion, and the communication codes is an unmistakably human breakthrough.

Durkheim documented the pan-religionism of primitive societies. Despite the distinctiveness of the profane aspect of activities, a primitive society is permeated with religious sentiments and activities. This includes not only religio-magical belief systems and ritual activities, but also the emotional excitement which pervades so much of the religious sphere.[21] Durkheim spoke of the *order of sacred* things in Australian society. Like kinship, it is prominent and elaborately structured. This elaboration apparently relates to the prescriptiveness of the socio-cultural system and is evident in the sacred order's ties to the kinship system. There are no independent cults which attract a clientele from a variety of kinship units. Rather, the significance of the *totemistic* components of the sacred conceptual order itself and of the actual organization of ritual perform-ances is that the totems are connected to clans as kinship units.[22] Fur-thermore, the totemic references are so formed as to symbolize the inte-

19. Talcott Parsons, "The Incest Taboo in Relation to Social Structure and the Socialization of the Child," in *Social Structure and Personality, op. cit.* Levi-Strauss, *Les Structures . . . , op. cit.;* also see chap. XV in Levi-Strauss' *Structural Anthropolgy* (New York: Basic Books, 1963).

20. Cf. Warner, *op. cit.*, chap. V.

21. Durkheim, *op cit.*

22. *Ibid;* Levi-Strauss, *Totemism, op. cit., passim.*

gration of the social unit within the total order of the human condition, since the totem is usually an animal species and thus sub-human as well as supra-human by virtue of being a sacred entity.[23]

Besides the totems, sacred things are significant at the tribal level. These figure in the origin myths that explain who the people are and how they came to be what they are. Again, they are directly integrated with the social structure. Wollunqua, in one aspect, symbolizes the corporate body of adult males who constitute the tribe, so far as this exists, not just a clan.[24] The Wawilak sisters symbolize, among other things, both the boys, who are absorbed into this corporate group through initiation, and the women, who are not initiated and remain permanently outside it. The story that Wollunqua "swallows" the sisters seems to involve *both* these symbolizations. Wollunqua is also related to certain conditions of the physical environment, especially the seasonal cycle which has contrasting rainy and dry seasons in that part of Australia. The incest theme is also in the Wollunqua-Wawilak myth. The mythical founders are thought to have committed incest—indeed living men are all, sufficiently far back, the product of incestuous unions. However, the *differentiation* of human society into organized kinship units precluded the continuation of this practice in both myth and actuality.

The religious ceremonials constitute a direct, dramatic acting out of the mythical beliefs in narrative form.[25] In Murngin tribal initiation ceremonies, the adult men, as a corporate group, play the part of the serpent Wollunqua, ceremonially swallowing the initiates—i.e., admitting them to membership. The adult man directly *participates* in the world of the sacred by playing the part of a sacred being. He actually *becomes* part of the totem or Wollunqua. This does not mean that the sacred beings are reduced to the status of secular social units, clan, or tribe. It means that *the statuses of sacred object and secular social unit have not been differentiated.*[26] A primitive institutional system must successfully

23. Later, we will see, especially in Egypt, that the religious use of animal symbolism is not confined to primitive societies, but extends well into the intermediate category. We may re-emphasize here that it is the diffuseness of the references in the sacred order and their structural correspondence to the social order, not the totemism *per se*, that seems to be the universal among very primitive societies. Cf. Levi-Strauss, *Totemism, op. cit.* and *Structural Anthropology, op. cit.*; also Leach, *Rethinking Anthropology, op. cit.*

24. *Warner, op cit.,* chap. IX, discusses the myth of Yurlunggur or Wollunqua and the Wawilak sisters, the central myth in many Australian systems of constitutive symbolism.

25. Cf. W. E. H. Stanner, *On Aboriginal Religion* (Melbourne: Oceania Monographs #11, 1964).

26. This proposition applies to the sacred object as a cultural object (part of a cultural system). The object is not itself "ultimate reality" but a "representation" of it, a term which Durkheim himself used.

consolidate all the organizational elements of a society at the cultural-symbolic level. Ritual generally includes a controlled permissiveness regarding behavior, beliefs, emotions, and so on, which are more regressive psychologically than those symbolically controlled by the ritual. The Australian case offers two examples. Participating in ritual, men *behave* as sub-human animals; they take the role of the totem species or the tribal serpent. Also, it is prescribed that they ceremonially do what is otherwise forbidden—namely, have sexual relations with members of categories of kin with whom marriage and sexual intercourse are forbidden as incestuous. However, this permissiveness, far from leading to reversion to precultural levels, serves as a mechanism for reinforcing commitments to maintain the cultural patterns.

Magic is understandable in this context. Religious beliefs and ritual practices are integrated with the social structure through common commitments (in the form of prescribed relational patterns) to either the largest significant collectivity or its segmental units—e.g., the clans. They promote the type of societal integration that Durkheim called mechanical solidarity. Magic is the ritualization of interests and activities which cannot be fitted into this framework, interests individualized in Durkheim's sense.[27] This is evident in regard to utilitarian problems of technology. In hunting, finding food, and (for peoples having settled agriculture) gardening, magic is a supplementary technique that ensures success.[28] It mobilizes supernatural forces from the realm of the sacred in favor of particular objectives but without mobilizing the collective solidarity of the community in the sense that religious ritual does. From such technological contexts, magic extends into areas, such as health, that involve integrative concerns. Illness is, from one point of view, the lapse of the sick person from his status as a fully integrated member of the relevant collectivities. Magical means help restore him to full functioning and are common throughout the primitive world. Black magic is the obverse; it is a primitive means, other than physical force, for exerting upon individuals the sanction of punishment or exclusion for deviant action. Magic's involvement with warfare and other forms of violence fits within the same paradigm. As Warner shows, warfare among clans is the most serious threat to the integration of Murngin society. When directed against presumptive enemies, warfare magic reinforces the internal solidarity of the warring group in order to promote its success but does not involve a set of ritual obligations held in common with the enemies. Internally (e.g., at the clan level), it may be effective both in promoting the clan interest and in minimizing the intervention of higher-order col-

27. Durkheim, *The Division of Labor in Society, op. cit.*

28. Cf. Bronislaw Malinowski, *Magic, Science and Religion* (Glencoe, Ill.: Free Press, 1948); and *Coral Gardens and Their Magic* (New York: American, 1935).

lectivities in the clan.[29] Such cases of magic fit the general framework of mechanisms furthering organic solidarity.

The functioning of any society, particularly a primitive one, requires the institutionalization of common normative codes, which contain rules for ordering the communicative aspects of social activities. In a society like the Murngin, the societal code system may be a less salient structure than kinship, religion, or technology—yet it is the cement that binds them all together.

Prescriptiveness[30] is characteristic of the undifferentiated Australian normative codes. Australian societies have a proliferation of kinship groupings, but these operate upon the individual's status-ascription so diffusely that he has a minimum of choices. Although individuals engage in a variety of concrete acts—e.g., technological work, religious and magical ritual activities, recreation, and so on—they do not perform these different classes of acts *in differentiated roles* in the sense true of individuals in more developed societies. Life in such a society is "a one-possibility thing" for the individual.[31] The relations among the various categories of acts which individuals perform are prescribed in terms of an undifferentiated intra-societal code. For example, all rules for hunting apply to the major elements of status in the society, especially sex, generational age, and kinship status. Once a kill is made, the normative order prescribes the way in which it should be distributed with reference to the same elements of status. The same elements also enter into the prescription of the ritual uses to be made of the hunt's proceeds, the persons to participate in the ritual activities, and the ways in which they will participate.

These facts consitute the core of the undifferentiatedness of Australian society. It embodies elementary differentiation of function by sex and age. By virtue of the latter, elders have more authority than their juniors, and there is a status distinction between uninitiated boys and initiated men. These bases of differentiation enter into the composition of the nuclear family, into its functions, economic and technological as well as socializing, and into the changes in family memberships at different stages of the life cycle. Beyond this, the society consists of *segments* distinguished from one another and bound together by the prescriptive rules and the practices they regulate, especially those pertaining to marriage alliances. The normative order is couched at a low level of

---

29. Warner, *op. cit.*

30. This use of the term "prescription" is an effort to build upon and generalize from Needham's and other anthropologists' usage. See Needham, *Structure and Sentiment, op. cit.*

31. W. E. H. Stanner, "The Dreaming," in William Lessa and Evon Z. Vogt (eds.), *Reader in Comparative Religion* (Evanston, Ill.: Row, Peterson, 1958).

generalization, though one compatible with the maintenance of cultural control over the relevant action process. Value patterns have to legitimize a role structure differentiated only by age and sex and by loyalties to four orders of collectivity—namely, nuclear family, lineage, clan, and the vaguely defined tribes. With the exception of in-marrying spouses, these membership loyalties are concentric, with the innermost implying the others, much as residence in American society implies belonging in a local community, a state, and the federal Union. The status of in-marrying persons is the only possibility for role-conflict[32] and is the most likely point for developmental change to take hold. Despite the rigidity of the prescriptive system, a look at this type of society reveals possible sources of instability and structual change.

THE TRANSITION
TO THE ADVANCED PRIMITIVE TYPE[33]

In the Australian societies, the core of the societal community is the affinal system regulated by prescriptive marriage rules. This complex of norms binds the segmentary lineages and clans together into a society, though not a sharply bounded one. I would expect structural change to become evident at this point, whatever its causes. A source of change arises when the status equivalence of the intermarrying kinship groups breaks down. A given group may attempt to improve its position for controlling resources by exercising preferences in giving or receiving spouses through establishing special relations with particular subgroups *within* the categories of prescribed affinal groups. That is, marriage alliances come to be made with a view to the advantages which the affinal groups may be able to bestow upon one another and hence involve an element of bargaining that cannot arise in purely prescriptive systems. Here, the potential for evolutionary advance depends upon the degree to which generalized grounds of status differentiation are institutionalized and are able to influence the preferences.

For evolutionary changes to emerge, these developments must be

---

32. *Warner, op. cit.,* chap. VI.

33. Because of limitations of space, the following section cannot follow through the processes of transition it surveys in terms of specific illustrative examples. It is more in the nature of an ideal-type construction than either the preceding section on Australian aboriginal society or the final section on the advanced primitive societies. Its purpose is to fill the gap so as to make the connection between the two stage-types comprehensible. It does not present a comprehensive analysis of any of the large number of societies that fall within this gap.

complemented by a generalization in the solidarity of the clan so that common identities prevent the more advantaged lineages from asserting themselves as independent clans. A lineage in one clan may develop special solidarity with a lineage in the prescribed alliance clan and effectively exercise systematic preferences for that lineage in choosing its spouses. In such transitional systems, the pattern of the circulation of spouses and of the alliance solidarities is the result of *both* prescriptive cycling and preferential subcycling.[34] However, the evolutionary tendency is toward the attenuation of the developmentally restrictive prescriptive regulations, which favor the generalized equality of categorical collaterals. Economic pressures may support this tendency. Australian conditions limit the manageable size of a band, and the band must enjoy autonomy from others in the clan. Settled residence, conditioned by agriculture and/or the use of domestic animals, tends to increase these pressures. Instead of vague rights to hunting and gathering in a large territory, specific kinship groups may come to hold more clear-cut *property* rights, often to the *exclusive* use of land tracts for cultivation and/or pasturing. The attendant economic advances may cause an increase in population, thus enhancing the pressure to lineage-segmentation. Furthermore, advances in economic organization and the crystallization of property rights increase the lineage's stake in effective control of territory and hence in the clarity of community and societal boundaries.[35]

If residence and utilization of land is to be stable, the predominant emphasis in defining the community must shift from the affinal aspect of kinship to independent territorial factors. To a new degree, the societal community must become endogamous in its *external* relations. Internally, however, it is problematic whether lineage segmentation will lead to status *differentiation* among lineages, rather than to multiplication of structually identical units. Some occupational specialization tends to emerge with these developments, although it does not become a primary basis of social differentiation until later in societal evolution. Within limits, certain lineages may differentiate themselves from others by undertaking specialized functions or controlling special resources. The most important of these involve trade, especially vis-à-vis the outside; warfare;

34. Needham, *op. cit.*; Leach, *op. cit.*; also *The Political Systems of Highland Burma* (Boston: Beacon Paperbacks, 1964); Jack Goody (ed.), *Developmental Cycles of Domestic Groups* (Cambridge: Cambridge Papers in Social Anthropology, 1958), especially Leach's chapter, "Concerning Trobriand Clans and the Kinship Category Tabu."

35. Cf. Meyer Fortes and E. E. Evans-Pritchard (eds.), *African Political Systems* (Oxford: Oxford University Press, 1940); I. Schapera, *Government and Politics in Tribal Societies* (London: Watts, 1956).

and special religious functions, such as the custodianship of sacred places.[36]

On the whole, the main line of growth for the primitive type of society involves not only such particular specializations but the differentiation of lineages on a generalized axis of prestige, advantage, and responsibility. Why is the lineage the crucial unit of differentiation? Perhaps because smaller kinship units—e.g., nuclear family, joint family, cognatic household, and so on, are too embedded in the articulations between the obligations of descent and affinity. It is unlikely that their members can sufficiently control their marriages—i.e., heads of the lineage or village, not just the parents, control the marriages of children; institutionalized control by the children themselves evolves only *much* later. In most cases some variant of the lineage type of organization serves as the society's *primary* agent of differentiation. It is strong enough to control the smaller kin units and to assure them sufficiently favorable marriage terms, unless it is on the downgrade itself. Also, it is not the main responsible guarantor of the traditional system, as the clan is.

Two forces support the emergence of differentiation among lineages. One—familiar in our traditions of social thought—is the tendency to differential advantage, property in land being its characteristic vehicle. Positions which are advantageous, whether by virtue of productivity, centrality of location or other factors, tend to be systematically preempted. Especially during periods of segmentation and population growth, the less advantaged lineages tend to be forced into inferior locations and to be deprived of resources. Despite the variety of bases of such advantage, it is difficult to maintain the egalitarianism presupposed by any system of the equivalence of clan collaterals once there are firm institutions of property. The other basis of differentiation arises from the growth in importance of the *societal* collectivity, including its tendency to become more definitely bounded. This involves the increased salience of its religious grounds of legitimation, of its territorial controls over its resource base, and of the common identity of its population. Hence, there is pressure to *symbolize* the collective identity of the society more explicitly and also to develop more effective instrumentalities for its functioning as a system, especially in governmental contexts.

The revelance of land and the territorial ordering of society, both in terms of external boundaries and internal land distributions, results from the importance of the physical world among the factors *conditioning* social action. Society-wide prestige and its relation to political leadership and the assumption of collective responsibilities generates leverage to *control* the conditioning factors. Furthermore, no ramified process of societal differentiation can consolidate itself unless the upper groups

---

36. Raymond Firth, *Primitive Polynesian Economy* (London: Routledge, 1939).

acquire generalized religious legitimation from the constitutive symbol system of the society as well as instrumentalities of power as such.[37] It is not crucial to assign priority to one or the other of the above factors. If different groups press their particular interests too fast and neglect the development of integrating factors, particularly religious legitimation, the society will break up, the relatively nonfavored elements seceding to form independent societies. If cultural or political centralization advances too far and if adequate bases of kinship and of economic-political member-ship units are not developed, the new level of cultural and political organ-ization cannot be maintained.

Thus, the most likely evolutionary development is a *stratified* society. There are degrees of stratification, but to emerge significantly a stratified society must break with the egalitarianism of a prescriptive affinal system based upon the equivalence of all same-category collaterals. Lineage units will tend to exchange spouses on a basis of *advantage*, high-prestige units allying themselves with other high-prestige units.[38] The high-prestige units become the focus of new elements of solidarity within the societal collectivity, elements which are likely to be at once political and religious, with varying emphases as between these two components. These develop-ments tend to become embedded in the kinship structure itself, involving the hierarchical principles that often inhere in lineage organization—e.g., seniority on the basis of generation status. The emergence of strati-fication tends to culminate in the elevation of a single lineage to privi-leged rank and perhaps of its senior member to a top authority and prestige position. That is, a tendency exists for the emergence of monarchy having both political and religious foundations. The basis of community must become redefinable to include the patterns of class and preferential marriage. The societal community comes to be conceived as an ethnic-territorial group. If descent is traced back far enough, all of its members are believed to be descended from common ancestors. But this com-prehensive descent-community is *not* backed by systematic intermarriage patterns that pervade the whole society. Common descent is likely to be associated with common culture in various ways—e.g., language, but especially religion. Furthermore, the emergence of differentiated political authority places a premium on the territorial aspects of community

---

37. There is a case which might seem to be an exception to this statement: namely, that in which a group subordinates another group by military conquest. This is not differentiation in the present sense. It has played an important part in process of social change, but usually the conquerors are a foreign group, not a structural segment of the original society. Furthermore, it is a limiting case when such a group eschews claim to religious legitimation and operates in terms of its naked self-interest alone.

38. Charles D. Ackerman, "Three Studies of Affinal Collectivity" (Ph.D. thesis, Harvard University, 1965); Leach, *Political Systems of Highland Burma, op. cit.*

solidarity. In short, the societal collectivity becomes a *tribe,* an ethnic group maintaining jurisdiction over a territorial area.

Once this transition has taken place, it becomes less possible to maintain the primitive coincidence between kinship status and residential location. The shift from prescription to preference is associated with increases in mobility and opportunities for dominance-dependency relations, Hence, the territorial sub-units of the society, from broad regions down to villages, tend to shift from uniformity toward pluralism and diversity. This is accentuated as stratification evolves to the point of monarchy, which involves a central seat of authority and prestige. Diverse elements are attracted to such a seat, either permanently or temporarily. Moreover, the principles for selecting the population of such a capital can hardly be confined to kinship terms.

An ethnic-territorial societal community requires a new, more generalized basis of legitimation both for its authority system and for the identity of the community itself. It is no longer a seamless web of kinship relations in which the primary units (e.g., clans) in principle are equivalent to one another. It is a system which has become *differentiated,* first by the varying statuses of its lineage units and then between kinship and non-kinship (e.g., region of residence) bases of status. This requires the institutionalization of more generalized constitutive definitions of who "we" are and of the natures of the diverse units included in the "we-ness." Kinship and locality units are independently variable, and a prestige scale interrelating both must be institutionalized—e.g., the lower-class resident of the capital community still enjoys a certain prestige as compared with the higher-class provincial.[39] Furthermore, the religious tradition is differentiated into elements associated with the societal leadership institutionalized in the upper groups (particularly the royal lineage) and elements which are particular to the local, parochial communities and kinship groups. Thus, the class dimension involves differential access to the *higher* elements of a new, more differentiated sacred order.[40]

In the most primitive societies, the societal community is based on affinal solidarities. The general processes of differentiation introduce a second axis into the community structure—which can be controlled by more complex integrative mechanisms. Territoriality bounds the community externally and grounds the institution of property in relation to territorial location (i.e., property in land) internally. Residential location and control of economic resources become *independent* of kinship; the operative unit—a lineage at some level—has *two* independent bases for its position in the system, kinship and property. Significant exchange

39. S. F. Nadel, *A Black Byzantium* (Oxford: Oxford University Press, 1951).

40. Daryll Forde (ed.), *African Worlds* (Oxford: Oxford University Press, 1954).

transactions are exchanges of spouses, directly or indirectly, in a circuit. As a consequence of differentiation, spouses come to be exchangeable for prestige and/or property advantage and vice-versa. Position in the system of stratification is the *resultant* of the interplay of two media of circulating valuables. In understanding this interplay, we must recognize that a marriage is a large, relatively infrequent unit of commitment for a small kinship group; to give a daughter or son to another group is a major expenditure of mobile resources. Similarly, the transfer of proprietorship in land-holdings is a transaction that can occur but seldom. What a marriage does is commit the wife-giving and wife-receiving units to continuing exchanges of valuable objects, starting possibly with a bride-price. These are usually balanced to compensate the wife- or husband-giving groups for its resource expenditure, although status differentials frequently complicate the exchange relations.

Property, at this level of evolution, is *not* a differentiated economic category but involves components of diffuse influence or prestige and political authority or power as well as control of economic resources. In some cases, the territorial involvements of landed property may make lineages practically into sovereignities within the larger tribal community. Thus, lineage is like a state within a federal nation, but is integrated into the larger system by informal mechanisms, particularly the interchange of spouses and the benefits of its diffuse property statuses. The components of the property complex are institutionally bound together in much the same way as the components of the primitive institutional codes. It does permit considerable variability in concrete action in addition to that deriving from the basic independence between the complexes of affinal and property relationships. The types of advanced primitive societies differ with the relative weight of the independent components of the property complex, the religio-cultural, the political, and the economic, as well as with the degree of differentiation between the affinal-kinship and property complexes. Hence, there is no neatly uniform, universal type.

In stratified cases, the royal lineages, which may become both large and compactly organized through the practice of polygyny, tend to acquire tight control of the more mobile economic and political resources throughout the society, largely by arranging politically shrewd marriage alliances. This seems to be an indispensable condition of such a royal lineage's capacity to discharge its responsibilities on behalf of the tribe as a whole. These responsibilities may include religious rituals, relatively secular ceremonials enhancing societal solidarity, the management of the political bureaucracy and the military organization, and the like. Stratification is the institution which makes possible an increase in the centralization of societal responsibility and, with it, collective effectiveness. At this evolutionary level, high status does not rest mainly on superior control of political power or economic resources. It makes possible the institutionalized concentration of such control which underlies such superiority itself.

Ultimately, two bases of prestige are crucial to the capacities of highly superior royal lineages to exploit their positions in the community, particularly its kinship structuring. First is the central role of the royal lineage in the more generalized religious system, a system which can legitimize a more differentiated and larger-scale society. Second is the freeing of resources from the ascription to kinship characteristic of primitive societies. The emergence of property in land as a structually independent element greatly enhances resource mobility. This mobility requires the establishment of equivalences in the input-output interchanges between lineage units—e.g., as regards the relative values of marital alliances and proprietary controls. It is prestige level in the stratification system that establishes the price at which such components can be interchanged. Institutional mechanisms for the flexible determination of this prestige element comprise a requisite of the advanced type of primitive society.

TYPES OF ADVANCED PRIMITIVE SOCIETIES

To conclude this chapter, consider the more advanced primitive societies, such as the African kingdoms, which present variety and have been thoroughly studied, mainly by British anthropologists.[41] Unlike the Austalian type, all advanced primitive societies are characterized by stratification and by some kind of central political organization based upon secure territorial boundaries. Furthermore, the political element involves a fusion political and religious components, which are relatively undifferentiated at this stage of evolution. There can exist, however, different emphases between the religious and political aspects, and this comprises the axis of variation.

An example of a people who have developed a monarchical institution with a paramount *religious* emphasis is the Shilluk of the upper-Nile Sudan. Established among the Shilluk is a divine kingship that is interesting because of its resemblance to the ancient Egyptian system and of the Sudan's proximity to Egypt. The Shilluk society is segmented, which is perhaps attributable to the fact that it is strung out along the east bank of the Nile.[42] There is also an institutional division between the northern

41. Most comprehensively reported in *African Political Systems,* edited by Fortes and Evans-Pritchard, *op. cit.,* and in Schapera, *op. cit.* I have also relied upon Evans-Pritchard's account of the Shilluk in his *Essays in Social Anthropology* (London: Faber and Faber, 1962); and on Nadel's account of the Nupe in his *Black Byzantium, op. cit.*

42. The neighboring Dinka and Nuer are similarly segmented, but lack a monarchical institution and are thus less advanced in our terms. Cf. E. E. Evans-Pritchard, *The Nuer* (Oxford: Clarendon Press, 1940).

and southern sectors of the society. Significantly, the capital and seat of the monarchy, Fashoda, is situated on the line between north and south, and the chiefs of the two sections help select new kings. The Shilluk upper class consists of descendants of former kings. By a variety of arrangements, their residences are dispersed throughout the territory, not concentrated in or near the capital. In part, this is a consequence of the matrilineal kinship system, but there is also a specific rule that princes (i.e., sons of a king's wife) should be brought up in the mother's natal community and never in the capital. The local chieftans reside side by side with the parochial lineage groups, a status shared by clans of royal retainers. They are not generally members of the royal lineage, but are heads of the local lineages. Moreover, they are nominated for their positions by their own lineages, not by royal appointment, though some kind of royal consent is customary. They do not constitute an administrative apparatus of the central government.

The royal institution is structured about the divinity of the king.[43] The current king is not only the heir but the incarnation of the divine mythical founder, Nyikang, who is the basis of the identity of the Shilluk as a people. When a king dies, Nyikang becomes incarnated in an effigy kept in his principal provincial shrine in the northern sector. About a year later, the effigy is ceremonially reincarnated in the king-elect, who is not only legitimized by Nyikang, but *becomes* Nyikang. The ritual procedures of the investiture stress not only the divinity of the king, but also his function in integrating the principal components of the society. He is nominated by the two chiefs of the northern and southern sectors, who *must* concur. Then representatives of all the main structual segments must ritually assent to the nomination. Shilluk religion represents a further generalization of the more primitive type of ritual order. The function of implementing the sacred traditions is centered in the royal lineage and upper class, particularly the institution of kingship.

Among the Shilluk, the integrative aspects of kingship have emerged without marked development of the more administrative and politically activistic aspects. They are settled and do have a higher-order economy than the Australians. Yet they conduct warfare by mobilizing their independent lineage units, not by virtue of the king's invoking standing military obligations that cross-cut the lineage structure and are at his disposal.

These structures constitute an early stage in the development of a type of society significant in subsequent societal evolution. This type rests on the integration of larger solidary structures through the association of basically equal sub-components. Only after further evolution can such components be individuals; in the earlier stages, they are always kinship

---

43. See Godfrey Lienhardt, "The Shilluk of The Upper Nile," in Forde (ed.), *African Worlds, op. cit.,* as well as the Evans-Pritchard essay noted above.

groups, generally lineages. The Shilluk divine kingship provides a sacred umbrella under which the segmental units can be consolidated into an associative structure, their divisive tendencies checked, and a positive solidarity developed. In a pattern similar to the Shilluk confederation of tribal units, ancient lineages associated to form more advanced societal structures of the small-scale *polis* type throughout the eastern Mediterranean and Mesopotamian regions.

The second principal type of advanced primitive societies is represented by a number of examples described in the *African Political Systems* symposium. In this type, the *political* component of the diffuse leadership institutions hold primacy over the religious component. The monarchical institutions are important to the differentiation of the upper class and institutionalize a diffuse precedence of societal solidarity over the interests of segmental units. A characteristic of this societal type is the development of a royal administrative apparatus which can be considered a government—which exists only in rudimentary form among the Shilluk. Fortes and Evans-Pritchard[44] emphasize *centralized* command of force in bringing this about. A factor here is the development of a military apparatus for conducting wars against outside societies with the line between defense and aggressive conquest or raiding being rather indefinite, as it frequently is in the history of warfare. Equally important is the use of the military to maintain internal order, especially to counteract the tendencies toward disolution and rebellion endemic in these societies. Significantly, *all* of them have histories of continual disorder, including frequent contests of the kingship among different branches of the royal line and different segmental groups. Perhaps the Zulu kingdom at its height was the extreme example of the tendency to militarization within societies of this type.[45]

However important the military factor and however great the possibilities for tyranny, the religious status of the monarchical institution and the authority system have been as crucial in this type as in the first. The uses of authority by the king and upper groups represent the collective interest of the tribe, as legitimized in the religious tradition. Compared to other primitive societal types, the religious tradition has usually been developed to a higher level of generality, particularly with respect to the divinities which concern the tribe as a whole, to the accentuated theme of the descent of the entire tribe from ancestors of an heroic past, and to the conception of the founder-king as the fountainhead of

44. Fortes and Evans-Pritchard (eds.), "Introduction" to *African Political Systems, op. cit.*

45. Cf. Max Gluckman, "The Kingdom of the Zulu of South Africa," in Fortes and Evans-Pritchard (eds.), *op. cit.*

socio-economic order and benefits.[46] Africa has been an area of pronounced mobility, and many contemporary kingdoms were founded sufficiently recently so that the successions of monarchs from the founders to the present rulers is traced circumstantially and maintained as tradition. That is, these societies have a history in a sense not true for the primitive Australian.

A characteristic of this type of society is the development of civil administrative systems differentiated from both military and religious organizations. The connection between the central administration and the chieftainships of regional and local lineage groups is a structural problem in these societies. Unlike the Shilluk, there is a tendency for local administrators to be appointed by the central authority. Moreover, they tend to develop powers of taxation, administration of justice, and the like, which are only partially controlled by the local groups. The central authorities of all these societies develop institutions for regulating the administration of justice—i.e., for ensuring that cases are treated in accordance with the accepted norms of the *central* tradition.[47]

Both military and civil bureaucracies of these types are points from which institutions can become increasingly differentiated from the kinship nexus. However, the political focus as distinguished from the religious focus tends to generate hierarchy. This inhibits the development both of associational solidarities independent of line authority and of unit autonomy that is more economic than political. A case of modest development toward the more political advanced primitive type is the Bemba tribe described by Audrey Richards.[48] The Nupe[49] approach, under Islamic influence, the borderline between a primitive society and an archaic one. It approaches what Weber called a patrimonial monarchy, having extensive administrative bureaucracy, organized handicrafts, controlled trade, and even the beginnings of a monetary system.

CONCLUSION

In this study of societies I shall be guided both by an evolutionary and by a comparative perspective. These perspectives conceive of man as integral to the organic world and of human society and culture as properly

---

46. Several chapters in Forde (ed.), *op. cit.*, are quite clear in these connections, perhaps especially "The Fon of Dahomey" by P. Mercier.

47. *Cf.* Schapera, *op. cit.*

48. Audrey Richards, "The Political System of the Bemba Tribe—North-Eastern Rhodesia," in Fortes and Evans-Pritchard (eds.), *op. cit.*

49. Nadel, *A Black Byzantium, op. cit.*

analyzed in the general framework appropriate to the life process. The principle of evolution is established as applying to the world of living things, and the social aspect of human life must be included. Such basic concepts of organic evolution as variation, selection, adaptation, differentiation, and integration are our concern—appropriately adjusted to social and cultural subject matter.

This chapter was concerned with primitive societies and the beginning of their long evolution toward modernity. Let me hasten to confess that, although I assume an evolutionary progression, I have no explanation for the emergence of primitive societies from primordial subhuman forms. I begin with primitive societies because, once the symbolic level of behavior was achieved by *homo sapiens,* a more rudimentary social organization was inconceivable. I confess further that I am able to say little about the detailed sequence of events in the course of which primitive socities begin their differentiation into more stratified societies. What I do say is that, given the pressure to adapt more successfully to its physical, biological, cultural, social, and psychological environments, a primitive society tends to develop a stratification system. Social differentiation is not inevitable, but if evolution occurs at all, it occurs through a process of differentiation.

However, differentiation does not occur alone. Differentiation is one of *four* main types of structural change which, interacting together, constitute progressive evolution to higher system levels. The other three processes are adaptive upgrading, inclusion, and value generalization (in application to societies).

Differentiation is the division of a unit in a society into two or more units that differ in their characteristics and functional significance for the system. To take a familiar example, the kinship-organized household in peasant societies is *both* the unit of residence and the unit of agricultural production. In certain societies, most productive work is performed in specialized units, such as workshops, factories, or offices manned by people who are *also* members of family households. Thus two sets of roles and collectivities have become differentiated and their functions separated. There must also be some differentiation at the level of norms and some specification of common value patterns appropriate for the different situations. If differentiation is to yield a more evolved system, each newly differentiated sub-structure (e.g., the producing organization in the above case) must have increased adaptive capacity for performing its *primary* function as compared to the performance of *that* function in the previous, more diffuse structure. Thus economic production is typically more efficient in factories than in households. This is the *adaptive upgrading* aspect of the evolutionary change. It applies to role and collectivity levels; the participating people, as well as the collectivity as a whole, become more productive than before as measured by some kind of output-cost relationship. These changes do not imply that the older residual unit will have lost function in all contexts of its operations. The household is no longer an important economic producer, but it may well perform its other functions better than in its earlier form.

Differentiation also poses new problems of *integration* for the system. The operations of two structural units must be coordinated where only one category existed before. Thus, in employment-occupational systems, the father of the household can no longer supervise production *in his kinship role*. Therefore, the producing organization must develop an authority system *not* embedded in kinship, and the producing and household collectivities must be coordinated within the broader system— e.g., through changes in the structure of the local community. Adaptive upgrading thus requires that specialized functional capacities be freed from ascription within more diffuse structural units. There is a reliance upon more *generalized* resources independent of their ascriptive sources. For these reasons, differentiation and upgrading processes require the *inclusion* in a status of full membership in the relevant community system of previously excluded groups which have developed legitimate capacities to contribute to the functioning of the system. The most common case concerns systems which have been divided into superior and inferior classes and in which the upper class has monopolized the status of real membership, treating the lower class, so far as it is conceived to belong at all, as a second-class citizenry. The processes of differentiation and upgrading make it difficult to maintain such dichotomies. Differentiation is especially likely to produce cases in which the necessities for integrating new sub-systems require including previously excluded elements.

The final component of the change process pertains to its relation to the value system of the society. Any value system, when institutionalized, establishes the desirability of a *general type of society*. By specification, such a general valuation is spelled out in its implications for differentiated sub-systems and various segmental units. Hence the value orientation appropriate to a particular collectivity, role, or norm-complex is not the general pattern of the system but a specialized application of it. A society undergoing a process of differentiation encounters the opposite problem from specification: the establishment of a version of the value pattern appropriate to the new *type* of system that is emerging. Since this type is more complex than its predecessor, its value pattern must be couched at a higher level of *generality* in order to legitimize the wider variety of goals and functions of its sub-units. The process of generalization often encounters resistance because commitment to the value pattern is interpreted by some groups as commitment to its particular content at the previous, lower level of generality. Such resistance may be called "fundamentalism." To the fundamenalist, the demand for greater generality in evaluative standards appear to be a demand to abandon the *real* commitments. Severe conflicts often crystallize about such issues.[50]

The state of any society and of a system of related societies is a resultant of cycles involving these (and other) processes of change. Such a result will tend to produce a fan-like spectrum of types that vary according to their different situations, degrees of integration, and functional locations in the broader system. Some variants within a class of societies having similar characteristics will favor additional evolutionary steps. Some others may be so beset with internal conflicts or other handicaps that they can barely maintain themselves or will deteriorate. But among these may be creative societies from the viewpoint of originating components of long-run importance.

When somewhere in a variegated population of societies there emerges a developmental breakthrough, the ensuing process of innovation will approximate the paradigm of evolutionary change. Such a breakthrough endows its society with *a new level of adaptive capacity*, thereby changing the terms of its competitive relations with other societies. This kind of situation opens four possibilities for the societies not sharing the innovation. The innovation can be destroyed by more forceful, even if less advanced, rivals. If the innovation is cultural, it is difficult to destroy completely and may become important later although its society of origin has been destroyed. Second, the terms of competition may be evened through adoption of the innovations. The present drive to modernization among underdeveloped societies is a case in point. A third alternative is the establishment of an insulated niche in which the society can continue to maintain its old structure undisturbed. The final possibility is the loss of societal identity through disintegration or absorption by some larger societal system. These possibilities are type concepts; any combinations of them may occur.

---

50. This analysis of the processes of evolutional change is a revision of the schema set forth in "Some Considerations on the Theory of Social Change," in *Rural Sociology*, September 1961, pp. 219–239.

CHAPTER 3
ARCHAIC
SOCIETIES
LEGITIMATION BY A
LITERATE PRIESTHOOD

The second of the three main stages of societal evolution is the intermediate stage, characterized by the development of written language. There are cases in which predominantly primitive societies interpenetrate with literate cultures, one instance being the Nupe following their conquest by the Islamic Fullani. The Nupe are peripheral to an essentially foreign religo-cultural complex, whereas in a fully intermediate society, an *indigenous* literate tradition is constitutive of the culture. We distinguish two principal substages of intermediate society, the archaic and the advanced intermediate. By archaic, we mean the first stage in the evolution of intermediate society, that of craft literacy and cosmological religion. The advanced stage is characterized by full upper-class literacy and, on the cultural side, by an historic religion, one which has broken through to philosophical levels of generalization and systematization.[1] Such religions develop for the first time conceptions of a supernatural order differentiated from any order of nature.

An archaic cosmological religio-cultural system systematizes the constitutive symbolism of the society more than the cultural system of any primitive society. *This cultural elaboration depends on the literacy of priesthoods and their capacity to maintain a stable written tradition.* The literacy is, however, still esoteric and limited to specialized groups—hence, it is craft literacy. Besides the religio-magical, its specialized use is for administrative purposes. Only in *advanced* inter-

1. Robert N. Bellah, "Religious Evolution," *The American Sociological Review*, June 1964.

mediate societies is literacy centering about the mastery of a literary tradition a characteristic of all upper-class adult males—e.g., the upper-caste Hindus or the Chinese gentry. A cosmological cultural system is usually interpreted for the society by temple priesthoods. The priesthoods administer *cults,* the ritual benefits of which are no longer rigidly ascribed to underlying kinship and local community structures as in primitive societies. The temple itself may become a focus of the social organiza-tion—e.g., in economic connections. In general, the function of cultural legitimation has become differentiated, generalized, and, though closely bound to the highest echelon of the society (e.g., the king), entrusted to the priestly groups.[2]

On the political side, there is a parallel differentiation. *All* archaic societies have an administrative apparatus elaborated beyond the level of such societies as the Shilluk or Bemba. Both priestly and administrative functions are usually controlled by lineages rather than appointed in-dividuals, particular statuses typically being hereditary. Moreover, the political and religious offices often overlap. They are, however, suf-ficiently distinct so that one can regard religious and secular stratification as being differentiated. Yet each tends to crystallize about a three-class pattern: the top, associated with the charisma of the monarch and the exercise of his combined religious and political authority; a mid-dle group responsible for the more routine functioning of the society; and the mass of the common people, who are tillers of the soil. The last also includes craftsmen and even merchants, who become increasingly prominent with further development, particularly as functionaries of the great households or temples, standing in client-like relations with the leading proprietary lineages.[3]

This further differentiation accounts for a shift away from the pattern prescribed by the two types of advanced primitive society we touched on at the end of Chapter 2. The two cases of archaic society which we will discuss in the present chapter, ancient Egypt and Mesopo-tamia, exemplify a reversal compared to the Shilluk and the Bemba. Egypt had a highly developed institution of divine kingship. At the same time, the structure of the society was not segmental in the Shilluk manner, but hierarchical and bureaucratic. In Mesopotamia, kingship was *not* fused with divinity, but the underlying base of the society was segmental. This segmentation developed in the form of the urban communities—

2. Cf. Talcott Parsons, "Evolutionary Universals in Society," *The American Socio-logical Review,* June 1964.

3. As archaeologists have emphasized, these developments usually also involve developments in urbanization. The comparative evidence on this point is summarized in *Courses Toward Urban Life,* edited by Robert J. Braidwood and Gordon Willey (Chicago: Aldine, 1962).

rather than kinship groups—that were the important member units of the society. The development of the intermediate level in the societal structures impelled this difference. Given the cosmological level of cultural symbolization, the organization of such a complex society (compared, for example, to the Shilluk) required a tightly controlled apparatus of both ritualization and political administration. In the case of Mesopotamia, however, the relative decentralization of the religious system permitted the constituent structural units greater autonomy. But the political apex of Mesopotamian society was not nearly so stable as that of Egypt. Archaic societies have emerged independently in many parts of the world, in the Indian subcontinent, China, Southeast Asia, and the New World (the Aztecs, Mayans, and Incas). I have chosen to examine Egypt and Mesopotamia because they have been so thoroughly investigated by archaeologists and because of their historic connections with advanced societies.

My treatment of advanced intermediate societies will be organized in two chapters, the distinctions between which are complicated but not arbitrary. Chapter 4 will deal with cases which achieved high organizational levels and maintained continuity in their basic patternings over some centuries, but which failed to generate the transition to the *modern* phase of social evolution upon their own resources and developmental potentialities. I view these societies in the perspective of Max Weber; the problem is why they did not develop the combinations of modernizing factors that appeared in the modern West.

Chapter 5 will deal with two cases of a different order—namely, Israel and Greece in critical periods of their development. Both were tiny societies compared with Egypt, Mesopotamia, or Persia; their political independence was precarious, and both lost it. They were not important in the civilizational complexes of their own time, yet both produced cultural innovations for the long-run future: the religion of Jahweh and the secular culture of Greece. In combination with other factors, these served to lay the foundations for the emergence of the modern societal type and deserve special treatment.

ANCIENT EGYPT

Egypt was literate, but in the sense of craft literacy. Literacy was used for maintaining religio-magical formulae and for administrative accounting.[4] Literacy and a corresponding level of education seem not to have penetrated the entire upper class, as it did later in postexilic Israel,

---

4. William F. Edgerton, "The Government and the Governed in the Egyptian Empire," *Journal of Near Eastern Studies*, July 1947.

Greece, Rome, Brahman India, or post-Confucian China. Egypt was bounded, both politically and culturally, a condition fostered by the geographical location of the Nile Valley, isolated east and west by deserts. Two boundaries were open, the Mediterranean Coast and the desert of the upper Nile.[5] The distance between these open boundaries, one bordering on Lower Egypt and the other on Upper Egypt, was important. Egypt's distinctive system, at once religious and political, was closer culturally to its more primitive neighbors in the upper Nile region than any others.[6] The Hebrews' sense of Egyptian culture's foreignness indicates how sharp were the differences at the Mediterranean boundaries.

Egypt had a system of stratification that included the lower classes. Conquest played a secondary role in Egyptian history. However authoritarian Egyptian rule may seem from modern viewpoints, all classes authentically belonged to the same society. Though differentiated, Egyptian society attained centralized integration which, except for a few periods of disorganization, remained intact for a long time.[7]

A distinctive feature of Egyptian society was the institution of kingship. Among the known institutions of monarchy, it accentuates not the divinization of the king but his actual *divinity*. The Egyptian conception was that to be the king *was* to be divine.[8] The two categories were inseparable—no human or ritual agency made the king divine, though he was concurrently regarded as human. The kingship was an aspect of the sacred order itself and of its functioning to regulate the cosmic order of both human affairs and of organic and inorganic nature.[9] Quite unlike the Greek or even the Mesopotamian gods, the Egyptian gods did not *intervene* in human affairs, did not rule them or manipulate the political leaders of human societies. The ruling of human affairs was integral to the divine order itself.[10] This does not mean that the Egyptians considered the human condition itself divine but the contrary. Compared to the primitive situation, the gap between divine and human was vast. Only through the divinity of kingship and its intimate associations could human beings relate themselves to the divine. Ordinary

5.   John A. Wilson, "Egypt," in H. and A. Frankfort, John A. Wilson, and Thorkild Jacobsen (eds.), *Before Philosophy* (Baltimore: Penguin Books, 1949), pp. 39ff.

6.   Among tribes we have mentioned, especially the Shilluk. Cf. Henri Frankfort, *Kingship and The Gods* (Chicago: The University of Chicago Press, 1948), Book I, especially chap. 14, on this general point.

7.   William F. Edgerton, "The Question of Feudal Institutions in Ancient Egypt" in R. Coulborn (ed.), *Feudalism in History* (Princeton: Princeton University Press, 1959).

8.   Henri Frankfort: *Ancient Egyptian Religion* (New York: Harper Torchbooks, 1961), p. 43.

9.   Unlike the Shilluk kingship, no lower-order human agency was required to legitimize the succeeding pharaoh.

10.   Frankfort, *Kingship and the Gods, op. cit., passim.*

people could not participate in the sacred order; they could only be articulated with it.

This articulation was accomplished mainly by a cult that spread throughout Egypt. The rituals of the cult related to myriads of gods conceived both on particularistic, local grounds and on general, cosmic grounds, and they were legitimized through the charisma of the pharaoh's divinity. The pharaoh delegated his charismatic powers to the corps of priestly officials.[11] This delegation was partly legitimized by the impossibility of the pharaoh's performing all the cult functions himself. The highest functionaries of this religious regime constituted part of the upper class, but others occupied positions at lower levels. The pharaoh's divinity was thus the basis of the system of temple priesthoods that held responsibility for the cults, administered immense economic resources, and interpenetrated with the political organization of the society.[12]

The primary principles of organization were probably linked both to kinship and to property in land. Closeness of kinship with the royal lineage was a prime criterion of status. Polygyny and large harems, maintained by the king, the members of his lineage, and other nobles, provided a pool of persons qualified by hereditary status for preferment; it was not unusual for a pharaoh to have two hundred actual sons.[13] The class structure, then, may have been symbolized by the pyramid itself, with closeness to the divine world being the criterion of status. Status was diffuse, cutting across the differentiation of later societies into religious and secular functions. Yet it could break through kinship ascription, making it possible for able people to be advanced from lower to higher positions of service. It could, hence, be more bureaucratized than any primitive society. Essential among these developments was a sharpening of the hierarchical distinction between the sacred and the secular worlds. The top was *more* sacred compared to primitive systems and the bottom *more* profane. This differentiation did not result in the generalized dualism characterizing the historic religions of Bellah's analysis.[14] Both spheres remained within a single system of order, neither "natural" nor "supernatural" in the sense meant in Western culture, the differentiation between them having not yet emerged.[15] The archaic development in-

11. Wilson, *op. cit.*, pp. 96–101.

12. John A. Wilson, *The Culture of Ancient Egypt* (Chicago: Phoenix Books, 1951), especially chaps. VIII and X.

13. Edgerton, *op. cit.*

14. "Religious Evolution," *op. cit.*

15. Here recall Durkheim's justification of his refusal to use the concept "supernatural" in discussing Australian totemism: Since an order of nature in the "historic" sense has not been defined, one cannot contrast a supernatural order to it. I have not adhered to this usage, but have allowed for the validity of the point.

volved differentiation between those aspects of a socially structured action system related to the sacred grounds of being and those related to it only secondarily, mediated through the king and the priests of the pharaonic cult.

The elevation of the pharaoh did not merely accord a special status to an individual but created a massive institutional structure, the royal lineage, to head an aristocracy that was tightly integrated. Apparently this aristocracy staffed the higher echelons of the two institutional structures that, besides the monarchy itself, were basically new—the elaborate religious cult system with its priesthoods and the civil bureaucracy both of which comprised many levels above the common people. In developmental perspective, the civil bureaucracy appears to be the greater innovation. Observers since Herodotus have never ceased wondering at the massive construction achievements of the Egyptians—the pyramids, the temples, the palaces, and the water-control and irrigation system of the Nile Valley. These feats depended on the organization of human services for collective goals on bases of legitimation that transcended kinship ties. Although the supervisory functions were exercised by an hereditary aristocracy, status in which was through kinship relation to, or direct appointment from, the royal lineage itself, skilled labor and massive manpower were mobilized for public works on bases other than those of kinship.[16]

Physical products, notably grain, could be mobilized in amounts great enough to permit their storage and territorial redistribution, establishing a means of support for the complex division of labor and for assurance against famine. Among ancient empires of comparable scope, Egypt seems to have been notably nonmilitaristic. Sheer assertion of superior force, leaving others no alternative to submission, was probably not the main process by which a lineage established itself in a position as preeminent as that of the pharaonic institution. The cultural aspects of the process were more important. Important though political power may have been, it must have been dependent on cultural legitimation.

Egyptian development also involved technological innovations.[17] Civilized Egypt was always a settled agricultural economy. The degree of literacy achieved was significant for bureacratic administration, and techniques of stone-working, metallurgy, and textile production advanced beyond earlier levels. The crucial innovation, however, pertained to manpower organization, the mobilization of human services for large collective enterprises. Its basis seems to have been the population's diffuse commitment to a welfare type of state, leadership of which focused on the king-

16. Edgerton, *op. cit.*

17. Wilson, *The Culture of Ancient Egypt, op. cit.*, chaps. II and III.

ship.[18] It was never a modern bureaucracy, because service within it was not perfomed in occupational roles. In Weber's scheme, Egyptian administration is best characterized as patrimonial, although this is only an approximate characterization. Manpower was requisitioned on the basis of the diffuse religio-political form of commitment and obligation. Although little is known about the conditions of service, remuneration, exemptions, and the like, the organizational pattern seems understandable.

Even the rudiments of differentiation that we take for granted in modern systems were not present in the Egyptian pattern. For those whose roles involved the performance of services, as distinguished from assumption of leadership responsibility, the main pattern was a response to the leadership's invoking obligations that were concomitants of the status of membership in the societal community and various of its segmental units. The modern analogy is military service performed by an ordinary citizen, except that the leader of the Egyptian bureaucracy did not need a special emergency to invoke obligations. Thus there was no private sphere within which the citizen was autonomous and which legally obliged the government to negotiate with him about the terms of his service. Service performances for Egyptian public programs were not hired from a labor force in the modern sense. People served under ascribed obligations, not feudally to particular aristocratic lineages, but communally to a whole society that was differentiated only between the kingship complex and the common people. It was a kind of archaic socialism. Leadership in the Egyptian bureaucracy did not constitute a civil service but a hierarchical ordering of ascribed positions of diffuse status and authority in which incumbents exercised the king's authority by virtue of participating at various levels in his charisma.[19] Such participation, as in the case of the priesthoods, was assimilated to kinship with the royal lineage. However, it is unclear how far this criterion could have been applied exclusively in such a complex system.

There existed a graded hierarchy of service. A religio-civil bureaucracy comprised the higher echelons with some differentiation, but its two aspects were not rigidly distinguished. Officials derived their legitimation and even their appointments from the king and his high officers. However, the criterion of a developed bureaucracy, a legal line between office and other personal statuses, did not exist. Bureaucratic office was a total status carrying many residual, non-administrative obligations and privileges, some requiring constant service, others invoked only on special occasions. The economic resources needed to conduct offices were centrally provided for, including the personal expenses of the officials and

18. Wilson, "Egypt," *op. cit.,* p. 90.

19. Frankfort, *Ancient Egyptian Religion, op. cit.,* especially p. 36.

their relevant kin and, perhaps, clients. We must not exaggerate the degree of this control. The lack of legal limits to official duties did not preclude different groups from having the power to affect the terms of their services, secure exemptions from services, or maintain property interests independent of official positions.[20] This last point relates to another aspect of fluidity in the system. There were tendencies, similar to those in feudal systems, for certain persons and kinship groups to control multiple offices, often both priestly and civil, and to shift from one type of office to another.[21] (Such pluralism supports effective checks on central authority.) Thus this system, like many others, was not immune to power struggles.[22]

Problems posed by particularistic interest structures were especially important at the lower levels of the administration and in local community organizations. Presumably, most craftsmen, temple scribes, and the like, held regular jobs in particular organizations, whether temples, administrative units, or local bodies. These positions were largely hereditary.[23] The masses of common people were peasants working the land, organized along traditionalized lines. Whether rural or urban, the population was also organized into territories ruled after the model of the pharaonic institution by governors appointed from the local aristocracy by the pharaoh and responsible to him. Within the territories, the national and territorial governments operated independently, utilizing separate means of organizational effectiveness.[24] Thus, Egyptian society contained many bases of solidarity independent of the main hierarchy emanating from the divine king. Not all particularistic elements were so atomized that the whole society was at the disposal of the royal leadership for any tasks that advanced national policy.[25] By modern standards, the possibilities for such mobilization were limited. However, such qualifications do not negate the difference in capacity for mobilization between Egypt and *any* primitive society. Throughout the society, immense human resources could be used for collective enterprises so long as the plan could be implemented from the top. The development of such capacity for organized collective effort was something new in social evolution. The

20. Edgerton, "The Question of Feudal Institutions in Ancient Egypt," *op. cit.*

21. Wilson, *The Culture of Ancient Egypt, op. cit.*, especially chaps. IX and X.

22. S. N. Eisenstadt, *The Political Systems of Empires* (New York: Free Press of Glencoe, 1962).

23. Wilson, *The Culture of Ancient Egypt, op. cit.*; also Frankfort, *The Religion of Ancient Egypt, op. cit.*, pp. 33–35.

24. Wilson, *The Culture of Ancient Egypt, op. cit.*; Edgerton, *op. cit.*

25. K. A. Wittfogel, *Oriental Despotism* (New Haven: Yale University Press, 1957), seems to have developed his argument largely from this erroneous viewpoint.

processes by which collective goals should be determined and collective leadership held responsible presented a new order of social problems.

The major integrative functions of Egyptian society centered about a scale of stratification which used the royal lineage as its reference point. Status in the system, which involved social prestige and authority, was ascribed to kinship in both its lineal and affinal aspects. However, because integrative mobility was essential in order to articulate specific statuses with service mobilization, pressures developed that made the affinal structures flexible—certainly more so than in primitive systems. When arranging marriages or making appointments, high officials of the court and the priesthoods had discretion in choosing among persons whose lineages were approximately equivalent in status.

The stratification hierarchy seems to have had a functional basis of differentiation, that between the religious hierarchy of priesthoods and the secular-administrative hierarchy. This differentiation derived from the mode in which the society was involved in action at the general level, the two hierarchies relating to the society's two functional references. One reference involved managing, first, the environmental conditions of well-being, focusing on the Nile as the source of agricultural fecundity and then the instrumental conditions of effective collective action, especially in regard to public order and public works. The other reference concerned articulation with the society's cultural foundations through the pharaoh's relation to the divine order and the *ritual* management of social and natural processes.

A feature of the Egyptian mode of relating the two hierarchies was the low degree of formalization of the legal system, especially when compared to the Mesopotamian codes. Justice, though religiously sanctioned in that its ideals were assimilated to the divine order, was the prerogative of the pharaoh and his officials in such a personal manner that the particularities of litigants' statuses were involved in all legal action. The few codes were scarcely more than the collections of wise decisions.[26] The religious aspect of the Egyptian system was its striking feature, bureaucratic effectiveness itself depending considerably on this aspect. I return to my keynote: Egyptian kingship was *at the same time* religious and political in a sense foreign to modern conceptions. Pharaoh was a kind of god, integral to the divine system. Hence, it is as essential to characterize the system of divinity as the king's position in it. We may regard Egyptian religion as symbolizing features of the human condition but also as asserting its differentiation from the divine substantially more than even the advanced primitive religions.

---

26. Cf. Sabatino Moscati, *The Face of the Ancient Orient* (Garden City, N.Y.: Anchor Books, 1962), pp. 145–146. This means that, in Weber's terms, law was governed by substantive, not formal, rationality, so far indeed as it was specially rationalized at all.

The theme affirmed by the religion was the *continuity* of the socio-cutural system, conceived as an integration of the divine order, human society, and subhuman nature.[27] Pharaoh, as both king and god (Horus), was the system's integrative center. Both divine and human, he was a link in the continuity of all meaningful phenomena. He was the son of Re, the Sun-god believed to be the source of all living things. More directly, he was also the son of more specific divine parents, the mother-goddess, Hathor, and his own royal father, as symbolized in the equation of Horus and the Bull.[28] Thus his humanity was linked to the general procreative order of animal life. He was also implicated in nature's cyclical processes—the seasons, the planting and harvesting of crops, and the Nile's annual flooding. Moreover, the kingship was a multi-generation institution that connected the living pharaoh with both his ancestors and his successors.[29]

To the psychologically aware, the explicit involvement of incest in the procreative order was impressive. Religious systems generally articulate in symbol with a socio-psychosexual base. The Egyptian case illustrates this through the occurrence of the incest theme at two levels. First, Egypt was one of the historic cases in which brother-sister incest in the royal family was mandatory for continuing the royal line.[30] However, the pharaoh and his sister evidently mated only on formal occasions and only to secure an heir to the throne. Otherwise, they were segregated. They were not married in the sense of sharing everyday life concerns and placing sexual relations in that context. Second, the incest theme recurred on a symbolic level. On his death, each pharaoh, as the god Horus, became Osiris, Horus' father, who stood for both the divine aspect of the particular king who had just died and *all* the dead pharaohs in Egyptian history collectively.[31] There were two features of the pharaoh's symbolic transition from life to death. First, he re-entered the womb of his symbolic divine mother, Hathor. But, concurrently, he procreated in her supernatural body the new pharaoh, who, in his divine aspect, was Horus.[32]

The continuance of the religious basis of society was grounded in

27. Frankfort, *Kingship and The Gods, op. cit.,* Book I, *passim* and *Ancient Egyptian Religion,* chap. I; Wilson, "Egypt," *op. cit.,* chap. II.

28. Henri Frankfort, *Kingship and The Gods, op. cit.,* chap. III and part III, *passim.*

29. Thus, unlike the Shilluk conception, the death of the pharaoh and the accession of his successor were conceived as phases of a *single* indivisible process on the religious level.

30. Russell Middleton, "Brother-Sister and Father-Daughter Marriage in Ancient Egypt," *American Sociological Review* (October 1962): 27:603–611.

31. Frankfort, *Kingship and The Gods, op. cit.,* part II.

32. *Ibid.*

incest. Modern psychology holds that brother-sister incest is the least disruptive of the three types possible in the nuclear family, incest between mother and son being the *most* serious. Significantly, the Egyptian system actualized the former institutionally, though in the confined context of assuring a proper royal succession, but yet enacted the latter symbolically to indicate the religious meaning of what Horus was doing when he became Osiris. Perhaps it was the divine reward he received with death in accepting the after-life. One may regard this as the nonfamilial top of a kinship-structured upper class, with the pharaoh's incestuous privileges and obligations symbolizing his special status.[33] Frankfort warns us not to rationalize Egyptian religious symbolism as if it were a philosophical theology—for example, the Egyptian conception that a fetus was the primary procreative agent seems irrational to moderns. The continuity theme has special references to the problem of death and to the king's mortality. The symbolic assertion that death was relative to a higher reality in the continuity transcending death is characteristic of all religions. But in this case, the pharaoh's relation to the cosmic order lends the assertion meaning at a unique level.[34]

The conception of this higher reality contrasts with those of historic religions, since it emphasizes man's erotic interests and their relation to kinship structure and procreation. The combination of reentry into the maternal womb and incestuous procreation equated birth and death symbolically in primarily *psychological* references. There was an exchange; as the old Horus became Osiris, the new Horus emerged from Osiris *cum* Hathor—the *balance continued.* Furthermore, the pyramid-tomb was in part a womb symbol, and mummification symbolized the indefinite preservation of a life-like form as a fetus, the state in which human organisms live was minimally disturbed.[35] The continuity of this equivalence was the thematic core of the cult of the dead—and a basis for conflict with the Hebrew orientation. It did not deny the reality of death—otherwise it would not be authentically religious in our sense—but it asserted continuity, not just of the human genetic strain, but also of its *social* organiation through psycho-social succession.

This constitutive cult, that of the continual *re*-creation of psychic and social life, was spun between the components of a conceptual system of order. First, it involved the conception of a cosmic just and proper order, termed *Maat.* The function of the pharaonic institution was to act

33. This is a special case of the principle that the origin of a differentiated system must, by *its* standards, be undifferentiated.

34. Frankfort, *op. cit.,* parts II and III; and Frankfort, *Ancient Egyptian Religion, op. cit.,* pp. 88–123.

35. Frankfort, *Kingship and The Gods, op. cit.*

in accord with *Maat* and to preserve it through action.[36] Distinctions between active and passive references do not seem to have emerged clearly. However, Egyptian society was permeated with beliefs confirming the importance of maintaining the cult. To infer that Egyptians believed that failure of the pharaoh and his priests to uphold the cult might jeopardize the cosmic constitution itself is not far-fetched. Thus, *Maat* was *not* a conception of order like that presumed in modern philosophy or even in the Book of Genesis.[37] It may be called a ritual order, for it contained much more projection of human interests and motives than do more advanced conceptions, such as those of the Hebrews and Greeks.

A second aspect of order was natural. It involved two themes: procreation and resurrection.[38] Procreation concerned the relation of human society to the animal world: the importance of cattle and, in that context, the relation between Egypt and the upper Nilotic societies, in which cattle also play a religious role.[39] Horus and Hathor were symbolized by the bull and the cow. Indeed, syncretism between men and animals was prominent in Egyptian art. This theme was related to the erotic complex of the constitutive cult; animal symbolism is often associated with erotically regressive elements in human motivation. The resurrection theme refers to a complex centered about the fertility of the soil and the seasonal cycle of the crops. With Egypt's lack of rain, the seasonal cycle, which depended on the Nile's annual flood, was basic to agriculture. These conditions were integrated into the religion; planting the seed symbolically represented the killing and burying of Osiris, and its sprouting under the flood's stimulus was his resurrection.[40] Thus, human continuity was reflected in organic life, in the seasonal cycle of vegetation as well as in the procreative immortality of animal species. The Egyptian ritual system managed not only human society, through the pharaoh and the gods, but also its relation to the organic world.

The divine order of Egyptian culture was not supernatural in the sense even of the divine order of early Judaism. Similarly, the procreative and resurrective themes should not be regarded as aspects of an order of nature in the sense of the late Greeks. Egyptian religion does present a hierarchy running from the sphere of the gods, through human society

36. *Ibid.*, especially part II; Wilson, *The Culture of Ancient Egypt, op. cit.*, chaps. V and VII.

37. Kenneth Burke, *The Rhetoric of Religion* (Boston: Beacon, 1961), chap. III.

38. Frankfort, *Kingship and The Gods, op. cit.*, part III.

39. *Ibid.*, chap 14; also, c.f., for example, E. E. Evans-Pritchard, *The Nuer* (Oxford: The Clarendon Press, 1940), and *The Divine Kingship of the Shilluk* (Cambridge: The Cambridge University Press, 1948).

40. Frankfort, *Kingship and The Gods, op. cit.*, chap. 15.

and the higher animals, to vegetation. The ordering of these levels, both internally and in their interrelations, did not, however, achieve a differentiation sharp enough to justify applying the terms supernatural and natural in the sense of Western religion and philosophy. Eisenstadt has suggested a parallel between Egypt and China in that both societies, each on its own terms, attained unusual levels of integration and structural durability.[41] I can treat this subject only after discussing China; the similarities between the two systems are embedded in differences regarding developmental level.

THE MESOPOTAMIAN EMPIRES

Egypt exemplified the more hierarchical type of archaic society, being structured in both religious and secular aspects about a series of ordered graduations from the pharaoh down. Indeed, the pyramid served as a symbol of the structure of the society itself. Though, like all societies, it was segmented on geographical (and some other) bases, it is difficult to see how a pattern of association between autonomous, presumptively equal units could be compatible with such a society.

The Mesopotamian cases present a contrast. They exemplified a pattern which, in a variety of forms, pervaded the region from the central Mediterranean through its islands, peninsulas, and coasts, eastward to the valley of the Tigris and Euphrates—namely, the development of autonomous urban communities. The broader, society-wide structures developed by processes of superimposition on these units in such a way that the units themselves were not totally absorbed. This more associative pattern of organization seems to have first developed in Mesopotamia and achieved there a scale and political effectiveness that went beyond Egypt. Mesopotamian society lacked the boundedness that characterized Egypt and lacked the latter's long-lasting stability. (This stability was an effect of geographical factors.) Though also centering on a river-valley in an arid area, the Tigris-Euphrates region is not so self-enclosed as the Nile region. Society there has a long history of contact, trade, and migration with the societies along the Mediterranean coast, in Persia, and in the Arabian and Syrian deserts.[42] And the delta on the Persian Gulf has always been open to foreign contact by sea.

From early times, the social structure took the form of relatively autonomous urban communities that controlled the agricultural territories surrounding them.[43] Their dominant elements were sets of upper-class

41. Eisenstadt, *op. cit.*

42. Sabatino Moscati, *Ancient Semitic Civilizations* (New York: Putnam, 1957).

43. Moscati, *The Face of the Ancient Orient, op. cit.*, chaps. II and III.

lineages with equal formal status. Formal authority rested in a council of elders comprised of the heads of these lineages. The centralized aspects of the authority structure were also pluralistic. On the local level there was even closer integration of functionally diffuse religious and political organization than in Egypt. The gods were conceived to be the ultimate proprietors of the land, and the temples were the major units of economic organization. Their religious legitimation was the source of flexibility in mobilizing resources, for allotments were controlled by the temple authorities, and manpower was mobilized for collective projects by temple corvées (labor obligations).[44] These temples were the focus of cults not as closely integrated wtih specific social units, either in kinship or territorial, as is usual in primitive societies.

Thus, the large city-state was formed by the confederation of several landholding temples, with the largest, presumably that of the main urban center, becoming *primus into pares* (first among equals). The chief priest of this temple then assumed the position of governor, and became responsible for the instrumental functions of the community, particularly operation of the irrigation systems and the management of trade relations with other communities.[45] The governorship seems to have been hereditary in the chief priest's lineage. The institution of kingship was gradually superimposed on this structure. The early Mesopotamian city-states did not have kings. They were elected by the councils of elders only to meet specific emergencies, generally military.[46] Perhaps the governor's religious status made military service unsuitable for him. Most Mesopotamian city-states were not provided with strong geographical defenses like the Greek *poleis,* which were situated on islands or small coastal plains surrounded by high mountain barriers. In any case, the early kings were expected to serve only for the duration of particular emergencies. However, situations tended to become defined as continuing emergencies. Gradually, kingship gained permanent and, indeed, hereditary status in particular city-states. Then the many city-states of the valley region were consolidated into empires under numerous dynasties. The institution of kingship continued to bear the imprint of its relatively *ad hoc* origin, which underlies its differences from Egyptian kingship.[47]

Mesopotamian society was archaic. Its literacy was confined to the craft level. The connection between the priesthoods and the management of economic affairs presumably relates to this. Probably the religious and

---

44. H. W. F. Saggs, *The Greatness that was Babylon* (New York: Hawthorn, 1962).

45. *Ibid.*

46. Moscati, *The Face of the Ancient Orient, op. cit.*

47. Frankfort, *Kingship and The Gods, op. cit.,* Book II, gives an extensive analysis of these differences.

accounting functions involving writing were often performed by the same people. Furthermore, Mesopotamian society held to a religious primacy different from any found at later phases of religious development. In the local, city-state organizations, the fusion of political and religious structures was as extensive as in Egypt and was symbolized by the governor's status as temple-priest. Though kingship originated in secular connections, its functions also were defined in religious terms. The king's election was attributed to the gods themselves. He was the mediator between society and the divine order, representing the gods to his subjects and interceding with the gods on behalf of his realm and people.[48] His major duties involved promoting the secular welfare of his realm.

Though it orginated in small city-states, the significance of kingship lay in its role in the eventual consolidation of the entire Mesopotamian region into an empire. Like Greece, Mesopotamia had, antedating the imperial phase, a common culture based on a polytheism which was unitary despite local variations. Hence, the great kings were able to become mediators between the pantheon of gods and all the societies under their domain.[49] No other institutionalized agency could fill this position since the city-states, their temples, and governors were inherently local. Given the tendency of an archaic society toward religious primacy, the emphasis on the king's religious functions at the supra-local level is not surprising.

The consolidation of the region under a single religio-political system stratified both the religious and the political spheres into a three-level complex in some respects parallel to that of Egypt. The typical Mesopotamian city-state had a gentry class of secular notables and priests standing above the common people—peasants, artisans, and, with greater prominence than in Egypt, merchants and traders. Around the king there develloped a central priesthood and bureaucracy. As in all archaic societies, the hereditary principle prevailed in this echelon, but there was scope for patrimonial relationships. The development of imperial institutions was accompanied by a generalization of major elements of the cultural tradition, particularly the constitutive symbolism. The status of the king was dependent on his religious legitimation by one or more gods in a pantheon that had attained pan-societal significance transcending the more local cults, though the latter continued to exist also. Indeed, they constituted a source of instability in the larger political structure through the political loyalties they continued to legitimize.

Underlying the kingship, there remained a plurality of local city-states maintaining independence more thorough than that of the Egyptian

48. Ibid.

49. Moscati, The Face of the Ancient Orient, op. cit. For the continued importance of such mediation, even to quite late times, see A. T. Olmstead, History of the Persian Empire (Chicago: University of Chicago Press, 1948).

territories.[50] This was an obstacle to the integration of the system. No dynasty could secure tight control in the face of so many crystallizing points for new regimes, especially in economically important cities of historical and religious significance.[51] Need for protection against the fragmentation of their empires was a reason why the kings emphasized their religious legitimation.[52] Despite this religious primacy, the Mesopotamian kingship was not typically defined as divine.[53] Some kings claimed divinity, but this was limited, sporadic, and of dubious legitimacy. There was no religious sanctification of the royal succession comparable to the Egyptian pattern. The royal line was never conceived to be divine, and conflicts over the succession were frequent; problems of competing lines aside, the many sons of a king with a harem often made trouble. The absence of ritual symbolization of royal continuity created problems. The funerary ritual for a dead king was dissociated from his successor's coronation. This was a difference from Egypt, where kingship was multi-generational.

The New Year ceremonies also indicate the kingship's lack of consolidation in the divine order compared to Egyptian kingship. These rites were supposed to re-establish the king's solidarity with the divine forces, the yearly renewal of which was essential to the prosperity of the realm.[54] Here, again, the human order appears contingent on divine favor rather than integrally involved with the divine order, as in the Egyptian case. Thus, compared to Egyptian conceptions, there was in Mesopotamia greater distance between the divine and the human and greater emphasis on *contingency* in the relation between those spheres. In Egypt the royal obligation was to *maintain* the established order of the relationship; in Mesopotamia it was to manage actively a precarious relationship. In this sense, the society lived in a continuing state of religious emergency, fraught with anxiety, the adequate coping with which was a duty of the king and the basis for legitimizing his institutional position. I consider this is a further step in the differentiation of religious and secular spheres.

Mesopotamia attained a higher secular development than Egypt. Although it underwent political vicissitudes, including the ascendancy of Sumerian, Assyrian, and Babylonian dynasties and foreign rule under the

50. Moscati, *Face of the Ancient Orient, op. cit.,* and Olmstead, *op. cit.*

51. Thus, it became usual to change the capital of the empire as new dynasties arose.

52. Olmstead, *op. cit.*

53. Thorkild Jacobsen, "Mesopotamia," in H. and H. A. Frankfort, John A. Wilson, and Thorkild Jacobsen (eds.), *Before Philosophy, op. cit.;* perhaps Frankfort, *Kingship and The Gods, op. cit.,* Book II, argues this point persuasively, especially in chaps. 17 and 19.

54. Frankfort, *Kingship and The Gods,* chap. 22.

Persians, this secular development made contributions to subsequent evolution, particularly in law and trade.[55] Written legal precepts in Mesopotamia go back into the third millenium B.C. The code of Hammurabi from the first half of the second millenium was foreshadowed by earlier compilations and was not so original as was long assumed.[56] It was not a code like the *Code Napoleon*, but a survey of legal topics on which, because uncertainties existed, authoritative statements were needed. Hardly a complete system in terms of coverage of subject-matter, it did treat a range of topics in private law, particularly property and contract and the family. Though not generalized in the sense of stating legal principles, it was universalistic in applying its rulings impartially to wide categories of cases.

Even the earliest Mesopotamian codes contained legal delineations of statuses. The development that emerged in the successive codes (like that essential to Greek and Roman civilization) was the conception of the free citizen of a city-state, who could hold land and property, enter into contracts and marriages, and expect reliable legal protection as a matter of right. Within the category of free citizens, the Mesopotamian codes made class distinctions between members of common and aristocratic lineages regarding legal rights and obligations, especially the punishments and penalties to be imposed upon those guilty of infractions of the laws.[57] The later systems extended the conception of aristocratic status in order to gain higher statuses and greater control over resources for the officials of the imperial bureaucracy.[58] A status of slavery, entered into by capture in war, slave raids, or by indebtedness, was also defined legally. In archaic and historic societies, substantial parts of the lower class were slaves.[59] This categorization of personal statuses established a groundwork for that developed by the Mediterranean society of Greco-Roman times.

The concept on which this legal system was based transcended the idea of retributive justice. The codes contained numerous statements asserting the king's obligation to uphold equitable standards and protect persons in weak positions, Economic references were prominent, an indi-

---

55. These two complexes are located primarily in the integrative and adaptive sectors of the society. The structural emphases of Mesopotamian civilization thus contrast with those of Egyptian society, which lay in the pattern-maintenance and goal-attainment sectors.

56. Moscati, *The Face of the Ancient Orient, op. cit.;* Saggs, *op. cit.*

57. Moscati, *op. cit.*

58. Saggs, *op. cit.*

59. In these, as in other intermediate societies, there were often shadings of statuses between members of an indigenous lower class and those who were deprived of rights of membership by virtue of being outsiders in ethnic or societal community terms.

cation of mobility of economic resources. For instance, the debt relationship was a salient problem. Unless resources were emancipated from purely ascriptive embeddedness, no opportunity could arise to exploit weaker parties through the debt relationship. Therefore, indebtedness was an index of resource mobility under contract and probably an index of considerable development of money. Concurrent with its enhancement of economic potentialities, resource mobility permitted injustices that could scarcely exist otherwise, however unequal ascriptive relations might be. Similar considerations apply to family law, which indicated a lack of prescriptiveness in affinal relations.

Mesopotamian society also made advances toward establishing procedural institutions. As with other problems, one must allow for variation over a long time and a vast region. Though in the empires, justice was ultimately the king's obligation, the city assemblies, consisting mainly of the aristocratic elders, did play a part somewhat like modern juries.[60] Sometimes only the assembly's officials functioned rather than the entire body, and then they are referred to as the assembly's "judges." However, there could not have been a fully institutionalized judiciary in the Roman sense. A kind of public law, extending to the international field, also developed in Mesopotamia. Indeed, the loose structure of the polity required continuity between tributary relations to vassal states and contractual relations to contiguous independent states with which stable ties were maintained.[61] This included agreements about the rights of trading groups established in, or passing through, the territories, and even the extradition of criminals. In sum, Mesopotamian society developed a normative order verging on the degree of systematization and universalism found in historic systems. Its shortcoming was its lack of a unified conception of the grounding of the meanings of the obligations it asserted. In many respects, however, the legal system was impressive. Mesopotamia had advanced beyond Egypt.

Economic enterprise also developed in Mesopotamian society beyond Egyptian levels. This is evidenced by contract regulations in the law, by the considerable use of money as revealed by government price-fixing for important commodities, and by the prominence of the indebtedness problem.[62] Trade and its personnel were regulated by the government and the temples, but some degree of economic independence seems beyond doubt.[63] Money was used in commercial transactions and loans were made

60. *Ibid.*

61. *Ibid.*

62. *Ibid.*

63. *Ibid.;* and Karl Polanyi, Conrad Arensberg and Harry Pearson (eds.), *Trade and Market in the Early Empires* (Glencoe: Free Press, 1957). Saggs criticizes Polanyi's thesis that market economy was virtually absent in Mesopotamia.

at interest, but the high interest rates suggest that the conditions of security constricted the volume of trade. Internal trade was considerable, the rivers being transportation routes. Considering the social and political conditions of the time, the extent of foreign trade was remarkable. It included both sea trade through the Delta and Persian Gulf and overland trade to Persia, Egypt, and the Mediterranean Coast. Indeed, through trade many elements of Mesopotamian culture were diffused as far west as Crete and perhaps to the Aegean and Greece.[64]

Very early, institutionalized market and credit types of exchange activity achieved independence from the ascriptive local organization of agricultural and craft production and from the central government. That they evolved as far as they did is related to the legal developments already discussed. Ventures beyond the ascriptive solidarities that maintained their independence of direct governmental function and mandate were hazardous. This situation could not have developed as extensively as it did without legal protection, an arrangement different from incorporation into the government itself. The development points up continuities with Greek and Roman society.

Finally, Mesopotamian society, compared with Egypt, achieved greater differentiation between the sacred and secular orders. Perhaps the clearest sign of this was the emphasis on *contingency* in the relationship between gods and men. This helps account for what impresses moderns as superstition—for instance, the development of astrology and the reliance on omens and their priestly interpretations—that is, reliance on magical components. The gods' actions were, in contrast to Egypt, conceived as unpredictable. The Egyptians lacked fear of god because they were embedded in an order so divinely regulated that it only required proper management. For the Babylonians, no such security existed. Continuing social evolution further involved creating systems of human order able to persist and develop within this basic contingent relation between the divine and human conditions.

CONCLUSION

Why is a written language necessary to societal evolution? Because along with stratification, a primitive society must develop *explicit cultural legitimation of differentiated societal functions* if it is to evolve, and a written language facilitates explicit cultural legitimation. Of course a written language does not mean universal literacy, not even upper class

---

64. Eric Voegelin, *The World of the Polis*, vol. II of *Order and History* (New Orleans: University of Louisiana Press, 1957), chap. I; Moscati, *Ancient Semitic Civilizations*, *op. cit.*

literacy. More usually, *craft* literacy develops, that is, literacy monopolized by a priestly class. Their control over written records gives the priests an intellectual advantage over other upperclass elements, including the political leadership. One use they make of this advantage is to legitimate the authority of the rulers (or to withhold legitimation). As long as a literate priesthood continues to provide legitimation for the political rulers, the rulers are able to exercise more effective leadership of the society than is possible in primitive societies. This does not mean that the leadership is used to direct the society toward "better" goals, only that it can be more effectively mobilized toward *whatever* goals are established. Bear in mind that increased adaptive capacity does not imply moral superiority.

CHAPTER 4
THE HISTORIC EMPIRES
FURTHER DIFFERENTIATION OF THE SOCIETY FROM ITS LEGITIMATING CULTURAL SYSTEM

The varieties of primitive and intermediate societies cannot usefully be regarded as comprising larger systems in the sense of the system of modern societies. This difference presents interpretive problems that will guide my discussion of advanced intermediate societies, problems the significance of which was demonstrated by Max Weber. The *range* of variation among advanced intermediate societies was wide—think of the contrast between the Chinese Empire at its height, the Indian caste system, the Islamic empires, and the Roman Empire! All these societies contained developed civilizations. Why, then, did the breakthrough to modernizations not occur in *any* of the Oriental advanced intermediate civilizations? Conversely, what constellation of factors were involved in its occurrence against the background of the most radical structural regression in the history of major societies—namely, the fall of the western Roman Empire and the reversion of its territories to archaic social conditions in the dark ages? This is the historical-interpretive perspective, as distinct from that of systematic theory, which will guide my evolutionary analysis.

This chapter will discuss four cases of the advanced intermediate type of society. All developed independent political organizations on a large scale and integrated large populations and territories, but they had varying success in achieving stability and maintaining independence. All of them depended in some way upon cultural developments which separate them from the archaic type of society discussed in Chapter 3. With the partial exception of China, they have been involved with the world religions in a sense not applicable to any archaic society. The genesis of these types of societies lies outside the scope of the present discussion. Certain regularities of pattern, both in level achieved and in their ranges of variation, will be our concern, along with the problem of why none of these societies, developing upon their own resources, attained modernity.

The systems selected for my study are China, India, the Islamic Empires, and Rome. They will be treated in that order, which is one of development toward the modern type of society. China and India were minimally influenced by the cultural movements which underlay Western society. India was influenced by Greek culture and by Judaism, via Islam, after the Islamic incursions, but such influences came late in its development. Islam and Rome were influenced by Israel and Greece.[1]

The societies treated in this chapter were characterized by the comprehensiveness of their cultural innovations at the level of constitutive symbolism. They were the direct heirs of cultural movements called philosophic breakthroughs. The common feature of these movements—one that crosscut their differences in orientation—was the attainment of higher levels of generalization in the constitutive symbolism of their cultures. This attainment posed problems concerning the coming to terms of the new cultural orientations with the societal structures in which they arose or to which they were diffused.

I shall not analyze the processes that generated these breakthroughs or attempt to assess the relative roles of various cultural and social factors. The breakthroughs occurred within a relatively short time span in several different societies from the eastern Mediterranean (in Greece and Israel), through India, to China about the middle of the first millenium, B.C. My concern is with the implications of these changes for institutionalization in large-scale societies—on the scale that the major powers of the time had already achieved. For the breakthroughs of China and India, these implications were direct; but for those of Israel and Greece, they concern heir-societies, including Islam and Rome. The direct processes in Israel and Greece will be discussed in the next chapter, and the Christian heir-societies will be considered in Chapters 6 and 7.

In the terms of our analytical scheme, the cultural breakthroughs—however they may have come about—affected the societal community structures of the societies in which they occurred or to which they were diffused. These cultural movements led to a differentiation between the order of representations of ultimate reality and the order of representation of the human condition. Any human being's pretension to divine

---

1. As a general reference source on these societies, as well as several others (e.g., Persia), see S. N. Eisenstadt, *The Political Systems of Empires* (New York: Free Press of Glencoe, 1963).

status became out of the question; hence the institution of divine kingship was terminated with the archaic period. But the sharpness of the newly posed dichotomy between the supernatural and the natural orders accentuated the problem of defining the relation of human elements to the higher-order reality. This undermined the archaic tendency—conspicuous in Egypt—to proliferate status gradations. It tended to introduce a dichotomy between the human elements having, and those who have not, the capacity to act directly in terms of the new conception of the ultimate order. Hence, a new type of *two*-class structuring of the human society was a consequence of these cutural innovations. Society came to be divided between those who are, actually or potentially, qualified for the highest human standing relative to the cultural definition of the transcendent order and those who are excluded from such qualification, either inherently or until they meet specific conditions of eligibility.

The imposition of this dichotomy upon established societies involved complex readjustments, which worked out in different ways in the different cases I will discuss. One generalization applies to all the societies in which this situation was introduced and in which its institutionalization was attempted on a large scale. There had to be eventual acceptance of the fact that the going society must include persons who could *not* meet the criteria of relatedness to the higher order of cultural standards that grounded the cultural definitions of desirable belonging. Chinese society had to include common people who were not "superior men"; India had the *Sudra* and outcasts who were not eligible for the discipline of religious enlightenment; Islam had the infidels who would not convert to the true faith; and Rome has the barbarians within her polity. By contrast, a trend in modern societies is the presumption of the possibility of including all persons subject to political jurisdiction in full membership status within the single societal community.

CHINA

Bellah[2] has stated that, among the historic religions, Confucianism was the most archaic. Associated with this archaic character was the fact that in China but not in the Islamic or Roman Empires the new cultural level became fully institutionalized in a unified large-scale society. Furthermore, China resembled Egypt in its basic stability and strong valuation of the bases of stability. The Chinese Empire took shape about 200 B.C. with its unification under the short-lived Ch'in dynasty and its subse-

---

2. Robert Bellah (ed.), *Religion and Progress in Modern Asia* (New York: Free Press of Glencoe, 1965), Epilogue.

quent consolidation under the Han dynasty, which lasted for nearly 400 years.[3] The Han established the distinctive institutions of the Empire, notably the scholar-bureaucracy.

The Empire was preceded by the *Chou* society, a system of patrimonial states resting upon a feudal base. Chou was an archaic society, although it differed from others in granting a preferred position to extensive patrilineages, the *Shih*.[4] The prince, like the archaic kings, was the senior head of the paramount lineage. Centering about his court, there gathered a class of retainers who were not kinsmen, but upon whom he relied for both ritual and administrative services. Furthermore, these men became sufficiently free-floating so that a proportion of them were available for service to different princes, moving from one employment to another as did the men who served different city-states during the Italian Renaissance. They comprised the class of scholar-officials (for whom Confucius was the most articulate spokesman) who set the tone for the new society. Such facts reveal that Chou China had become a *system* of patrimonial societies which, though warring with one another, maintained integrative relations. To a degree, they shared a common culture with a common written language and an accumulating body of classical documents having both a ritual and a philosophical character. This common culture constituted a condition for the establishment of a politically organized society, the Empire, over a vast area.

Confucius considered himself to be the codifier of this cumulative written tradition; he denied making innovations but wanted only to transmit the "wisdom of the ancients."[5] But by the acts of codifying the tradition and adding aphoristic commentaries, Confucius and his followers produced a new ordering of the material. Thus, despite its repudiation of metaphysical speculation as vain, Confucianism became a *new* cultural system, one legitimately regarded as rooted in a religion. The Confucian codification became the basis of Chinese classical education. Institutionalizing this education involved the transition from craft literacy to the literacy of a *whole* upper class—i.e., of its adult males. Thereafter, the Chinese gentleman was a scholar in the Confucian classics.

The institutionalization of the Confucian tradition in an educational system came to include the requirement, grounded in the examina-

3. John King Fairbank, *The United States and China*, 2nd ed. (Cambridge, Mass.: Harvard University Press, 1959) gives a brief treatment of the essentials of Chinese history, see especially chaps. 2–6. More detailed is Kenneth Scott Latourette, *The Chinese: Their History and Culture* (New York: Macmillan, revised 1946).

4. H. G. Creel, "The Beginnings of Bureaucracy in China: The Origin of the Hsien," in *The Journal of Asian Studies*, February 1964.

5. Cf. Fung Yu-lan, *A Short History of Chinese Philosophy* (New York: Macmillan paperback, 1962), chap. 4.

tion system, that holders of imperial public office (except the emperor himself and special categories of courtiers) should be qualified through the discipline of this education—hence through the societal significance of the cultural tradition itself.[6] The mandarins, then, became a governing class whose status was defined in cultural terms. This was something new in societal evolution. In archaic societies, cultural legitimation was more dependent on the structure of the society. The impact of the Chinese legitimation system did not concentrate at the top, as did the Egyptian system focusing about the pharaoh. The Chinese emperor held only the vague Mandate of Heaven. Rather than integrating the many levels of a cosmos, from the gods to physical nature, as did the Egyptian ruling elements, they imposed a culturally defined, ultimately grounded pattern on the society.

To see how this arrangement worked, one must follow two strands outward from the scholar-official's status. The first concerns the nature of the cultural system. The second concerns its articulation in the structure of the society, involving both the positive integration achieved and the limits on such integration. Confucianism was close to being archaic in its special conception of boundedness. It held a sinocentric view of the human world and, beyond that, of the cosmic system. China was the Middle Kingdom, the center of the world. The various systems of order, whether cultural or social, general or specific, constituted concentric circles around this center. Yet, in the upward direction, this center was linked to a cosmic reference, to the system of a *Tao* and *Yang* and *Yin,* in a manner requiring the ritual management of human relations to these ultimate forces or, in Granet's term, "emblems."[7]

The emperor was a kind of pope. He was not himself divine, but he did hold a divine mandate. His societal functions were more specifically ritual than those of the pharaoh, leaving more freedom to his governmental subordinates. The supernatural sphere was sufficiently differentiated from the societal order so that it was not necessary to claim direct sanction by the highest legitimating authority for every act of government. The mandarins, as a class, undertook responsibility for specific governmental acts. They were accountable for the discharge of governmental duties, but they were autonomous in the *way* in which they governed. Heaven, in the Chinese sense, was not a policymaking agency.

The cosmic order and the human social order were conceived to be similarly bounded and essentially congruent with each other through likeness in form. Their principles of order, rather than being rationalistic

6. Max Weber, *The Religion of China* (Glencoe, Ill.: Free Press, 1951), chaps. V and VI.

7. Marcel Granet, *La Pensée Chinoise* (Paris: La Renaissance du Livre, 1934); Fung Yu-lan, *op. cit.,* chaps. 12 and 15.

in the Western sense (i.e., deriving from Greek thought), were symbolic-ritualistic. Order was a matter of the proper relations among diffuse entities defined as being multiply involved with one another. At the cosmic level, the *Yang-Yin* dichotomy was identified with more specific ones—e.g., South-North, Warm-Cold, Male-Female, Upper Status-Lower Status, Left-Right, and so on. *Tao* was the principle of maintaining a proper balance among such entities, with due regard to the various situations in which different ones were predominant and in which cyclical alternation was the pattern of relationship.[8] To the analytically minded, it is striking that the dimensions of superiority-inferiority and of qualitative functional difference without hierarchical distinction were not distinguished. *Yang* elements were in general *superior* to *Yin* as well as being qualitatively different.[9]

The imperial institution provided ritual articulation between the cosmic and the human; in this respect it was similar to Egyptian kingship.[10] The human society was organized around a harmony of differentiated, opposing, and cooperating entities. Its order was diffuse and particularistic, with the exception of one structual feature, the break between its upper and lower echelons. The *social* equivalent of *Tao* was *Li,* the observance of proprieties. Each element in the society had its proper place. It should be given its due within that place but should not be permitted to break away from it. The institutional embodiment of *Li* was the educated class, particularly its minority selected for appointment to government offices. The educated class carried the responsibility for implementing the mandate of the emperor to keep the system in harmonious balance. His was the ritual responsibility vis-à-vis the supernatural, cosmic order; its was the practical responsibility involving the conduct of human affairs. The two aspects were never sharply differentiated, and the magistrate carried on both practical administrative and ritual responsibilities, linking the locality of his particular office with the society-wide system in both respects.

The social structure interpenetrated with the cultural system. The culturally qualified group took over control of the society (in a sense not true of *any* archaic society) by virtue of its embodiment of the ideal cultural patterns. Yet, it could never become the corporate entity that defined the society as a whole, for it was only a body of "superior men" with a combination of prestige and governmental authority. But a line

8. *Ibid.*

9. Such isomorphism between the cosmic and the human social orders and such lack of differentiation are not typical of more advanced socio-cultural systems, but represent aspects of the archaic note in the Chinese system.

10. Cf. Marcel Granet, *Chinese Civilization* (New York: Meridian Books, 1958), pp. 92 ff., pp. 377 ff.

was drawn between them and the common people so that classical China remained a two-class society. To be sure, it was possible for individual sublineages to cross the line through upward (or downward) mobility—and they often did so, though with varying frequency in different periods.[11] In terms of social structure, however, there was no possibility of including the lower groups, especially the peasantry, in the positively valued societal community. The nature of this class barrier involved China's special approach to kinship, both actually in human society and symbolically in the cultural system. The kinship level of organization was not transcended, as it was in other historic systems. To be sure, the bureaucratic system involved a universalistic emphasis. Office was open to all who were qualified by education, as tested by the examination system. But this was a differential joint, the flexibility of which made possible the maintenance of kinship particularism above and below it in the social structure.

The Confucian ethic established a microscopic-macroscopic congruence between the family and the society as a whole. The doctrine of the five relationships included three which were specifically familial—father-son, husband-wife, elder brother-younger brother—all exemplifying the fusion of hierarchical and qualitative differences. (The other two were superior-inferior in official contexts and friend-friend, one being a senior friend who was a kind of patron.) The doctrine held that, if these relationships were properly ordered from the viewpoint of each individual, then the whole society would be properly orderd. In modern societies the family and its particularistic environment *cannot* serve as a prototype of the social structure as a whole.

As a social class, the gentry could not rest solely on its performance of governmental service, partly because of the selective principle in the appointment system. There had to be more qualified candidates than offices to fill; otherwise selection of the best would have been meaningless. From the perspective of the individual, the long process of education had to be taken at a risk—he might or might not have a successful career. The institutional development that marked the transition from *Chou* feudalism to the imperial system was the establishment of the *Hsien,* generally translated as "county" or "district."[12] The *Hsien* was the lowest order unit of imperial administration occupied by an appointed magistrate. For the magistracy and higher positions, the organizational principle was bureaucratic—the encroachment of kinship and other particularistic ties was excluded by elaborate precautions, such as the three-year term for holding

11. Robert M. Marsh, *The Mandarins: The Circulation of Elites in China, 1600–1900* (Glencoe, Ill.: Free Press, 1961); Ho Ping-ti, *The Ladder of Success in Imperial China* (New York: Columbia University Press, 1962).

12. Creel, *op. cit.*

a particular office and the prohibition against serving in the province in which one's lineage resided.

The town that was the seat of the *Hsien* magistracy was also the residence of the local gentry, who lived in large households with many servants. Typically, their economic base rested in proprietorship of agricultural land in the surrounding areas, though many also conducted artisan workshops and mercantile enterprises. They constituted a rather informal corporate group with which the magistrate had to come to terms in implementing policies and vice versa.[13] That they were town-dwelling, though usually land-owning, made them different from medieval and post-medieval European upper-class groups. In China, no bourgeois class could become independent of the principal land-owning classes, the feudal nobility, through political control of the towns. The gentry household, the *chia,* was basically a *three*-generation unit,[14] not a nuclear family household of the modern type. It included a parental couple—often complicated by plural wives and/or concubines—their sons, the sons' wives and children, any unmarried daughters, and servants, including artisans. The institution of basic equality among sons, especially in inheritance—a contrast with the primogeniture of Japan and most of Europe—should be credited to the Han dynasty. On the death of the parents, the sons usually separated and divided the household property.

The interposition of *Hsien* magistracies and the equality of inheritance among sons broke the power of feudal lineages at the *Shih* level and made the gentry into an upper class more like the Western than that of any feudal or archaic system. At the same time, the position of the gentry, grounded in both the *Hsien* town and the peasant villages of the countryside, prevented the universalistic bureaucratic institutions from developing effective routine organizational contact with the mass of the people.[15] For example, taxation was not based upon centrally established rates. Rather, each magistrate was responsible to his provincial governor for a certain sum each year. The taxes were not levied on individuals but on the *chia* units, and with much politicking between the *chia* and the magistrate and among the *chia.* How the magistrate collected taxes from the *chia* and the peasants was up to him, and he defrayed administrative expenses and took his own remuneration from what he could collect.[16] Although he exercised police powers and possibly military enforcement,

13. Weber, *The Religion of China, op. cit.;* Chang Chung-Li, *The Chinese Gentry* (Seattle: University of Washington Press, 1955).

14. Cf. Marion Levy, *The Family Revolution in Modern China* (Cambridge, Mass.: Harvard University Press, 1949).

15. Chang, *op. cit.*

16. It was taken for granted that a magistrate would enrich himself as far as possible.

he had to rely upon his working relations with the local gentry to collect taxes and to secure support and services for governmental operations. They had control over the masses of the lower groups, a control reinforced by their relations with the governmental system.[17]

The masses of common people were peasants, living in corporate villages and tilling the soil. They maintained the same patterns of *chia* organization as the gentry, but usually in truncated form, since economic pressures kept them from establishing large households.[18] Formally, land could be freely sold or transferred, and the peasants were not serfs, but legally free. Gentry ownership, however, was so widespread that although conditions varied by period and region, large numbers were tenants rather than independent proprietors, and, short of tenancy, there was much dependency through chronic indebtedness. Yet, it was possible for peasant lineages to rise into the gentry class through accumulation of landed property. If they had the economic base, they could give their sons a classical education, the great *desideratum,* and adopt the gentry way of life—the scholar's long gown symbolizing that its wearer did not perform physical labor. Kinship particularism was reflected in the ancestral cult. Effective solidarity in economic contexts was never strong beyond the *chia* level, but ritual solidarity was maintained through the ancestral system. Since ancestors were not divine in the Confucian system, the Western term "worship" is inappropriate in describing the cult. Rather, the ancestral cult was the basis in ritual propriety (*Li*) for the status of a *chia* unit in the larger system.[19] In more modest ways, the peasants also practiced the ancestral cult.

Creel overstates the case in claiming that the Chinese imperial system developed a full bureaucracy.[20] Its limitation lay in the nature of the qualifications for office (education in the Confucian classics) as compared to the Western traditions of training in the law, which had a bearing on organizational competence, or in science-based forms of professional competence. The scholar-official was a cultivated gentleman, not a professional in the Western sense.[21] Nevertheless, the administrative system was the mainstay of an imposing socio-political structure which was unique in scale, stability, and durability until the modern era; Rome was com-

---

17. *Ibid.;* Fairbank, *op. cit.,* chap. 6.

18. Fei Hsiao-Tung, *Peasant Life in China* (London: Dutton, 1939), and *Earthbound China* (Chicago: University of Chicago Press, 1945).

19. Cf. Francis L. K. Hsu, *Under the Ancestors Shadow* (New York: Columbia University Press, 1948).

20. Creel, *op. cit.;* Cf. Max Weber, *The Theory of Social and Economic Organization* (Glencoe, Ill.: Free Press, 1947), pp. 329 ff.

21. Weber, *The Religion of China, op. cit.,* chaps. V, VI, VIII.

parable in scale, but not in durability and cohesiveness.[22] China proved capable of defense—though it was not a militarized society. When, as during the Mongol and Manchu conquests, its defenses broke down, it demonstrated its cultural power by Sinifying its conquerors. It mounted vast public works, the Great Walls, canals, palaces. Yet China had two evolutionary limitations.

First, rationalization of law and legal procedure was scarcely superior to that of Mesopotamia and was not comparable with that of Rome. This relates to the character of the cultural tradition. Though *Li* provided a basis for a kind of law, it was subject to substantive rather than formal rationalization and reflected particularistic themes. This is evident in Confucius' aphorism about the propriety of protecting one's father from the authorities in the name of filial piety even though he had stolen sheep.[23] Second, China failed to differentiate specialized economic structures. Although it achieved high productivity, centralized its resource exploitation, as in the transportation and storage of grain, and probably exceeded Egypt in requisitioning manpower for large enterprises, its economic institutions were deficient in two respects. The Chinese never developed the monetary institutions necessary to support a ramified market system on the scale that the Greeks and Romans did.[24] Also, China did not develop a *legally* defined and protected order which could make economic activities independent of requirements for particularistic political protection. Only politically powerful groups could conduct extensive economic enterprises. Another index of the lack of legal support for economic development was the tendency (that emerged whenever central authority was impaired) for the economic-political order to break down into warlordism and, on a smaller, more local scale, banditry.

INDIA

The Confucian cultural system and its mode of institutionalization prevented Imperial China from breaking through archaic particularism in reorganizing the society, especially in including the masses of the population in the reorganized system. Weber closed his analysis of religion and society in China by contrasting Confucianism with Puritanism: "Confucian rationalism meant rational *adjustment* to the world"; Puritan rationalism meant "rational *mastery* over the world."[25] Confucian ad-

22.   Cf. Eisenstadt, *op. cit.*

23.   Creel has pointed out the significance of this aphorism, *op. cit.*

24.   On the Chinese economy in general, cf. R. H. Tawney, *Land and Labour In China* (London: Allen and Unwin, 1932).

25.   Weber, *The Religion of China, op. cit.*, p. 248, italics added.

justment accepted the unalterability of the societal substructure, especially its anchorage in the soil, in primordial kinship relations, and in their cultural accompaniments—above all, magical beliefs.

India's cultural development went farther than China's in producing a rationally consistent pattern of orientation toward ultimate reality. It did so, however, in a way that radically dissociated the modes of implementing the belief system from concern with the structure of the society. If Confucianism did not sufficiently differentiate the cosmic order from the social order, Hinduism and Buddhism differentiated them so radically that they could not be articulated in a way that would promote institutional change. In India, a two-class structure much like that of advanced intermediate societies preceded the central cultural development. Although an archaic civilization existed in Northwest India previously, the Aryan invasions from the North—probably infiltration over a long period around the middle of the second millenium B.C. rather than sudden conquest—brought in a new language, Sanscrit, and a new religion centering about the Vedic gods. Both language and religion were related to those of Greece and Rome; they were Indo-European.

Throughout this period, the descendants of the invaders comprised the upper group, while the indigenous peoples, often called Dravidian, constituted the lower group.[26] The class difference included a color factor. As the new religious system developed, the upper group divided into three *varnas,* the Brahmans, the priestly class; the Ksatriyas, the warrior-nobility; and the Vaicyas, the landowners and merchants. Together they constituted the twice-born, the bearers of the main Vedic cultural tradition eligible for its privileged religious statuses. The lower groups, the Sudras, were excluded from cultural advantages; they were tillers of the soil, servants, and the occupiers of humble statuses. This division remained constant down to Gandhi, although the full caste system did not crystallize until after the Buddhist period. For theoretical purposes, the duality is more significant than the subdivision of the upper group.[27]

In emphasizing this duality, I am not ignoring the variegated character of the Indian caste system. The outline, in terms of the three twice-born castes, the pure and impure Sudra, and eventually the Untouchables, was clear-cut. However, the effective unit was not the Varna itself but the caste or subcaste collectively, which was local or regional. There was often uncertainty about the exact ranking of such units, especially in the form of regional variations in the ranking of units that claimed to belong to the same Varna. There was also, over considerable periods, appreciable caste mobility in the Varna hierarchy, usually ac-

26. Charles Dreckmeier, *Kingship and Community in Early India* (Stanford, Calif.: Stanford University Press, 1962).

27. Max Weber, *The Religion of India* (Glencoe, Ill.: Free Press, 1958), chap. I.

companied by Brahmanic genealogies of dubious authenticity. The system was tightest at the top and became looser as one descended the status-scale, at least down to the line between the Sudras and the Untouchables, the latter being totally excluded; respectable Brahmans would perform no ritual services at all for them. My point is not that Indian caste presented a polarized two-class system but that the duality central to its religious legitimation was never transcended in the direction of the inclusion of the nonprivileged in a more equalized societal community.

The Vedic religion centered on a polytheistic pantheon but also on a sacrificial cult that shared features with the cults of Mesopotamia and Palestine. The Brahmans were its priestly group, functioning in terms of ritual sacrifice. But the distinctive cultural development was the philosophical speculation about the *meaning* of the sacrifices in which they engaged, along with the nonpriestly Aryans.[28] From this speculation came the conception that the world of life consisted of a myriad of timeless, metaphysically ultimate entities, or souls, undergoing an endless series of incarnations and reincarnations. Not only was individual death (or birth) not considered ultimate, but everything terrestrial was relativized. The world of zoological life—why plants were excluded is mysterious—was comprised of incarnated souls, not only of man, but of all species, even the insects or worms. Above man was the realm of the gods, who were also mortal incarnations of souls, though perhaps living for thousands of years. Only souls and the ultimate grounds of being of the universe, Atman or Brahman, were exempt from mortality and relativity in this sense.

The ultimate meaning of temporal process was formulated in the concept of moral causation, *Karma,* according to which the consequences of every act of every living being was attributed to the responsible individuals. On this basis, souls were thought to be rewarded for meritorious acts by being promoted on the scale of being in their subsequent lives and punished for reprehensible acts by being demoted. This system was inherently hierarchical, ranging from the gods, through the graduations of human society, to the lower animals.[29] Such relativization raised acutely the problem of the meaningfulness of the individual human life. This problem was addressed through a doctrine of salvation.[30] The religious goal was to go beyond optimizing one's fortunes in the round of rebirths and escape completely from the wheel of karma, attaining absorption into the ultimate.

28. W. T. de Bary, S. N. Hay, R. Weiler, and A. Yarrow (eds.), *Sources of Indian Tradition* (New York: Columbia University Press, 1958), chap. 1, especially pp. 15–18.

29. Heinrich Zimmer, *Philosophies of India* (Cleveland: Meridian Books, 1956).

30. Weber, *The Religion of India, op. cit.,* chaps. IV and V.

Besides its philosophical sophistication, two features of this religious orientation have significance for my purposes. First, given that the cultured Indian was permeated with these beliefs and that he would desire salvation, this orientation precluded his doing so in the ordinary course of secular life. The path to salvation lay through withdrawal from secular associations and responsibilities to practice ascetic exercises or mystical contemplation. There was no equivalent of the Confucian valuation of the ethical obligations of public life, to say nothing of a Puritan-type conception of a calling. To be sure, social responsibility was religiously sanctioned, but as *second* best, not as a prime obligation of life. Second, the doctrine was *radically individualistic* at the religious level. There was no pattern of a collectivity parallel to the People of Israel or the Christian Church. Each person sought his salvation on his own, with the tutelage of a spiritual guide, a *guru*.

Underlying these two characteristics was a devaluation of life in this world. In the form in which it was developed by certain of the philosophical schools, the conception emerged that concrete existence was itself an illusion (*maya*), and that appreciation of reality was possible only through turning one's back on the world.[31] The consequences of such a view depend on its perspective on the nature of the world. In the relevant periods of Indian history, concrete human society was relatively devalued. I find Weber's thesis incontrovertible: that, in the circumstances, this meant *traditionalized*. However, the fact that Brahmanic religion was not ascetic for the ordinary man but only for the religious virtuoso contributed to the viability of this traditionalizing ethic.

The society in which this new cultural movement developed was an advanced archaic society, not so different from Mesopotamia. There were patrimonial principates, capital cities of considerable size and complexity, development of craftmanship and of certain arts, public works on a large scale. But the variation at any given time was considerable. Continuity and communication with Mesopotamia, via Persia, was probably important. The question is why, in an area of comparable social conditions, the constellation of factors necessary for further societal evolution came together on the western periphery but not on the eastern periphery. Whereas Confucianism consolidated the *cultural* institutionalization (in the cybernetic sense, control) of the Chinese social order, the Indian religio-philosophical movement, which in cultural terms was more advanced than Confucianism, drained away cultural impetus for social development, leaving the society at the mercy of relatively archaic social configurations.

Developing in the upper classes, especially among the Brahmans,

---

31. *Ibid.;* also Max Weber, *The Sociology of Religion (Boston: Beacon Press,* 1963), chaps. IX–XII; and Zimmer, *op. cit.*

the cultural movement divided into three branches in the classical period —Hinduism, Jainism, and Buddhism—all of which departed from common ground. Jainism developed a position as a sectarian subgroup within the society, in some respects parallel to that of the Jews in the Diaspora, though not so widespread. As Weber pointed out, Jainism was important as the basis of a commercial class.[32] Buddhism, the most radical of the three religions, was extruded from India, but became one of the three great proselytizing religions in world history, extending throughout Asia south and east of India, though it did not fully displace the indigenous culture in China and Japan.[33]

Hinduism, led by the Brahmans, became the basis of the later cultural and organizational framework of Indian society. But, instead of promoting a corporate societal collectivity of the twice-born, which could be extended to include the entire society, it consolidated the religious other-worldliness and individualism of the Indian tradition at the societal community level. This legitimized a hierarchical order of secular society on the religious level. Thus, secular society was regarded as the human arena for the operation of *karma* and transmigration in such a way that merit relative to *karma* coincided with *dharma,* the performance of the traditional obligations of caste status.[34] The individual was a good citizen insofar as he observed the traditional obligations of his ascribed station in life. If meritorious, he would move upward in the *next* incarnation; otherwise, downward. The social structure was one of hereditary groupings, largely occupational, but with cross-cutting tribal divisions and with village communities that symbiotically included members of a number of castes and provided a framework for broader organization in the largely agrarian society. The criteria of status were ritual criteria in terms of the Brahmanic conception of the world. For these reasons, the Hindu orientation could not legitimate any major movement for social change. The system for attaining salvation articulated with the *dharma* system through the institutionalization of other-worldly asceticism and mysticism on an individual basis. Ideally, the high-caste individual was to pursue radical other-worldiness in the later stages of his life after he had met his traditional obligation and left a son old enough to continue the kinship line.[35]

Hinduism consolidated after the rise of the Buddhist movement, which was more radical in devaluing life in this world in favor of contemplative-mystical withdrawal. Buddhism did not sanction caste in the

32. Weber, *The Religion of India,* op. cit., chap. VI.

33. Cf. Hajime Nakamura, *Ways of Thinking of Eastern Peoples: India, China, Tibet, Japan* (Honolulu: East-West Center Press, 1946).

34. Weber, *The Religion of India,* op. cit.; Zimmer, *op. cit.*

35. Zimmer, *op. cit.;* and de Bary *et al., op. cit.,* part III.

Brahman manner but treated all secular affairs as of little consequence. It did develop a collective structure, a form of monastic community, the *Sangha,* in which monks lived together in withdrawal from the world. But its sense of religious community did not extend to the ordinary person; there was no Buddhist parallel to the Christian laity. Moreover, its monastic life was dissociated from social usefulness. This applied even to the monk's maintenance—the strict monks could not even grow their own food but had to beg for it, since work was defiling.[36] No long-term, stable large-scale political organization was established on the Brahmanic base. Although India developed many principalities and kingdoms, only one Hindu empire gained considerable size and duration: the Gupta dynasty of the fourth century, A.D.

There was, however, an *attempt* at political consolidation under the king, Ashoka, of the Maurya dynasty (fourth century B.C.). Although Ashoka eventually joined a Buddhist monastery, he was not really a Buddhist.[37] Rather, he attempted to mold a general social order (his system of *Dhamma*) by combining various elements of the tradition, Brahmanic, Buddhist, and Jain. This was as near to a general upper-class culture similar to Confucianism as appeared in Indian history. Ashoka's synthesis disintegrated both politically and culturally after his death. After that, the consolidation of Hinduism and the caste system proceeded apace under leadership from the Brahmans who, as a group, had reacted against Ashoka. The Buddhist movement gradually weakened and was eventually extruded from India.

Some centuries later, the Islamic movement spread into India. With varying comprehensiveness and duration, political structures emerged under Muslim rule. The last was the Mogul Empire, which controlled India for approximately two centuries prior to the advent of the British. History indicates that India was vulnerable to foreign rule. Nevertheless, the Muslims did not manage to convert the majority of India's population to Islam but had to accept a compromise between an Islamic minority and a Hindu majority.[38]

36. *Ibid.,* chaps VI and VII; also Nakamura, *op. cit.*

37. Peter Pardue, "The Enigma of the Ashoka Case" (Doctoral thesis, Harvard University, 1965); also A. L. Basham, *The Wonder That Was India* (New York: Macmillan, 1954).

38. The history of Buddhism outside of India is complicated. In China, Buddhism exerted influence, but only after the Empire was consolidated. Although Buddhism, somewhat like Taoism, played a role in China, it never threatened to displace Confucianism as the cultural focus of the society. It served an interstitial, safety-valve type of role. For example, it was at times prominent at the imperial court and, more generally, among upper-class women. For many groups, it was associated with the circumstances of death, with funerals and memorial observances of various kinds. The differences between the kinds of resistance to full institutionalization of Bud-

THE ISLAMIC EMPIRES

In China and India, the decisive cultural developments were indigenous to the societies in which they evolved and on which they had
their impact. In the Islamic societies and Rome, this was not the case.
Though Islam arose about a millenium after the prophetic age of Israel
and several centuries after the beginning of Christianity, it was, nevertheless, a product of the same Semitic cultural traditions. Similarly, the flower-
ing of the Greek culture had come and gone some three centuries before
Roman political authority penetrated its area, enabling it to become influential on Roman society. However, Rome's development depended less
directly on the Greek heritage than did that of Islam on the Israelitic
heritage; it was a case of independent variation from a common base, the
polis system.

Islam and Rome, following Israel and Greece, both developed a
pattern of societal community that contrasted with the patterns found
in the Orient.[39] In this pattern, the membership of the community was
not a class in the sense of the Chinese gentry or the Indian "twice-born,"
but the *entire* corporate entity, which bore the cultural tradition. In early
Israel, this entity was the *Chosen People,* corporately bound together and
to Jahweh by the *Covenant.* Its members maintained relations with non-
members, but the concept, People of Israel, remained the reference point
for their sense of societal belongingness. In Greece and Rome, the corporate body of the city-state, *polis* or *urbs,* comprised the societal community,
the category of membership being the status of *citizen.* This body often
maintained complicated relations with non-citizens, both within and outside the territorial limits of the city-state, but the polis remained the focal
entity of the society. In both the Semitic and the Greco-Roman cases, the
community entity was potentially a total society. This was not so for the
upper classes of either China or India. Furthermore, by the nature of their
cultural traditions and their societal communities, these Western societies
were oriented more actively than the Oriental societies toward institutionalizing the value-patterns of their cultures as constitutive of the society.

Islam recognized its cultural derivation from Israel by acknowledg-
ing the validity of the Hebrew prophets, especially Abraham and Moses,

---

dhism in China and of Islam in India are suggestive of the differences between the
religions and the societies involved. On the diffusion of Buddhism, see Nakamura,
op. cit.; Robert N. Bellah, *Tokugawa Religion* (Glencoe, Ill.: Free Press, 1959) contains discussion of Buddhism in Japan.

39.   Max Weber, *The City* (New York: Collier Books, 1962).

and also Jesus.[40] It had the same basic character of an associational societal community. Originally, the associated societal community centered on
the leading lineages of Medina and Mecca, which acknowledged Mohammed's leadership as the prophet of the one true God, Allah. This community, whose members were at once *believers* and solidary with each
other through their common allegiance, was the *Umma*. From the beginning, it was both a religious and a political community.[41] But, unlike
early Israel, it did not for long claim jurisdiction over a traditionally
settled territory or population. It began to expand, first over the Arabian
peninsula and then outside it. The question arose of the relation between
the full members of the religio-political community and non-members on
whom it impinged. This was defined neither in terms of class status in
the Confucian manner, nor in terms of special religious qualifications in
the Brahmanic manner, but was a matter of accepting the faith and giving
allegiance to Allah and his Prophet, Mohammed.[42] Those who did not
were infidels and could not be granted the privileges of the faithful. This
is the Islamic version of the two-class system.

One difficulty for Islam as it expanded its rule rapidly over a large
part of the civilized world was combining under unified rule two aspects
of the Islamic community, the *Umma* of the faithful and the political,
territorial community. In the first phase of expansion, Arab ethnicity and
language provided a basis of unity, but thereafter the tendency to identify
Islam with Arab culture became a hindrance in integrating non-Arab
populations into the community.[43]

Mohammed had envisioned a single *umma* that was also a politically organized society. With Islam's expansion, this ideal failed to be
implemented. First, it proved impossible to convert all the masses of the
conquered populations to Islam while at the same time maintaining adequate political control *over* them. Almost everywhere (as I have already
noted for India), large non-Muslim population elements remained, and,
over time, consolidated their positions as non-Muslims. Gradually, realistic hope of their conversion was abandoned.[44] Furthermore, there was
nominal, diluted Islam containing religiously dubious strains of other

40. H. A. R. Gibb, *Mohammedanism* (New York: Galaxy Books, 1962), especially
p. 50.

41. *Ibid.*, chaps. 2 and 3.

42. Cf. Reuben Levy, *The Social Structure of Islam* (Cambridge: Cambridge University Press, 1962), especially the Introduction and chap. I. Levy's discussion shows
this pattern to have been the predominent tendency despite difficulties of institutionalizing it.

43. Cf. Gustave E. von Grunebaum, *Medieval Islam* (Chicago: Phoenix Books, 1961),
especially chap. VIII.

44. *Ibid.*, chaps. V and VI.

traditions.[45] Second, it proved impossible to maintain political unity. Under the strain of its rapid spread, the Islamic system broke up into a plurality of politically independent units by a process analogous to that which occurred in Western Christendom when the Holy Roman Empire fragmented into feudal-national states. Thus, the Moorish, the Arab, the Persian, the Indian, and eventually the Turkish political systems became independent.

Muslim theory required that there be a single religious head, a successor to the Prophet, who should also wield political power over all Islam. The institution of the Caliphate, however, was never stabilized, but became the subject of rival claims and the occasion of many intra-Islamic wars over several centuries. At issue were competing principles of legitimation, which, though based upon differing claims about descent from the Prophet, involved normative problems that were never authoritatively resolved.[46] Islam, like Israel, emphasized the religious *law*. It was preeminently a religion of the *Book*, the *Qur'an*, the revealed word of Allah through the Prophet, supplemented by what were traditionally regarded as his sayings, the *Shari'a*, and the interpretive glosses of many generations of legal experts. Indeed, the rigid monotheism of Islam inhibited concern for theological subtleties and placed the emphasis in religious culture on the law. The law became the basis of unity for the religious community, as it became for Israel.

However, Islamic law failed to develop the kind of basis for a normative order that developed in Rome. Islam had no corporate body to which the authoritativeness of its law referred, not even a people in the Hebrew sense, since it had abandoned its ethnic identification with its expansion, though aspects of Arab primacy lingered on informally. In general, the law was universalistic in applying ideally to all the faithful equally. But in the absence of a corporate reference, it had to rest on the loosely integrated tradition of the *Qur'an*, the *Shari'a*, and the glosses. Although it was maintained by a group of experts, they never held an organized status in a corporate entity in the fashion, for example, of the canon lawyers in the Mediaeval Christian Church.[47] This condition permitted the group of legal experts, and actually the law itself, to fragment into several competing schools, thereby making the authoritativeness of legal controls still more problematical.[48] But the underlying difficulty was that the *Umma* did not comprise a corporate entity in the Christian sense.

Furthermore, Islamic law remained legalistic in the sense also true

---

45. Cf. Clifford Geertz, *The Religion of Java* (Glencoe, Ill.: Free Press, 1960).

46. Grunebaum, *op. cit.*, chap. V.

47. *Ibid.*; and Gibb, *op. cit.*, chaps. 6 and 7.

48. In turn, this made differentiation among the political, religious, and legal foci of societal organization still more difficult.

of the Jewish law, especially in its Talmudic phase. The *Qur'an* and, even more, the *Shari'a* were aphoristic and unsystematized. The Islamic tendency was to elaborate particular precepts and prohibitions on relatively *ad hoc* bases, adapting them to the various circumstances in which the faithful found themselves. Thus, Islamic law was characterized by ingenious casuistry rather than integration about clearly formulated legal principles;[49] compared to the Roman use of the conception of natural law, it had hardly any philosophical grounding.

A basic dualism was never successfully transcended and became characteristic of all Islamic societies. On the one hand, legitimized by the religious mission of Islam, there was a continual drive to unify the faithful politically. But, on the other hand, there was the anchorage of the Islamic masses in traditional agrarian or nomadic societies, organized about kinship and particularistic local solidaries that were never thoroughly structured to match the religious universalism—or even that attained by the highest political authorities and the law. Indeed, the particularism often penetrated the higher echelons.[50] Religiously, this duality was clear. Orthodox Islam adhered to a theological rigidity that could not legitimize any mediation with the diversity of human interests and motives. But these human elements gave rise to the popular Sufist movements that fostered emotionalism, mysticism, and magic and undermined the institutionalization of any distincitvely Islamic pattern in large-scale societies.[51]

Besides the heritage it shared with Israel, Islam also drew upon the heritage of classical antiquity. It was from the Arabs that many classical texts, such as those of Aristotle, were recovered in the West, and in such fields as mathematics they advanced classical culture considerably. Indeed, the impact of the classical heritage led to a major crisis in Islamic culture, reaching its climax with the work of Al Ghazzali, the Thomas Aquinas of the Islamic Middle Ages. The negative response to this impact, however, was the opposite of that of Christian Europe. Islamic orthodoxy, in protecting the purity of the Prophet's tradition, failed to exploit classical philosophy as a means of integrating secular culture into its system and thereby cut itself off from another constituent of modern societies.[52]

Unlike China and India, Islam developed a radically activistic orien-

---

49. *Ibid;* and Levy, *op. cit.*, chaps. IV and VI.

50. Cf. Eisenstadt, *op. cit.*

51. On the general point of such dualism particularly, but also for the whole sketch on Islam, I am especially indebted to the work of H. A. R. Gibb. See especially his recent volume, *Studies on the Civilization of Islam* (Boston: Beacon Press, 1962).

52. Bellah emphasized this point in a personal communication. It is evident at many points in E. I. J. Rosenthal, *Political Thought in Medieval Islam* (Cambridge: Cambridge University Press, 1958).

tation. Acting upon a culturally defined base, it attempted to transform human society into a religiously ordained ideal pattern. It must be judged an historical failure in that it did not even thoroughly Muslimize much of the population under its political control; the Christianizing of Europe offers a contrast. Beyond that, its cultural tradition and societal normative order did not undergo the processes of differentiation, inclusion, and upgrading that could have transformed the *Umma* into a total society permeated by universalistic norms. Hence, rather like China and India, the Islamic societies remained, despite their imposing achievements, traditionalistic and segmented into a variety of particularistic groupings operating under a veneer of common Islamic culture. The adaptive shortcoming of the Islamic societies was the failure of the *Umma* to become *institutionalized* as a corporate societal community comprising the whole population of the society. This can be partly attributed to Islam's tendency to direct action—i.e., to take political control, usually through military means, and attempt to Muslimize the society from that vantage point. In later chapters I shall stress the difference between this process and that which provided the basis of modern Christian society.

Features of the religious tradition underlay Islam's evolutionary limitations. Islamic monotheism, despite its purity, was embedded in a good deal of archaic cultural content, particularly in the *ad hoc*, unsystematized Koranic law, much of which was parochial to Arab culture or even idiosyncratic to Mohammed himself. Still more fundamental was the lack of a philosophical grounding for both theology and law. In its *use* of philosophy, Islam was not on a level comparable with the Indian religions or Christianity. Thus, despite the majestic transcendence of the conception of Allah, the line between the worldly and the other-worldly was not clearly drawn, but resembled the pattern common in archaic religions.[53] For example, the pleasures of the Harem seem to have been disproportionately prominent in the Islamic conception of the after-life. Its inability to accept the rationalizing resources of Greek culture probably made the full institutionalization of Islam's activistic ideal patterns impossible.

THE ROMAN EMPIRE

Roman society, in common with the Greek *poleis,* surpassed the Israelitic conception of the People and the Islamic conception of the *Umma* in developing a pattern of societal community having a specifically *corporate* character. Resting on the ancient traditions of city-state organization, the Greek and Roman city-states developed as small, politically

53. Grunebaum, *op. cit.,* chaps. III and IV.

independent, territorial units, the original cores of which were comprised of aristocratic partrilineages. The heads of these lineages—e.g., the original Roman *paterfamilias*—were presumptive equals *asociating* themselves, their kinsmen, and their clients into a corporate entity, the *polis* or *urbs*.

In Rome's early phase, before its political expansion, the originally aristocratic structure of the *urbs* was democratized, a process common to most of Greece and Italy.[54] The distinction between patricians and plebians gave way to a common *citizenship* status in which all adult males were presumptive equals. A factor in this development in both Rome and Greece was common involvement in military service—the citizen body (i.e. corporate Rome) was also an army. The urbs also established a system of elective offices, a citizen assembly with political power, and a universalistically selected senate composed of former magistrates. Although the population governed by the community of Rome did not consist only of citizens with full political rights and their families, citizens comprised the core of the societal community. Not only a corporate citizen body and elective office but also an effective, authoritative law were characteristic of Rome from an early stage. The legal system underwent an internal development parallel to that of the political system, especially in the extension of legal rights from the *paterfamilias* as a lineage head to the individual male, who became *sui juris* (possessed of full legal capacity to act in his own behalf.)[55]

Like early Islam and many other empires, this originally small corporate society embarked on expansion, successively conquering its immediate neighbors, the whole of Italy, and virtually the Western civilized world, including the entire Mediterranean Coast and extending as far as Britain in one direction and Mesopotamia in the other. With this immense territory, the early Empire comprised a population estimated at about 60 million,[56] large indeed for the time. Rome's expansion, from the late Republic on, cannot be explained solely by her superior military organization. However important that may have been in taking over new populations and territories, the stabilization of Roman rule was dependent on the legal system which provided its institutional framework. By the time this expansion occurred, Roman law had been systematized

---

54. Cf. William Warde Fowler, *The City-State of the Greeks and Romans* (London: Macmillan, 1921) for a treatment of the political and legal aspects of the democratization process.

55. This carried the de-institutionalization of kinship solidarity one step farther than the Chinese system did. The male head of the nuclear family household, not merely the 3-generation *chia*, became *sui juris*.

56. Cf. Adolf Harnack, *The Mission and Expansion of Christianity* (New York: Harper Torchbooks, 1962), p. 8.

upon the principles of the Stoic philosophy of the law of nature. In particular, the *jus gentium* and the Roman concept of empire itself could not have developed without this philosophical systematization.[57]

Thus, by utilizing the principles of Greek philosophical generalization, the Roman system of legal order came to be formulated in universalistic terms applicable to all men and based on general views of normative order which could be institutionalized as common to the civilization of classical antiquity. The religion of early Rome was relatively parochial and could not alone have developed and legitimized such a legal order. The contrast between Rome and Islam with respect to legal rationalization brings out the importance of this feature. Law was essential to Rome, not only for its ordering of relations among private parties, but also for the constitutional capacity it gave the Roman state to mobilize resources and act with rationality and consistency in various contexts.

Whatever may be said about the justice or humanitarianism of Roman rule, it had unique institutional features. As a conqueror, Rome did not simply rule over its subject peoples in an imperialist manner but accepted elements of them into her corporate structure, mainly by the extension of Roman citizenship, first to elite elements and then to more common people; first in Italy, then in Greece, Gaul, Spain, North Africa, the Middle East, and so on. Finally, all free men of the Empire were accorded citizenship, though its significance had by then become so diluted as to be meaningless politically. A means of extension was the grant of citizenship to all men, whatever their origins, who had honorably served a six-year term in the legions. This was a process of democratization, for it cut across the internal stratification of the subsocieties involved. Extension of citizenship involved, *ipso facto,* the extension of the rule of law because the central legal system, the *jus civilis,* applied to all citizens, whether resident in Rome or not. Furthermore, the legal tradition was so strong that an additional system of law, the *jus gentium,* was developed for the peoples under Roman jurisdiction who were not citizens, in order to regulate their relations with Roman authority and with one another.[58] The *jus gentium* articulated with the central law and extended universalistic regulations to the entire population under Roman rule. These concerned the rights of persons vis-à-vis government and in relation to one another in the fields of civil rights, property and contract, freedom of movement, and the like.

Besides the system of substantive rules, Rome also developed an elaborate system of judicial procedure. The courts were presided over by

57. Cf. Ernest Barker, "The Conception of Empire"; and F. de Zulueta, "The Science of Law," in Cyril Bailey (ed.), *The Legacy of Rome* (Oxford: Clarendon Press, 1923).

58. Zulueta, *op cit.*

the *praetors,* who were not legal professionals, but regular magistrates engaged in political careers. In the later period, there did appear legal professionals, the jurisconsults, who advised clients and judges about technical points of the law but were not regular attorneys in the modern sense. This was the most developed, largely secular system of law that evolved in *any* society until early modern times. Under its governmental and legal system, Roman society became cosmopolitan and individualistic. Both persons and property were mobile throughout the Empire. A money, credit, and market institutional complex encouraged the development of non-political economic enterprise. In the cultural spheres, the ethnic and cultural heterogeneity of the population contributed to an immense range of religious and cultural freedom and mobility. Quite probably a movement like Christianity could not have spread through proselytization in other advanced intermediate societies. Thus, its legal system, rather than its political control of large territories and populations, was Rome's distinctive achievement.

In the course of Rome's expansion, its complex of citizenship and law encountered difficulties in meshing with the rest of the social structure. First, under Roman conditions, the extension of citizenship in the legal context involved a concomitant dilution of political content. Expanded Rome *could not* function as a political democracy. There are many reasons for this, especially Rome's failure to develop *representative* institutions, which was partly due to the unitary character of governmental authority, the *imperium.*[59] Effective political power and influence came to be concentrated in a small upper group, the senatorial class,[60] and became subject to arbitrary intervention by military elements, not only because of the coercive power of the military establishment, but also because military units were traditionally units with political powers. When the tendencies to concentrate power eventuated in a monarchy, Rome never managed to institutionalize a solution to the problem of succession. Political concentration was related to stratification though not identical with it. The senatorial class became, *de facto,* mainly hereditary, though it remained open to "new men," especially from the provinces. Along with some auxiliary groups, like the tax farmers, the senatorial class came to amass, especially for political use, concentrations of influence, power, and wealth for which there were apparently no effective countervailing means of control. This eroded the position of the Empire-wide citizen body as the core community of the society.

Given the nature of the indigenous Roman religion and the cultural diversity of the Empire, the development of a secular law and a political

---

59. Cf. Martin P. Nilsson, *Imperial Rome* (New York: Norton, 1964).

60. Ronald Syme, *The Roman Revolution* (Oxford: Clarendon Press, 1939).

authority administered with relative impartiality over so many different ethnic, cultural, and religious groups generated a crisis in cultural legitimation. The Imperial cult was weak, for the cultural sophistication of the Empire had passed the stage of god-king. Yet, the Empire had developed no adequate alternative for meaningfully articulating the *moral* basis of the legal-political order with the ultimate grounding of the system of moral commitments.[61]

Each of these difficulties limited the institutionalization, on the scale of the Empire, of the underlying Roman conception of the societal community as a corporate body of citizens. The greatest success in overcoming the difficulties was achieved at the legal level. But the extension of the legal status of citizenship involved a dilution of its political aspects and probably also of legal security. The *jus gentium* was, in the circumstances, a double-edged sword. As a universalistic normative order developed among distinct ethnic groups, the *jus gentium* was institutionalized more thoroughly than any previous system of comparable scope. But the fact that the *gens* ("people" or ethnic group) was recognized as a unit requiring a legal relation to other units of its type diluted its inviolability. It was through membership in recognized *gentes* that individuals not citizens of Rome held legal rights in the Roman system—the *gens* was the external parallel to the *familia*.[62]

This background throws light on the structure of Roman political authority and especially on its unitary character. The formula *Senatus Populusque Romanum* (the Senate and citizenry of Rome) balanced the democratic and aristocratic principles, even though in constitutional law the Senate was an organ of the people, consisting of former magistrates who, as magistrates, had been popularly elected.[63] The system became *de facto* aristocratic in that the magistrates were recruited from senatorial class lineages. However, the senators came to be drawn from broad ethnic and geographical groups so that the Senate ceased to be exclusively Roman or even Italian. Yet, the Roman state remained unitary, resting ultimately on the concept of a citizen body.[64] Its resistance to differentiation is illuminated by its failure to differentiate the civil executive, the military, and judiciary as functions of specialists. Roman magistracies carried the *imperium* (authority) of the state as a diffuse whole, having the right to exercise any aspect of the governmental powers and being differentiated only by rank.[65] Although the judicial functions were exercised by

61. A. D. Nock, *Conversion* (Oxford: Oxford Paperbacks, 1961).

62. Parenthetically, I suggest, the West's radical solution of this problem derived, above all, from the drastic spiritual individualism of Christianity.

63. H. Stuart Jones, "Administration," in Bailey (ed.), *op. cit.*

64. Syme, *op. cit.*

65. Jones, *op. cit.;* Nilsson, *op. cit.*

the *praetor*, he was not a lawyer but a politician occupying the praetor-ship as a step in a public career that had probably begun with a junior military command.

The *consuls* exercised supreme military command, not in the general sense in which the American President, as Chief Executive, is also Commander-in-Chief, but because during the Republican period, they were expected to serve as field commanders. Thus, there was no class comprised specifically of professional military officers. The case of the consulship illustrates the problems which differentiation posed for the system. Pressures to differentiate military from civil responsibility were such that frequently one *consul* acted as field commander while the other directed the civil government. Yet the two *consuls*, having identical powers, were incumbents of one category of office, not of two separate offices. Any differentiation was based upon informal agreement, not constitutional provision. These facts reflect the obligation of the entire citizenry of Rome—as of most Greek *poleis*—to render military service. One may say that Rome did not *have* an army as much as it *was* an army. For this reason, service in the legions was a major means of extending citizenship. The civil and military bases of status were closely linked.[66]

The legislative function, insofar as it was exercised separately from other political functions, belonged to the people. However, the effective institutionalization of their rights became increasingly difficult. Thus, legislation tended to center in the Senate, though much of the unruliness of the city's populace and the tendency of the legions, notably the Praetorian Guard, to intervene in politics, reflected the people's lingering claim to the ultimate sovereignty. The Senate became not so much a representative body as a council of elder officials having a *de facto* aristocratic base. Its relation to the *princeps* was ambiguous and difficult,[67] a condition that was exacerbated by the principate's tendency to become hereditary *de facto* but without firm institutionalization. Such resistence to differentiation, manifested in many contexts, is a keynote of the Roman political structure. This structure was a powerful solvent for primordial solidarities because of its all-or-none character and the links between the unitary authority system and the legal structure of citizenship. Yet, it also tended to use political control to press the pluralistic element of the heterogeneous society into a mold. This tendency could be seen in the case of the early Roman family and the concentration of its rights in the status of *paterfamilias;* since the married women could not be the legal representative of an autonomous collectivity, she was denied all legal status. The family had to have a *potestas* (the rights to use power) as unitary as the state's *imperium*.

66. Nilsson, *op. cit.*

67. Syme, *op. cit.*, pp. 365 ff. and 407 ff.

This problem was more serious for the *gentes* of the *jus gentium* because they were larger units. For example, the large Jewish diaspora communities, as in Alexandria or Rome itself, were treated largely as units, being held to collective responsibilities by the state—e.g., for payment of taxes and maintenance of order among their members. Despite the many contrasts with China, there was a common limiting element, the failure to absorb important segments of the system into the universalistic framework. Especially outside Italy, unabsorbed, particularistically structured socio-cultural elements remained.[68] In this respect, Roman society resembled the Islamic Empires in India—there were numerous large Hindu elements beneath the Islamic political authority.

Roman society encouraged significant developments in public administration, trade, and various sorts of cultural activity. Particularly in the Antonine period, it provided political order and peace, protection of individual liberties, and economic prosperity that was unequalled for both the area and population controlled and the thoroughness of control for many centuries. The limitations I have sketched, however, not only reflected failure to attain modern levels of structural differentiation but also created instability that made the Western Empire shorter-lived.

These considerations support Weber's analysis of Rome's economic decline. Weber emphasized the system's dependence on slavery, especially for providing agricultural products on the scale required by its urban populations and wealthy classes.[69] The slave population was recruited mainly from prisoners of war. Their organization in barracks on the *latifundia* (plantations) precluded family relations and prevented the slave population from sustaining itself by natural increase. So, with the pacification of the outlying parts of the Empire, the slave supply dwindled. Family relationships had to be granted to the slaves. This led toward a semi-independent peasant agriculture and destroyed the basis of plantation production. Certain features of the Roman political and legal system complicated the slavery problem. The unitary character of *imperium* was shared by the legal category of property. Something was or was not an object of possession. Hence, there was a tendency to constrict the many possible shadings of "unfreedom"—men who were not free were treated as slaves in the most drastic sense. Slavery, however, was economical only on a special basis of social organization, and when that basis was threatened, a reversion to less advanced forms ensued. Role differentiation relative to kinship and property rights was insufficient for

68. Eisenstadt, *op. cit.*

69. Max Weber, "The Social Causes of the Decay of Ancient Civilization," in *Journal of General Education*, October 1950.

a formally free, individualized labor force.[70] The proprietary unit of a traditional kinship-based agriculture could break through to the employment of individuals only by categorizing employees as slaves. When this became untenable, a situation ensued in which security could be gained only by re-traditionalization.

It is often said that the genius of Rome was legal, political, and military rather than cultural. Properly understood, this seems correct. Indeed, Roman religion was, relative to that of classical Greece, more archaic in most respects. As political rule and the legal order were extended and the political content of citizenship was attenuated, the problem of legitimation became increasingly acute. During a critical period, Hellenization of the upper classes of the whole Empire, not just its Eastern half, filled the gap.[71] The lasting contribution of this development was the philosophical grounding that the Stoic conception of natural law provided for the Roman legal system.

Rome drew heavily upon aspects of Greek classical culture in organizing a vast imperial society. Nevertheless, it lacked the capacity to develop a dynamic religious system which could legitimize the expanded societal community. The archaic attempt to deify the emperors was a symptom of this— it was treated with open ridicule by some of the intellectuals of the time. The need for a higher order of moral direction was evidenced by an unstable welter of exotic cults, sects, syncretistic belief systems, and religious movements, many of which offered some kind of salvation to the individual. They were not, however, adequately grounded in the general culture, nor did they mesh the religious needs of the individual with the nature of the society as a whole, particularly in regard to the legitimation of government.[72] Like Islam, but in a somewhat different sense, Rome was overextended in these respects. It failed to build a viable societal community, support its government, and prevent the alienation of its best citizens on the requisite scale.

Sir Ernest Barker has suggested that a reason for Christianity's eventual adoption as the state religion was a need for cultural legitimation which the previous religious culture could not provide.[73] Certainly Christianity was a religious movement with the potential to fill this need. In the early stages of its development, however, it was too other-worldly to

---

70. In "Sociological Categories of Economic Action," *The Theory of Social and Economic Organization, op. cit.,* part II.

71. Charles N. Cochrane, *Christianity and Classical Culture* (New York: Galaxy, 1957).

72. See Nock, *op. cit.* and Franz Cumont, *Oriental Religions in Roman Paganism* (New York: Dover Books, 1956).

73. Ernest Barker, "The Conception of Empire," in Bailey (ed.), *op. cit.*

help integrate *any* society—Gibbon's verdict that Christianity was a *disintegrative* force in Roman society is probably correct. Even later, it could not simply graft into the framework of Roman society, for the Empire involved too much that was alien to Christian principles. Societal regression was necessary before the religion could *grow with* the structure of a new society, before its legitimizing and regulating potential could fully develop.[74]

CONCLUSION

This chapter has been concerned with the consequences of differentiating the cultural and social systems beyond the level found in archaic societies and the implications of such differentiation for the nature of the societal community. In *all* four cases discussed, the patterns of the cultural system penetrated deeper into the societal structure than in *any* archaic system. Yet the cases divide into two pairs.

In China and India, the cultural system became the focus of status for well-defined upper-class groups, the scholar-gentry and the "twiceborn," who collectively set the tone for the society, though without corporate organization. In both cases, the societal penetration of the cultural élites was limited by a combination of their own characteristics and those of the broader societal matrices. This left a mass of undigested primordial populations and structures that could not, in the circumstances, be engaged in the socio-cultural patterns defined as ideal by the élite traditions in more than a superficial sense.

Islam and Rome involved more world-oriented conceptions of societal community that were, in principle, extendable to all who could enter the cultural-social community—and neither emphasized ascriptive barriers. However, given the nature of the obstacles inherent in their social situations and the problems of *scale* which full institutionalization of their ideal patterns would have imposed, the success of both was incomplete. Islam never succeeded in adequately integrating the vast *Umma* and a comparable political community. Rome failed to coordinate its extended citizenship with the political, stratification, and legitimation requirements necessary for such a large body of citizens to become the effective integrative core of a viable society. Many of the ingredients of modernity were present in these societies despite their failures to evolve into modern societies. Their failures were not at the level of values but in the problems of integrating values with the differentiated conditions of a complex society in a complex environment. Incapacity to cope with these conditions imposed limits upon the development of more advanced cultural patterns.

74. Cf. Ernest Troeltsch, *The Social Teachings of the Christian Churches*, vol. I (New York: Harper Torchbooks, 1961).

CHAPTER 5
CULTURAL LEGACIES FOR LATER SOCIETIES
THE HEBREW AND GREEK CONCEPTS OF A MORAL ORDER

The lower a system stands in sociocultural evolution, the more co-extensive and less independent are its societal and cultural systems empirically. This may explain why some anthropologists fail to distinguish between societies and cultural systems analytically and speak of a society as "a culture." The relation between social and cultural systems is always complex, partly because so many components of cultural systems can vary independently. In Egypt, such co-extensiveness was greater than in Mesopotamia. China exhibited the greatest co-extensiveness among the historic civilizations, though some of its culture proved exportable to Japan and other parts of East Asia, and it imported Buddhism from India. The Mediterranean world consolidated under Roman rule, on the other hand, was notably cosmopolitan in cultural terms. Yet, in the societies discussed so far, the institutionalization of cultural elements, particularly the normative order, occurred predominantly within the concrete population, territory, and historical period in which the cultural developments first emerged—due allowance being made for the time that processes of institutionalization take. Buddhism is a cultural complex that had its influence *outside* the society in which it originated. But because it did not lead toward modernity and because it had little significance for Western society, I have not discussed it extensively.

Two societies, though having small consequence in the sociocultural systems of their time and place, were the agents of cultural innovations that have proved crucial for societies that were not their evolutionary sequels—namely Israel, the originator of the religion of

Jahweh (or Judaism), and Greece, the originator of a famous, secular culture. I shall analyze these two cases; they illustrate a contribution to the evolutionary process which has not been emphasized in previous chapters. These societies present two problems: to define the societal conditions which made their cultural innovations possible and to explain how the cultural products became sufficiently dissociated from their society of origin to have consequences for subsequent societies.

With respect to the first problem, Hebrew and Greek cultural innovations were so radical that their bearers could not have established them over the vast territory of the large-scale empires of the period. The processes had to occur in small-scale societies with unusual bases of independence. In both cases, furthermore, the innovation had to involve, under the leadership of the important classes, a differentiation of *the society as a whole* from the others to which it was related. It had to become a new *type of society*, not merely a new sub-system within an existent type.[1] With respect to the second problem, both cases involved a loss of political independence and the transfer of prestige within the relevant populations to elements not carriers of political responsibility at the societal level but specialists in the maintenance of the cultural systems themselves.

With these considerations in mind, let us review the facts and then attempt to formulate the factors common to both examples of this type of evolutionary process. I shall not be concerned with the cultural contribution of each and its specific relevance to subsequent evolution. My concern will be with the nature of the process by which radical cultural innovations arise and are then differentiated from the societal matrices of their origins.

ISRAEL

Israel started as a tribal confederation in the fringe area between Palestine and the desert.[2] The social factors that transcended tribalism in the early period fused religious and political components in an archaic manner. How far back the universalistic monotheism of Jahwism dates is controversial, but it is unlikely that a principled monotheism arose before the Mosaic period and probably not even then.[3] Nevertheless, the

1. Thus, if these two cases had a common background in the New Eastern societal type of the period, as Cyrus H. Gordon has claimed in *The Common Background of Greek and Hebrew Civilizations* (New York: Norton, 1965), it had to be a *background* that preceded the breakthroughs that each made, and *from* which each broke.

2. Moscati, *Ancient Semitic Civilization, op. cit.*

3. Theophile James Meek, *Hebrew Origins* (New York: Harper Torchbooks, 1960), chap. 3.

characteristics of the Hebraic religion that enabled it to break through the archaic type of cultural order was already visible in the Mosaic patterns of conceptualizing God and his relations with his historical people.[4] The early Jahweh was the God of the *political* confederation of Hebrews and was minimally implicated in the internal structure of the tribes, for which other gods continued to be significant.[5] As Weber emphasizes, Jahweh was the God of foreign policy, war interests being a feature of his worship, as the appellation "Lord of Hosts" suggests.[6] During the captivity in Egypt and the conquest of the Promised Land, Jahweh was not yet conceived of as omnipotent, as able to guarantee his Chosen People success against human enemies and their divine sponsors.

Israel's social development in Palestine was from a pastoral and agricultural patriarchalism to a loosely structured society of city-states. Apparently, these were similar to those of Mesopotamia and the Syrian-Lebanese coast, having upper classes in which member lineages were basically equal—Job seems to have been an elder in such a community. The lower classes were clients of the upper groups, though we should not impute too rigid a particularism to this dependency relation. Later, when monarchy emerged, Israel became a small empire not different in basic social structure from the much larger-scale Mesopotamian type. It was not stable or well integrated. Although the reigns of David and Solomon consolidated the people of Israel into a single kingdom, it soon split into northern and southern kingdoms. In the culminating reign of Solomon, the kingdom was a petty oriental monarchy with a national temple cult, a patrician class, a patrimonial, centralized bureaucracy, a rudimentary legal system, a semi-free peasant and artisan class, considerable market trade, a corvée for mobilizing manpower, and nomadic fringe groups that posed threats to political security.[7]

What was distinctive about the Israelites was their conception of Jahweh and the people's relation to him based on a *Covenant*. This conception of a Covenant developed through several forms, notably those attributed to Abraham and Moses. The Covenant was conceived on the model of treaties between vassal states and Great Kings of dominant empires in the Near East, particularly the Hittite Empire.[8] Thus, it bal-

4. Martin Buber, *Moses* (New York: Harper Torchbooks, 1958).

5. Meek, *op. cit.*

6. Max Weber, *Ancient Judaism* (Glencoe, Ill.: Free Press, 1952), chap. IV.

7. W. F. Albright, *From the Stone Age to Christianity*, 2nd ed. (Garden City: Anchor Books, 1957).

8. George E. Mendenhall, *Law and Covenant in Israel and the Ancient Near East* (Pittsburgh: Biblical Colloquium, 1959).

anced three themes—the absolute sovereignty of God, the mutuality between God and His people, and relations among the people.

The first theme accentuates the chasm between the divine and the human that marks their more generalized differentiation. However much later development there was, this theme is the point of entrance for the concept of a transcendent God, which eventually made His attributes inconceivable in human terms. Thus, His plans and will were not to be evaluated by human standards. Although staying on the right side of Jahweh in the sense of propitiation of Him was necessary, more crucial was that His people lived to do His will as a collectivity. This belief is the substance of the shift in relations with the divine, from religious bartering with it—typical of archaic religions—to serving as *its instrument*.[9] Among the themes of Egyptian religion, creation took precedence for Israel, while procreation and resurrection receded to insignificance. The Chosen People were by God's creative act endowed with a divine *mission*, a conception involving a step beyond not merely the Egyptian but also the Mesopotamian belief system.

Thus, no Israelitic King could legitimately claim divinity within the bounds of strict Hebrew religion. He was merely the human leader of a human community that took its mandate from God, but in no way participated in the divine. Indeed, a tendency of Solomon to claim some sort of divine status was a factor in the Prophets' opposition to the monarchy.[10] The trend of Israelitic thought established a gulf between the divine and the human that was as unbridgeable for the higher human echelons as for the lower ones. This relates to the fact that a special prestige status was never firmly institutionalized for the Israelitic priesthood. The king having no godhead himself, had no special priestly charisma, unlike his Mesopotamian and his Egyptian counterparts. The Covenant had significance for the organizational development of religious action. A religious focus on cult was characteristic of archaic civilizations. This was not absent in Israel, but the developmental trend of religion based on the Covenant was to ethical instruction and to law.

In early times, Jahweh's sacrificial cult was practiced by all dignitaries, particularly the patriarchs, heads of lineage groups.[11] Eventually, the cult, which (following the terms of the Covenant) came to mediate between God and the people of Israel collectively, was centralized in the Temple at Jerusalem and practiced by its priesthood. Numerous cultist elements did remain scattered about the countryside, but they were diffusely embedded in other statuses, mostly of intra-tribal significance,

9. Weber, *Ancient Judaism, op. cit.*

10. Frankfort, *Kingship and the Gods, op. cit.*, concluding chap., "The Hebrews."

11. Meek, *op cit.* chap. 4.

and often were independent of Jahweh worship or, like the Baal cults, were even opposed to it.[12] Thus, Israel lacked extensive priesthoods constituting a structurally distinct, high-status sector of the society, as in Egypt or Mesopotamia. This feature of the society resulted in an interest structure open to anti-traditionalist influences. During the period of political independence, the sacrificial cult came to be centered in the Temple at Jerusalem and was effectively eliminated from the constituent units, such as lineages and local communities. Yet Solomon's Temple, as the central symbol of Israel, was an archaic element. The experience of having to live in the Diaspora without a temple cult—particularly during the Babylonian captivity—prepared the way for the later form of Judaism. This emerged after the destruction of the Temple, when the cult element disappeared entirely, but without destroying the ethnic and cultural identity of the people of Israel.

Concurrently with this de-emphasis on cult, Judaism developed a second distinctive characteristic, namely, the belief in the special significance of the *law* distinguished from the cult. This emphasis, which emerged only after Moses, followed from the belief that the religious obligation was less to worship Jahweh than to *obey* him. The law, grounded in the Mosaic Decalogue, became increasingly the charter of the people. Their acceptance of it and, through that, of their special relation to its divine author constituted their identity as an ethnic community.[13] Important legal developments had occurred in Mesopotamia. Except for specifically religious items, such as the First Commandment, the Israelitic law was not so different in content from such developments, although it did eliminate class differences in legal rights and obligations.[14] Its unique quality lay in the *meaning* attributed to it. Not simply the king's exercise of authority over relations among his subjects or between his regime and his subjects, it constituted the *content* of God's will for his people. It was Jahweh's Commandments.

Therefore, whatever the human organization of political authority, the normative order governing human relations was *independent* of it. The king, insofar as the kingdom was Israelitic, was to act *under* the law and be the agent of its implementation, not its source and origin. Under non-Israelitic rules, the Jew's first obligation was to the Jewish law, not to the political authority[15]—this is the point of the episode involving Daniel and his associates in Babylon. The religious and secular components of

12. *Ibid.;* Weber, *Ancient Judaism, op. cit.,* chaps. VI and VIII.

13. *Ibid.*

14. Moscati, *Ancient Semitic Civilization, op. cit.;* Albright, *op. cit.*

15. Martin Buber, *The Prophetic Faith* (New York: Harper Torchbooks, 1960), *passim.*

this normative order were not yet differentiated, and both aspects of the developing law were particularized in substance. Indeed, they became continually more so in post-Exilic times.[16] Further advances occurred only much later under different conditions.

Despite legitimizing the law of the community on religious grounds, the Hebrew system maintained its relevance to practical human affairs. The transcendence of the source of legitimation did not imply that only otherworldly action could be acorded religious merit, as Indian doctrine tended to hold. Jahweh's will for his people involved their proper management, as a social community, of this-worldly, quite ordinary, affairs. The status of the law as the means of relating to Jahweh provided the basis for the special nature of the Hebrew societal community, usually designated as the *people*. The people were defined both by having been chosen and by having voluntarily associated themselves. Thus, mutual commitment, both to Jahweh and to one another, defined their solidarity. This conception of the people provided the constitutive symbolism for maintaining the societal identity that survived not so much persecution as the absorbent pressures of societies organized on a much larger scale than Israel. The stories of Joseph and Potiphar's wife and Daniel in Babylon illustrate the significance of this communal identity.

This identity was also the basis of an internal leveling tendency. The Kingdom of Solomon was stratified according to the pattern of the times. As Israel's special nature became more salient, pressure developed to define all Hebrews as having the same problem.[17] Hence, the distinction between belonging and not belonging became emphasized rather than differentiations within the community of Israel itself. The *basis* of commitment, not only (as in Job's case) toward Jahweh, but also toward the community of Israel, became troublesome and had to be resolved on *voluntary* grounds. Adjacent societies offered numerous and attractive opportunities for defection from the community.

The focus of Judaism was the conception of the people as the societal community that possessed a distinctive culture. However, the leveling tendency and the note of voluntary adherence also developed religious individualism, which grew in later periods and fed into the stream of Christian individualism.[18] The covenant relation thus motivated positive loyalties to the religion of Jahweh and to the community

---

16. Rudolph Bultmann, *Primitive Christianity in its Contemporary Setting* (Cleveland: Meridian Books, 1956), pp. 59 ff.

17. Weber, *Ancient Judaism, op. cit.,* Part IV; and Buber, *The Prophetic Faith, op. cit.*

18. Bultmann, *op. cit.;* Eric Voegelin, *Israel and Revelation,* vol. I of *Order and History* (New Orleans: Louisiana State University Press, 1956), chap. 13, especially part 3.

of the people without converting the Hebrews into a band of special, fissive devotees or a small sectarian order that could not involve a whole ethnic community.

Although Jahweh's transcendence so surpassed humanity that a human contract could not bind Him, essential to the Covenant were His favorable promises to the people contingent on their fulfillment of His Commandments.[19] Faith in Jahweh could not be sustained if His conduct were conceived as totally arbitrary—i.e., if divine promises were not morally binding so that the man or community who did not live faithfully according to the law could have no legitimate complaints if punishment rather than reward resulted. This was the problem raised by the Book of Job. There was a complementary expectation that an individual's seed would be rewarded for his faith if *he* were not. Nevertheless, some expectation of reward for faithful execution of Jahweh's Commandments is required as an incentive for motivating people to higher achievements. Thus, a Covenant by which Israel was chosen, but which left Jahweh morally free to treat His people as He saw fit, regardless of their behavior, could not have been meaningful in terms of this orientation, however meaningful it has been since, as in the theology of Augustine and the early Church Reformers. Equally essential, however, was the concept that the Jew was not to count upon *immediate* reward.

Until the Prophetic Age, Judaism was the religion of a politically independent community standing in a precarious position between the great powers, Egypt and Babylonia.[20] Not only small and weak, it appeared pretentious, claiming to be the Chosen People of a supreme god, if not *the* supreme God. On such a basis, an alternative to extinction was the course later taken by Islam—expansion and absorption of its neighbors. This was not a realistic possibility in the circumstances. Israel took a different course through the Prophetic movement. Basically, this course was the renunciation of the *right* to political autonomy: the Babylonian conquest was accepted not only as inevitable but as legitimate—a punishment handed down by God on his people for their failure to keep His Commandments. Although a reaction against the monarchy and the upper classes, the Prophetic movement did not attempt to take over from them, as is normal for revolutionary movements, but rather to deflect the line of social development in a different direction.[21] It projected fulfillment in a land of milk and honey into the remote future, accepting an indefinite period of penitent purification in the Diaspora state.

Thus, whatever the respective contributions of internal tensions and

19. Weber, *Ancient Judaism, op cit.,* chap. V, IX, XII.

20. *Ibid.*

21. *Ibid.;* also, cf. Buber, *The Prophetic Faith, op. cit.*

of threats of invasion from Mesopotamia, the Prophetic movement tended to shift the problem of meaning from here-and-now rewards to the eventual fate of Israel. This involved deflating optimism about the immediate future and interpreting the unfavorable situation in terms of the people's guilt for not having kept Jahweh's Commandments. Bringing Babylonia into the system made it necessary to accentuate the conception that Jahweh was not just the Israelites' God but *the* universal God, who could manifest His will and power by using the Babylonians to chastise His people for their sins.[22] Through processes related to these developments, Israeli culture attained a new level of literacy. The reference for the community's constitution was its Covenant relation with Jahweh. The meaning of this relation was increasingly found in the content of the God-given law. This placed a premium on knowledge of the law, which required emphasizing its authoritative documentation. Israel, thus, became a people of the Book.[23]

In early times, the Levite tribe exercised ascriptive control over correct sacrificial ritual, although in the patriarchal period they did not themselves officiate as priests—this role was performed by the patriarchal lineage heads.[24] They acted analogously to the parliamentarian of a convention, being expert on correct procedure. It was difficult to draw a line between such ritual concerns and the elements of law regulating ordinary social relationships. A premium was placed on knowledge of the law in general, not only its specifically ritual elements, and it became impossible for any group to monopolize relevant legal knowledge. This function was universalized. In the hands of the Rabbinate and the Pharisees, learning in the law eventually became independent of ascribed positions or special offices.[25] Moreover, *all* responsible community members shared a legal competence. This depended on their being literate and able to discuss relevant problems with the rabbis or Pharisees. Thus Israel was among the first societies to develop a fully literate upper class, practically all of whose male adult members were schooled in the basic religious documents.

Despite the particularism of the Chosen People concept, Israel, as a societal community, regulated itself and defined its identity according to a normative order that was divinely bestowed. This order was objectively contained in canonical documents, knowledge of which confirmed the legitimacy of the patterns of human relations, including political authority. Furthermore, the belief that Jahweh was *the* universal God, not

22. Voegelin, *op. cit.;* Weber, *Ancient Judaism, op. cit.,* chap. XII.

23. *Ibid.,* especially chaps. III, XII, and XV.

24. Meek, *op. cit.,* chap. IV.

25. Bultmann, *op. cit.*

merely Israel's God, meant that his normative order should be applicable to *all* mankind. This resulted in the conception of a moral order governing human affairs that, being controlled by a transcendental God, was independent of *any* particular societal or political organization. Jahweh could punish indigenous kings and use nonbelieving emperors as his instruments. Such beliefs sustained the dispersed Jewish community when it lost political independence, even after the realization that this loss was permanent and even after the sacrificial cult was extinguished by the Temple's destruction.[26] This peculiar cultural complex: first, a transcendental legislator god; second, a moral order prescribed by him; and third, the idea of a holy community executing his mandate was able to survive the ending of a politically independent Israel and eventually to become independent of the Israelitic community's dispersed units and be transferred to non-Israelite societies and collectivities; this was Israel's contribution to social evolution.[27]

GREECE

The social and cultural continuities among ancient Near Eastern societies have been underestimated. Available evidence indicates that there was continuity in city-state structure from Mesopotamia to the Greek mainland and islands, including Cyprus, Crete, and the Syrian and Aegean shores of Asia.[28] The Dorian invasion of Greece introduced a less drastic break than was long believed. But the Greek city-states were the only highly civilized small units, aside from certain Phoenician communities, that maintained *political* independence.[29]

The tiny *polis* was the primary societal unit. Nevertheless, the Greek *cultural* pattern coalesced about the language and a certain written heritage involved in it, particularly the poems of Homer and Hesiod.[30] This linguistic-literary culture was borne by many politically independent *poleis*, which, during the classical period, did not develop beyond the

---

26. *Ibid.*, pp. 80 ff.

27. Weber, *Ancient Judaism, op. cit.*, chaps. XIV and XV.

28. See, for example, Gordon, *op. cit.*; Olmstead, *op. cit.*; Eric Voegelin, *The World of the Polis* (New Orleans: Louisiana State University Press, 1957), especially chap. I; Donald Hardin, *The Phoenicians* (New York: Praeger Paperbacks, 1962; and Martin P. Nilsson, *Minoan-Mycenaean Religion and its Survival in Greek Religion*, 2nd ed. (Lund: Gleering, 1950).

29. Victor Ehrenberg, *The Greek State* (New York: Norton, 1964), chap. I.

30. See especially, Werner Jaeger, *Paideia: The Ideals of Greek Culture*, vol. I (New York: Oxford University Press, 1945), Book One, Chap. III, "Homer the Educator."

city-state level of organization. The interaction of a common culture with a multiplicity of units contributed to the special creativity of Greek civilization. The uniformity among the Greek city-states was thus *primarily cultural*, although it also included such politically relevant elements as feelings for the distinction between Greeks and barbarians. Beyond that, it involved interaction. Though Greeks fought Greeks in continual inter-polis warfare, there also was friendly visiting, official and unofficial. There were elaborate diplomatic relations and alliances against outsiders, particularly against Persia during the crisis of the early fifth century. Certain international institutions, particularly the Oracle and Shrine of Delphi and the centers at Olympia and Epidaurus, were unifying features. At these sites, masses assembled from the Greek world on varieties of errands and occasions.[31] Each of the centers concerned the religious culture common to all Greeks but had its special emphasis. Delphi, which commanded the greatest dignity, was religio-political in focus—the United Nations of the Greek world. Olympia was oriented to the cult of physical fitness and beauty and Epidaurus to that of health.[32]

The religion on which this Greek international order was based was polytheistic and hence pluralistic, in contrast to Judaism, which emphasized the whole community's relation to *one* God and his unitary will for its role in His creation. Nevertheless, the consequences of the Greek and Israeli patterns converged in one respect. Because it was pan-Hellenic, Greek culture, like Hebrew culture, transcended any single politically organized community. In Greece as in Israel, no king or assembly of citizens, whether constituted aristocratically or democratically, could claim sovereignty in the sense in which it was claimed in Egypt, or even in Mesopotamia, in the sense that *this* actual polity could be identified with the ultimate source of universal order.[33] The Israelites had a transcendent normative authority, the will of Jahweh, to which they had to *adapt*. The Greeks conceived such authority not as the will of any particular deity but as an order divinely existent and imposed upon them, which eventually came to be formulated as the order of nature. This was independent of the politically organized community in a sense unknown to archaic societies. Indeed, it bound the gods themselves.[34]

---

31.   Martin P. Nilsson, *Greek Folk Religion* (New York: Harper Torchbooks, 1961).

32.   As a psychiatrist told me after a visit there, "Perhaps the best mental hospital of historic times."

33.   Voegelin, *The World of the Polis, op. cit.*, especially his discussion of the *Iliad*, which shows how the actions of even heroes and gods were transcended by principles of the normative order.

34.   *Ibid., passim.*

This conception of order was a condition of the distinctive Greek pattern of social organization. It carried the equality of the city-state's constituent elements farther than any previous cultural pattern. The earliest Greek *polis* structure was continuous with the general city-state pattern of the Near East, including Mesopotamia. In each case, it was formed by a religiously grounded confederation of lineages that constituted the upper class of a two-class system.[35] The male heads of the upper-class lineages were formally equal. The kings of the pre-classical period, like Agamemnon, Menelaus, or Priam in the *Iliad* were considered first among equals.[36] Furthermore, under Greek conditions, such a king could never obtain by conquest the paramount positions in other city-states, as Mesopotamian kings commonly did.

Although classical Greece was divided into aristocratic-oligarchic and democratic *poleis,* every *polis* was a corporate group of citizens within which formal equality was supposed to prevail in regard to basic citizenship rights, including some participation in government.[37] Even oligarchs and tyrants were spokesmen for the community of citizens; indeed, the tyrants played roles in democratizing certain *poleis.* On the basis of this corporate principle, a number of *poleis,* notably Athens, developed full democracy for the male citizenry with equality of the franchise and other basic rights before the law, including rights in litigation before a jury of peers.[38] To be sure, such democracy often approached benevolent dictatorship in order to maintain cohesiveness and effectiveness, as occurred in Athens under Pericles; but this does not diminish the achievement. In line with the general characteristics of historic intermediate societies, this relatively egalitarian corporate community, the citizen body, comprised an upper class within a larger system, much of which was denied full rights of membership. The *citizens* of the *polis* were normally a minority. It is estimated that the Athens of the Periclean Age had only about 30,000 citizens, including women and children, in a total population of about 150,000. The remainder were slaves and metics, resident aliens, some of whose ancestors had been resident for many generations. Complete inclusion in a societal community on a full-membership, democratic basis had to await early modern types of society, though in one

---

35.   Martin P. Nilsson, *A History of Greek Religion* (Oxford: Clarendon Press, 1949), chap. VII, especially pp. 244–249.

36.   W. Warde Fowler, *The City-State of the Greeks and Romans* (London: Macmillan, 1921), chap. II.

37.   Ehrenberg, *op. cit.,* chap. II, especially part V.

38.   C. Hignett, *A History of the Athenian Constitution* (Oxford: Clarendon Press, 1952).

aspect it developed in Rome.[39] Outside the territorial limits of the Greek political system, as well as of the particular *polis,* were the barbarians, who were lower class in terms of Greek values.

Because, as an upper class, it devoted so much of its time to government and war, the citizen group was economically dependent on these subordinated groups, even under such simple economic conditions. Moreover, the *poleis* had to be simple governmentally, not requiring much bureaucratization, because safeguards preserving the interests of the citizens encumbered administration, both civil and military.[40] Indeed, Sparta, in specializing as a military *polis,* became the principal agency in the system's disintegration, for loosely organized Athens could not compete over the long run with Sparta's military efficiency. Internal *stasis,* or class conflict, and inter-*polis* warfare were the immediate factors that destroyed the *polis* system.[41] It was vulnerable to intervention by an outside expansionist power, squeaking by the threat of Persia narrowly and, only a century later, succumbing to Macedonia. Its independence during the creative phase was short.

Let us consider the principal developments of the Greek cultural pattern. Its religious emphasis was different from Israel's. Israel exalted divinity above the level of archaic polytheism and gave it transcendence, unity, and coherence, so that the human level, sharply differentiated from the divine, was endowed with its own special independence and dignity. The Greeks humanized the gods, even attributing to them ordinary human failings, such as vanity and jealousy. However, they conceived both gods and men as subject to a binding order of nature that was normative. This conception of order underwent development and generalization.

Significant is the juxtaposition common in all classical thought, particularly its drama, between an archaic and a more advanced conception of order.[42] For example, in the Oedipus trilogy of Sophocles, the conception concerns the ineluctable consequences of the normative order with respect to the problem of incest. The pathos in Oedipus' situation re-

39. Internally, the Jewish Diaspora community probably came closer to the concept of full inclusion than any Greek *polis*. However, it was not a society, but an ethnic enclave within a host society. The Gentiles, although they were the power-holding majority of the host society, were, from the Jewish point of view, the disqualified lower class. Elaborate ritual measures maintaining separateness from the Gentiles were a salient feature of post-exilic Judaism. Cf. Weber, *Ancient Judaism, op. cit.*

40. W. C. Beyer, "The Civil Service of the Ancient World" in *Public Administration Review* (1959): 19, 243–249.

41. Olmstead, *op. cit.;* Ehrenberg, *op. cit.*

42. Voegelin, *The World of the Polis, op. cit.;* E. R. Dodds, *The Greeks and the Irrational* (Boston: Beacon Paperbacks, 1957).

garding his fate is comparable to that of Job's (and that of Calvinistic predestination). And, as with Job, intentional motivation to violate the order is ruled out: Oedipus could not have known that he had killed his father and married his mother. Nevertheless, the consequences of infraction inexorably follow these acts, regardless of their motivation. Sophocles then generalizes this moral order to a new normative level through the intervention of Theseus, who symbolizes Athenian civilization. In death Oedipus is absolved from his sins, apotheosized as basically guiltless, and admitted to the holy fraternity of Athenian citizenship. Sophocles was saying that the *polis'* kinship-incest-based archaic order had been superseded by an order based on civic relationship.[43] The latter became dissociated from the kinship aspects of the normative order except, in the Athenian case, for citizenship eligibility, which remained ascribed to kinship—but even this was symbolically broken through in Oedipus' case.

Similar themes were formulated by the philosophers. Socrates' polemic against the Sophists concerned their relativism. He asserted the ultimate propriety of a civil justice that transcended the Sophistic relativisms—e.g., the right of the stronger—and also rejected the traditional norms from which the Sophists had emancipated Greek thought.[44] The "justice" of Socrates and Plato was grounded in a universalistic conception of general order. This order, accessible to understanding through reason, was superior—in conceptual generalization and in the potential for social development that would be realized from its institutionalization— to morally nihilistic acceptance of civic struggle (as propounded by Thrasymachus) and to the archaic traditionalism of the type that plagued Oedipus with ascriptive obligations and admitted the meaningfulness of whimsical acts from the gods.[45] It was the first formal conceptualization of the normative framework for human life that abstracted moral obligations from the nonhuman elements, including the divine, involved in the condition of action. It was later reformulated by the Stoics as the Law of Nature.

As the political thought of Plato and Aristotle shows, the universalistic potential of the Natural Order concept was not institutionalized in the political organization of the time. Both philosophers believed the small *poleis* to be the only ethically acceptable political organizations, all larger-scale polities being barbaric in form. Yet, Aristotle's private thoughts on the political goals of his employer, Philip, and his pupil, Alexander, would be interesting, as it seems unlikely that he considered their visions of a large-scale polity *simply* as barbarous. Greece, then, like the people

43. Kenneth Burke, *Poetics* (unpublished manuscript).

44. Jaeger, *op cit.,* Book I, chap. 9; Book II, chap. III.

45. Jaeger, *Paideia: The Ideals of Greek Culture,* vol. II, *passim.*

of Israel, developed a distinctive cultural system by a process that involved the differentiation of the *whole* societal unit from other societal types. The *polis* developed into a *corporate* body of citizens, which became (especially in the case of Athens) a body of equals, though non-citizen residents were excluded and remained a lower class. During this development, the Greek world enjoyed a precarious freedom from intervention by great powers. This condition encouraged fragmentation and also continual internecine wars. Such autonomy on the part of the individual *poleis* was probably an *essential* condition for the development of their special social and cultural patterns. Largely because of it, however, Greece was nearly conquered by Persia and actually succumbed to Macedonia a century later.[46]

The Greek development was more complicated than Israel's in that its cultural complex was borne through the period of its emergence by a number of small independent societal units. The cultural preeminence of Athens gave coherence to the movement, since Athens attracted talent from all over the Greek world. Greek culture was separated from its original cultural matrix as an eventual result of the Macedonian conquest, after which the Greek *poleis* never regained their political independence. The process was different from the Hebrew case. Philip and Alexander were marginal Greeks, and the Hellenistic kingdoms made Greek the language of their courts and, eventually, of their educated classes generally. Thus, the Septuagint (the translation of the Old Testament into Greek) was occasioned because the educated Jews of Alexandria read Greek more generally than Hebrew. Greek culture became paramount throughout the whole eastern Mediterranean region and extended far into the East. Its eminence continued throughout the Roman period. It was spread thinly over the welter of other traditions in the area, which were never fully absorbed into the Roman community. Indeed, until the rise of Christianity, there was no cultural tradition that could compete successfully with Greek philosophy for the interest and allegiance of the intellectual elite.[47] Hence, it was in a strategic position to exert a massive impact on any process of cultural innovation occurring in that area. It become one of the constituents of the Christian movement, particularly through the influence of the Alexandrian school of theology.[48] The

---

46. Max Weber, in an exchange with the ancient historian Eduard Meyer, argued that a Persian victory at Marathon or Salamis would have changed the course of Western history. It would have cut short the development of Greek secular culture, which then could not have become a constituent in Hellenistic, Roman, and modern Western society. (Cf. Max Weber, *Gesammelte Aufsatze zur Sozial- und Wirtschaftsgeschichte* (Tubingen: J. C. B. Mohr, 1924), chap. I, sections 4 and 5.

47. A. D. Nock, *Conversion, op. cit.*

48. Werner Jaeger, *Early Christianity and Greek Paideia* (Cambridge, Mass.: Harvard University Press, 1961).

mobility and individualism of the Hellenistic and Roman societies were conditions of this influence.

From the Macedonian era, the societal bearer of Greek culture was no longer the individual *polis* or system of *poleis*. To be sure, Athens retained its intellectual prestige throughout the Roman period. For example, it was fashionable for Roman artistocratic families to send their sons to Athens as to a kind of finishing school; and Greek teachers, many trained in Athens, were an intellectual influence throughout the Empire. Gradually, the intellectual center of gravity moved to Alexandria, which was the center of the development of Greek science. Thus, although there was no Greek Diaspora, conditions were equivalent. Emerging from both Jewish and Greek culture were scholar classes—the rabbis and philosophers—that did not command the same order of political status and responsibility that had been carried by pre-Exile Hebrews and fifth-century Greeks. Their social status in their communities became the societal anchorages of relatively independent cultural traditons.

CONCLUSION

The interrelations between a society and a cultural system requires the *legitimation* of the society's normative order. Legitimation systems define the reasons for members' rights and for the prohibitions incumbent upon them. For instance, the use of power requires legitimation. The concept of legitimation need not imply the adjective "moral," in a modern sense. It does imply that it is right that things be done in accord with the institutionalized order. The function of legitimation is independent of the *operative* functions of a social system. No normative order is *self-legitimating in the sense that* the approved or prohibited way of life simply *is* right or wrong and admits of no questions. Nor is it adequately legitimized by necessities imposed at lower levels of the hierarchy of control— e.g., that things *must* be done in a *specific* way because the stability or even survival of the system is at stake.

But societies differ in the kind of morality used to legitimize its institutions. Modern societies tend to use universalistic legitimation, what Bredemeier and Stephenson call the "morality of principle" as contrasted with the "morality of loyalty."[49]

> The "morality of principle" consists of the expectation that one should treat everyone according to the same abstract, general, *universal* principles. The "morality of loyalty" is the expectation that one should treat people differently

49. Harry C. Bredemeier and Richard M. Stephenson, *The Analysis of Social Systems* (New York: Holt, Rinehart and Winston, 1962), p. 17.

depending on their *particular* relationship to one. Principle morality or universalism, for example, says that if you see your best friend cheating, you should report him to the professor. Loyalty morality or particularism says that you should lie to the professor to protect your friend. Particularism says, "My country—may she ever be right; but right or wrong, my country!" Universalism says, "May she ever be right—if she wants my support."

The development of a cultural system emphasizing generalized universalistic norms was a complex evolutionary breakthrough. One source of this universalistic morality was Roman law, which was discussed in the previous chapter. This chapter has considered two other universalistic influences on modern society: the Hebrew and the Greek concepts of a moral order. Although the Hebrew concept was religious and the Greek secular, each constituted a step toward greater universalism. The outcome of these steps was not the successful institutionalization of a morality of princple in Hebrew or Greek societies, because these societies disintegrated. But their cultural innovations survived and contributed a necessary ingredient to modernity.

CHAPTER 6
THE RELIGIOUS LEGITIMATION OF SECULAR SOCIETY

The development of cultural innovation in the seed-bed societies of ancient Israel and Greece depended on conditions under which cultural advances could develop and become dissociated from their societal origins. These two models were chosen because of their contributions to later social evolution. Elements derived from classical Hebrew and Greek sources, after undergoing further development, are cultural components of modern society. Their focus was Christianity. As a cultural system, Christianity proved able to absorb components of the secular culture of antiquity and to form a matrix from which a new order of secular culture could be differentiated. Christian culture— including its secular components—was able to maintain more consistent differentiation from the societies with which it was interdependent than either of its forebears. Because of such differentiation from society, Christian culture came to serve as a more effective innovative force in the development of the sociocultural system than had any other cultural complex that had yet evolved.

A cultural system does not institutionalize itself; it must be integrated with a social environment that can fulfill the functional requirements for a viable society. Evolution involves continuing *interaction* between the cultural and social systems, as well as among their respective components and subsystems. Social prerequisites of cultural effectiveness not only change but also may at any given stage depend upon *previous* stages of the institutionalization of cultural elements. In this perspective, the Roman Empire takes on dual significance. It constituted the social environment in which Christianity developed. Because

Roman society owed a debt to Greek civilization, Greek influence entered the modern system not only culturally, through Christian theology and the secular culture of the Renaissance, but also through the role structure of Roman society, especially in the East where the educated classes remained Hellenized after conquest by Rome. Second, the heritage of Roman institutions was incorporated into the foundations of the modern world. Greek influence and the Roman institutional heritage were significant for the *same* structures: The legal order of the Empire, a necessary condition of Christian proselytization, reflected elements of Roman law in the canon law of the Church and in the secular law of medieval society and its successors.

I shall begin with the two social bridges between the ancient and modern world: Christianity and certain institutions of the Roman Empire. Then I shall skip a number of centuries to the immediate background of modern society: feudal society and its culmination in the high Middle Ages. Finally, I shall discuss the Renaissance and the Reformation.

EARLY CHRISTIANITY

Christianity originated as a sectarian movement within Palestinian Judaism. It soon broke with this religio-ethnic community when St. Paul decided that a Gentile might become a Christian without joining the Jewish community and observing Jewish law.[1] The early Christian Church evolved into an associational religious group independent of *any* ascriptive community, either ethnic or territorial. Its focus was specifically religious, the salvation of the individual soul; in this respect it became differentiated from any secular social organization. It gradually spread throughout the Roman Empire through the proselytizing of the apostles and other missionaries. Its early success was among the humbler urban population—craftsmen, small merchants, and the like—who were bound neither by the traditionalism of peasant groups nor by the upper classes' vested interests in the status quo.[2]

In terms of religious content, the elements of continuity with Judaism were transcendental monotheism and the conception of a covenant with God. A sense of having been chosen by God for a divine mission continued. In classical Judaism, the people of Israel had enjoyed this status; in Christianity the company of professing *individuals* gained access to eternal life through their adoption of the faith.[3] Salvation was to be

1. A. D. Nock, *St. Paul* (New York: Harper, 1938).

2. Adolf Harnack, *The Mission and Expansion of Christianity* (New York: Harper, 1961).

3. Rudolph Bultmann, *Primitive Christianity* (Cleveland: Meridian, 1956).

found in the Church, especially after the sacraments had crystallized. The early Church was a voluntary association quite antithetical to a people in sociological type. The individual could be a Jew only as a *total* social personality: one of the "people"; but one could be *both* a Christian *and* an Athenian or Roman on the level of societal participation: a member of both the Church and an ethnic-territorial community. This step differentiated both role and collectivity structures.

This definition of the basis for the religious collectivity and its relation to secular society was legitimated theologically by the concept of Christ, who was more than another prophet in the Jewish tradition; such figures had always been purely human. Christ was *both* divine and human, the "only begotten son" of God the Father but also a man of flesh and blood. In this dual aspect, his mission was to offer salvation to mankind. The transcendence of God the Father was the source of the differentiation between the spiritual and temporal spheres. The basis for their integration was the relation of souls to God, through and in Christ and His Church, which was defined theologically as the "mystical body of Christ" and partook of the divinity of Christ through the Holy Spirit.[4] Christ not only offered salvation to souls but also freed the religious community from previous territorial and ethnic ascriptions. The relations among the three persons of the Trinity—and of each to man and the other aspects of creation—were complex. A theological ordering of these relations required intellectual resources not present in prophetic Judaism. Late Greek culture contributed such intellectual resources. The Christian theologians of the third century (especially the Alexandrian fathers Origen and Clement) mobilized the sophistication of neo-Platonic philosophy to handle these intellectual problems,[5] thus establishing a precedent for drawing upon secular culture in a way that has been closed to other religious movements, notably Islam.

The conception of the Christian Church as both divine and human was of theological origin. Its conception as a voluntary association, with overtones of egalitarianism and corporate independence relative to the social environment, owed much to the institutional models of antiquity. St. Augustine's use of the term "city," in the sense of polis, was a striking symbol.[6] Certainly the Church was an association of religious citizens parallel to the polis, particularly in the local congregation. Because the Empire could be regarded as a federation of city-states, it too provided a

4.   A. D. Nock, *Early Gentile Christianity and Its Hellenistic Background* (New York: Harper, 1964).

5.   Werner Jaeger, *Early Christianity and Greek Paideia* (Cambridge, Mass.: Harvard University Press, 1961).

6.   Charles Norris Cochrane, *Christianity and Classical Culture* (New York: Oxford University Press, 1957).

model as the movement came to require structures of authority for stabilizing relations among its local congregations. Centralization seemed appropriate, and the gradual establishment of the Roman papacy was the solution. Although the Church became differentiated institutionally from all secular organizations, it also became structurally more congruent with the society of its environment.

There was *sharp* differentiation of the Christian Church from secular society: The early Christians lived in the secular world but were not of it. The larger society was pagan and appeared to Christians devalued as a world of sin unredeemed. The admonition "render unto Caesar the things that are Caesar's" should be understood as a recognition of Caesar's being a pagan monarch, the symbol of a pagan political and social order. As an acceptance of Roman authority, it expressed Christian passivity in relation to all worldly things. As Troeltsch has emphasized, early Christianity was not a movement of social reform or revolution. Acceptance of Caesar was not an expression of positive integration, for it was rooted in eschatological expectations of the immediacy of the Second Coming, the end of the world, and the Last Judgment.[7]

The Christian movement contained a duality in its orientation toward the secular world largely as a heritage of Judaism. On one hand, it asserted the primacy of eternal life over *all* worldly concerns. It emphasized devotional and ascetic means to salvation. On the other hand, Christ and His Church, like the people of Israel, had a divinely appointed mission *for this world,* which meant for human society. Although the situation of the Church within imperial society necessarily subordinated this secular component, it had great evolutionary potential. Christian aloofness from secular concerns was threatened as an increasing proportion of the population converted, particularly among the higher, socially and politically more responsible, classes.[8] This process culminated during the early fourth century in a new imperial religious policy, reflected in the Edict of Milan (which proclaimed the toleration of Christianity), the conversion of the Emperor Constantine, and the adoption of Christianity as the state religion.[9] This culmination was simultaneously a triumph and a source of strains within Christianity, for the Church was in danger of losing its independence and becoming an instrument of secular political authority. During this period monasticism was established.[10] The Pauline

7. Ernst Troeltsch, *The Social Teachings of the Christian Churches,* vol. I (New York: Harper, 1960).

8. *Ibid.*

9. Hans Lietzmann. *A History of the Early Church* (Cleveland: Meridian, 1961), esp. vols. II and III.

10. Paul Tufari, "Authority and Affection in the Ascetic's Status Group: St. Basil's Definition of Monasticism," unpublished doctoral dissertation, Harvard University.

admonition to "remain in that station in which you are called" had seemed insufficiently radical to a minority of Christians who renounced the world totally to become anchorites. This dynamism was now harnessed to the establishment of organized communities devoted to the fully religious life in withdrawal from the world under vows of poverty, chastity, and obedience.[11]

Although it was a seed-bed movement carrying potentials for *future* societal change, Christianity could not transform the Roman Empire because the necessary conditions for its institutionalization were absent. But the monastic movement established another kind of seed bed *within* Christianity, exerting increasing evolutionary leverage on both the "secular" church and secular society. The institutional structuring of the Christian mission for the world, in which monasticism played an important part, was an aspect of differentiation between the eastern and western branches of the Church. Partly as a result of the weakening of secular authority in the West, including the abandonment of Rome as the imperial capital, the Church had more opportunity to become independently activist there. In organizing itself for the whole body of Christians, lay as well as clerical, the Western Church consolidated a universal episcopal system centralized under the see of Rome.[12] During the Dark Ages and the later medieval period, this organization was more effective than was any in the secular realm, through the long-run effects of three developments.

First, a more nearly legitimate place was established at the highest theological level for the "city of man," as distinguished from the "city of God," partly through the influence of Augustine. In contrast to the total alienation from secular society common under early Christianity, Augustinian thought tolerated society, allowing its moral improvement through Christian influence as a legitimate endeavor.[13] Augustine also went farther than his predecessors had done in accepting the secular culture of the ancient world. Second, with the establishment of the Benedictine order, Western monasticism turned to a much greater concern with worldly matters than did Eastern monasticism. This shift accelerated with the establishment of other orders in the Western Church, for example, the Cluniac monks, the Dominicans, the Franciscans, and the Jesuits. Third, the organization of the Church was cemented through the sacraments, which reached their final form before the Middle Ages. Priesthood was transformed into an *office* independent of the personal

---

11. Herbert B. Workman, *The Evolution of the Monastic Ideal* (Boston: Beacon, 1962).

12. Lietzmann, *op. cit.*, esp. vol. IV.

13. Cochrane, *op. cit.*; and Troeltsch, *op. cit.*

quality of the incumbent and therefore of his particularistic connections.[14] The Western Church achieved a higher level of bureaucratic independence for its secular priesthood than did the Eastern Church, whose bishops came to be drawn from the monastic orders and whose parish priests were involved in local communities.

The Institutional Heritage of Rome

Imperial Rome declined from the highest levels of civilization. Political authority in the West disintegrated into shifting tribal and regional groupings and authorities accompanied by the virtual disappearance of a monetary and market economy and by reversion to local self-sufficiency and barter.[15] When revival began, a new relation between church and secular authority emerged. The legitimation of Charlemagne's regime revolved around its relation to the church, as symbolized by his coronation by Pope Leo III in A.D. 800. This ceremony provided the model for the later Holy Roman Empire, which, though never a highly integrated polity, served as a legitimating framework for a unified Christian secular society.[16] Within this institutional framework, the medieval synthesis was characterized by *differentiation* between church and state— in the special medieval sense of the state. This differentiation was defined as that between the spiritual and the temporal arms of the Christian mission. The special mode of differentiation and integration formed the core of the first conception of a Christian Society.[17] As a result, the institutional elements of Roman origin that survived through the Middle Ages were connected with the development of the Church.

The universalistic structures of Roman law had been undermined during the migrations period by the principle of the personality of law, the judgment of a man according to the law of his own particular tribe.[18] This particularistic reference to tribal allegiance could only be overcome in jurisdiction and enforcement by the gradual revival of a *territorial* principle, for the particularistic aspect of law was an aspect of the status of territorial political authorities. Although the secular law of the newly defined Empire was Roman law, the Empire was too loosely organized to constitute an effective agent of the detailed enforcement of law. The legal

14. Max Weber, *The Sociology of Religion* (Boston: Beacon, 1963).

15. H. St. L. B. Moss, *The Birth of the Middle Ages* (London: Oxford University Press, 1935); and Ferdinand Lot, *The End of the Ancient World and the Beginnings of the Middle Ages* (New York: Harper, 1961).

16. Henri Pirenne, *A History of Europe* (2 vols.; Garden City, N.Y.: Anchor, 1958).

17. Troeltsch, *op. cit.,* vol. I.

18. C. H. McIlwain, *The Growth of Political Thought in the West* (New York: Macmillan, 1932).

tradition therefore tended to exert a cultural pressure, through its legitimating action, toward the establishment of territorial jurisdictions less extensive than the Empire as a whole.[19] Nevertheless, law meant Roman law, and the legal system of imperial Rome continued to be in force, even in English Common Law, which was less a new legal system than the adaptation of Roman law to English conditions.[20] Furthermore, the Church adopted much of Roman law for the regulation of its own affairs through the canon law and developed a class of legal experts within the clergy. Perhaps the bureaucratization of the medieval Church was less significant than was its ordering in terms of a universalistic legal system.

The territorial basis of political institutions, another essential component of modern societies, owes more to the Roman heritage than to any other source. Despite the many differences between Roman and modern institutions, the Roman model provided the point of departure for the development of the early modern European state, not least through the legitimation inherent in assumed continuity of organization.[21] Still another institutional heritage of the ancient world was the pattern of municipal organization. The Roman *municipium* had been derived from the city-state of earlier times: the Greek polis and the *urbs* of Rome and other Italian provinces. The *municipium* had lost its political independence, yet it retained many of the old institutional patterns, in particular, the conception of its core as a corporate body of citizens. In certain respects the citizens of a *municipium* constituted a body of equals with shared legal and political rights and such obligations as military service. Although the *municipia* followed Rome in developing aristocracies of citizens with prestige and wealth, who monopolized public offices, their associational character was sufficiently preserved to contrast with rural society, especially under feudalism. The survival of these communities constituted a difference between premodern Europe and any Oriental society of comparable development.[22]

MEDIEVAL SOCIETY

The period of uneven development between the end of the Middle Ages and the crystallization of modern society resulted from the combination in medieval society of features favoring modernization and features

19. *Ibid.;* and Otto von Gierke, *Political Theories of the Middle Ages* (Boston: Beacon, 1958).

20. F. W. Maitland, *The Constitutional History of England* (Cambridge: Cambridge University Press, 1908).

21. J. B. Morrall, *Political Thought in Mediaeval Times* (New York: Harper, 1962).

22. Max Weber, *The City* (New York: Free Press, 1958).

basically incompatible with modernity. As a type, feudal society was antithetical to the more advanced types that preceded and succeeded it. It represented regression of the components of Rome's advanced society toward more archaic forms. Yet, once the point of maximum regression had been reached, recovery was rapid. A key to this development is that feudalism, the product of retrogression, received only secondary legitimation. Although feudal loyalties were romanticized and indeed blessed by the Church, this recognition was limited. These loyalties were easily superseded by alternative claims with deeper roots in the culture, components of which remained highly rationalized. From the eleventh century on, elements that could evoke primary legitimation began to assert themselves, initiating the process of differentiation; related developments eventually produced the modern structual type. The general *direction* of this evolution was determined by advances within the bridge structures already discussed: the orientation of Western Christianity, the functional specificity of the Church's organizational structure, the territorial principle of political allegiance, the Roman legal system, and the associational structure of the urban community.

The fragmentation of imperial Roman social organization had given way to the decentralized, localized, and structurally dedifferentiated type of society called feudalism.[23] The trend of feudalism was the elimination of a universalist base of order in favor of particularistic loyalties, originally tribal and local. Concomitantly, the old elements of relatively egalitarian associational individualism tended to give way, at least at the level of political and legal rights, to diffuse hierarchial relations based on the inequality of the reciprocal duties of vassalage, protection, and service. The feudal hierarchical relationship began as contractual, in that the vassal agreed, through his pledge of fealty, to serve his lord in exhange for protection and other advantages.[24] It became hereditary so that only when a vassal lacked a legitimate heir could his lord select a new man to succeed him in a fief. For the peasants the feudal system established hereditary unfreedom through the institution of serfdom. One criterion of aristocracy was, however, recognition of the legitimate heredity of status. Provision for physical security was probably the most pressing problem of the time. Beside the original barbarian invasion of the Empire, disorder throve on long-continuing incursions (for example, by the Muslims on the east and south, Huns on the east and north, and Scandinavians on the north and west) and internecine strife induced by political fragmentation.[25] A premium was thus placed on the military function, the basis of

23. For authoritative discussion relevant to sociological analysis, Marc Bloch, *Feudal Society* (Chicago: University of Chicago Press, 1961) is the most useful single source on feudalism.

24. F. L. Ganshoff, *Feudalism* (New York: Harper, 1961).

25. *Ibid.*, part I.

protection being military safeguards against violence. With support from the traditions of antiquity, a predominately military class became ascendant in secular society and secured its position through the hierarchical institution of vassalage.

It became less possible to maintain clear feudal hierarchies, however. Relations became so ramified that many people held feudal rights and obligations within several potentially conflicting hierarchies. The liege relationship took precedence over other obligations and was an attempt to solve this problem; the institution of kingship had not been completely feudalized but was reasserting its paramount prerogatives.[26] After the eleventh century the territorial organization of the state, bound to the principle of kingship, gained steadily in importance. Europe's increasing population density, economic organization, and physical security shifted the balance from feudal bases of organizational allegiance toward territorial bases. Concomitantly, there was a crystallization of the institution of aristocracy, which was a compromise between the territorial and feudal principles of organization.[27] In its full flower, aristocracy was a late medieval phenomenon. It represented at the macrosocial level the two-class system from which modern national secular social stratification developed.

Interdependent with the political feudalization of the early Middle Ages was economic retrogression. The societal resource base became increasingly agricultural in the institution of the manor. The manor was a local, relatively self-sufficient agricultural unit worked by an hereditary labor force dependent, in legally unfree status, on a feudal lord, generally an individual but sometimes an ecclesiastical corporation like a monastery or cathedral chapter. The functional diffuseness of the manor was exemplified in the lord's status, which combined the roles of landlord, political leader, military commander, judicial authority, and shaper of economic organization.[28] Such diffuseness was suitable to the manor as a security base in the midst of feudal disorder but prevented it from providing the local organization necessary for modernization. That organization was more closely approached in the towns.

The social structure of the Church was the primary institutional bridge between ancient and modern Western society. In order to influence evolution effectively, however, the Church had to articulate with secular structures at strategic points. The European urban community offered such a strategic point.[29] In Church contexts, differences of social class were downgraded, though not eliminated, within urban communities.

26. Bloch, *op. cit.*

27. *Ibid.*

28. *Ibid.*, part V; and Henri Pirenne, *Economic and Social History of Mediaeval Europe* (New York: Harvest, 1937), part III.

29. Weber, *The City.*

The mass was open to the whole urban community without basic distinctions.[30] The nature of the religious component in urban organization was demonstrated by the cathedral, which was never simply a building; it was an institution that, as both the seat of a bishopric and the focus of the cathedral *chapter*—a collegial element in the Church structure—articulated two levels of Church organization.[31] The participation of the guilds in financing and building cathedral chapters and churches indicates that religious organization was associated with the economic and political aspects of the rising towns.

The secular associational phenomenon in the towns was the emergence of an urban version of aristocracy, the patriciates—town-dwelling upper groups constituted as corporate entities. The significance of these groups was their principle of organization, which ran counter to feudal principles of hierarchy.[32] They were organized in guilds, merchant guilds being particularly influential. But the guild, itself following the pattern of the polis and *municipium*, was an *association of equals*.[33] Although there were guilds at various levels of prestige within the same urban community and although the town could be variously located within the political structures of feudal society, the urban communities presented organizational patterns conflicting with feudalism but consonant with the course of later development.[34]

An evolutionary development in the early medieval period occurred in the Church, the structure sufficiently inclusive to affect institutional patterns throughout Europe. The papacy of Gregory VII in the late eleventh century was the turning point. The Church had renewed its interest in the philosophical-theological issues involved in establishing a Christian body of knowledge that could serve as a guide to realizing the Christian society.[35] The first of the Scholastic syntheses was in the offing. The revival of systematic studies in the canon law and the Roman secular law—which Gregory himself encouraged—had begun. A critical develop-

---

30. In rural areas the pattern was for the lord of the manor to attend mass in his chapel whereas the commoners in his service attended church in the village or at a nearby monastery or town, if at all. Any noble of consequence had a priest as his own chaplain. It is significant that Thomas Aquinas held that the urban way of life favored Christian virtue more than the rural way of life could. See Troeltsch, *op. cit.*, vol. II, p. 255.

31. R. W. Southern, *The Making of the Middle Ages* (New Haven: Yale University Press, 1953), pp. 193–204.

32. Bloch, *op. cit.*, p. 416.

33. Henri Pirenne, *Early Democracies in the Low Countries* (New York: Harper, 1963).

34. Henri Pirenne, *Mediaeval Cities* (Princeton: Princeton University Press, 1925), esp. chapter II, "Municipal Institutions."

35. Southern, *op. cit.* and Troeltsch, *op. cit.*

ment at the level of social structure was Gregory's insistence on a monastic degree of religious discipline in the church as a whole combined with his general assertion of Church interests in secular society.[36] He and some of his successors pushed the power of the Church to points that opponents believed asserted its hegemony over secular structures. Such hegemony would have been inconceivable in the Byzantine Empire.

In some respects Gregory's innovation was his insistence that the *secular* clergy observe celibacy.[37] Just when hereditary elements, as distinct from the more personal element of fealty, were gaining in the feudal system, he removed the priesthood, especially the bishoprics, from the possibility of hereditary consolidation. Whatever the sexual morality of secular priests, they could not have legitimate heirs, and their priestly offices could not become institutionalized functions of kinship status, as monarchy and aristocracy were becoming. This insulation was not destroyed by the common practice of appointing the higher clergy from the nobility. Although priests, bishops, and popes continued for many centuries to be chosen largely for their kinship affiliations, efforts to *legitimate* such choices on kinship grounds were repudiated even though the hereditary principle was becoming entrenched in many secular contexts. The tension between the Church's spiritual universalism and feudalism's temporal particularism prevented Western society's settling into a comfortable traditionalism.

THE DIFFERENTIATION
OF THE EUROPEAN SYSTEM

So far I have discussed medieval society in terms of component structures considering their differential arrangement in various geographical areas within the system. Let us now consider the extent to which the differentiation of Europe as a system was foreshadowed in premodern stages by the varying distribution of institutional components throughout Europe.[38]

The social environment of the European system consisted of relations to other societies.[39] The social environment of the Northwest was

36. Morrall, *op. cit.*

37. Henry C. Lea, *History of Sacerdotal Celibacy in the Christian Church* (New York: Macmillan, 1907).

38. Bloch, *op. cit.*, suggested that such a pattern can, with the appropriate modifications for developmental changes, be extended past the first stages in the development of the modern system.

39. See Oscar Halecki, *The Limits and Divisions of European History* (Notre Dame, Ind.: University of Notre Dame Press, 1962). Halecki gives a general survey of the evolution of geographical-social differentiation in Europe.

not problematic, for it was protected by the Atlantic frontier, which at that time was not an arena of significant societal and political interchange. In the south and east, however, the social environments were significant. Spain was partially occupied by the Moors for most of the medieval period and maintained relations with the Saracens in the eastern Mediterranean throughout the Middle Ages. To the southeast lay the Byzantine Empire, which at the end of this period fell to the Turks; Orthodox Christianity extended northward into what eventually became Russia. The eastern boundary was a zone of struggle on the two axes of religion and ethnic affiliation. The Poles, Bohemians, and Croats became primarily Roman Catholic, whereas the Russians and most of the southern Slavs became Orthodox. From Austria northward there was an unstable border between the Germanic and Slavic peoples, a line that did not coincide with the religious boundary. A strategic enclave just east of the German area was the Hungarian ethnic group, a precipitate of the Hunnic invasions.

There was thus an east-west difference in the bounding environments of Europe, involving physical differences, the extent of previous penetration of Roman influence, and the consequences of the split between the Western and Eastern Churches. There were also north-south differences, based on the physical barriers of the Alps and the Pyrénées. Italy was the seat of government of the Roman Catholic Church but *never* of the Holy Roman Empire. Although Latin culture, grounded in language, penetrated Spain, France, and a few other border regions, the bulk of trans-Alpine society was ethnically not Latin. Italy played a special role in the constitution of medieval society for two reasons. First, it contained the seat of the Church and as the area where the Church's influence was concentrated. Second, Roman institutions were firmly established there and were thus able to recover rapidly after feudalism.

Under medieval conditions the Church became politically and economically entwined with secular society to a point beyond that in modern times. An aspect of this involvement was direct governmental jurisdiction of the popes in what became the Papal States. At the same time the general decentralization of medieval society permitted the urban component of the Roman heritage to become strongest in Italy. North of Rome, Italy came to be organized predominantly in city-state form. The upper classes of the northern urban communities developed into an amalgam of rurally based, initially feudal aristocracies and of urban patriciates. They became a *town-based* upper class, however; even though its members owned most of the agricultural land, it was a different class from the feudal aristocracy of the North.[40] These circumstances inhibited the emergence, first, of a predominantly feudal structure and, later, of territorial states that could not be controlled by a single central city. As the wider application of

40.   See F. Schevill, *The Medici* (New York: Harcourt, 1949).

Roman law in secular society depended upon the development of territorial states, law did not flourish there until later. As had the city-states of antiquity, the Italian units eventually proved unable to maintain political integrity in a great-power system. Nevertheless, Italy was the principal *pattern-maintenance* subsystem of European society at that stage, an essential seed-bed for later developments in secular as well as in ecclesiastical culture.[41]

The eastern frontier was the most feudal part of the European system, although it had a variegated pattern of its own, particularly in Germany.[42] Eastward from the Rhine Valley and northeast from the Baltic Sea, the urban component became attenuated to the lowest level in Europe. Economic and cultural conditions were more primitive than elsewhere, and the proximity of the frontier encouraged a military emphasis. The feudal structure and social stratification generally were more hierarchial than in the West, providing the basis for authoritarian regimes. Hierarchial differentiation and political authority thus outweighed economic development and the extension of culture. The resulting hierarchial political centralization was a special development of resources for political effectiveness that had implications for the future of the system. The eastern frontier areas, then, played an *adaptive* role in the European system, developing organization to protect it from threats of a sociopolitical and cultural character.

Social and political innovation began primarily in the Northwest. Paris was the center of the Scholastic philosophy, and the university developments at Oxford and Cambridge fostered cultural innovation. This geographical area also promoted a double social development. On the one hand, England and France became the early versions of the territorial state—distinct from feudalism, though its development had feudal underpinnings.[43] On the other, there was a blossoming of urban communities in the Rhine Valley from Switzerland to the North Sea. Both developments owed much to the organizational looseness of the Empire. Given the peripheral location of England and France, their kings were able to ignore allegiance to the Emperor. Many of the continental urban communities became "free cities" of the Empire with substantial exemptions from the feudal structure and the developing territorial monarchies.[44] As these towns were generally also the seats of cathedrals, this position of strength was reinforced by alliance with the Church.

41. J. H. Plumb, *The Italian Renaissance* (New York: Harper, 1965), esp. chap. 10.

42. Bloch, *op. cit.*

43. Charles Petit-Dutaillis, *The Feudal Monarchy in England and France* (London: Routledge, 1936).

44. Even today Hamburg and Bremen are "free cities" within the West German Federal Republic.

The processes that centered first in England and France constituted the earliest differentiation of the modern form of *societal community*. Developments in the free cities, in association with the Italian cities, initiated the further differentiation of the economy from political structures and from the societal community as such. Neither of these forms of structural differentiation was compatible with a predominantly feudal organization. The early kings were kings in the later sense and also feudal magnates. Theoretically they were vassals of the Holy Roman Emperor; their barons were in turn their feudal vassals-in-chief. As such, the feudal classes not only exercised governmental authority within their fiefs but also constituted the core of the societal community; the nobility was both the highest-prestige stratum and the symbolic focus of societal solidarity. The network of feudal solidarities that clustered about them constituted the main societal structure. The lower classes were bound into it through their unfree status on the manors; they were beholden directly only to their own lords. Virtually no civil administration reached down to the level of the lord of the manor, to say nothing of the serf. An early exception was the king's prerogative of keeping the peace, institutionalized, for example, in the English court system, through which he could intervene locally in major criminal matters and in quarrels between two feudal lords.[45] The multiplication of allegiances as feudalism developed encouraged further royal intervention and facilitated national integration.[46]

The feudal baronage evolved into what became the aristocracies of early modern societies. The crucial political development was the assumption by royal governments of two prerogatives, first, of military command without feudal dependence upon contingents under the control of barons and, second, of direct taxation, bypassing intermediate feudal echelons. The successors of the baronage, however, remained socially the class with the highest prestige, articulated with the monarchy, in that the king was always the "first gentleman" of the realm and the head of the aristocracy. With these developments, land-holding moved away from the land*lord* status, which included political control of the people as well as of the land, even though it remained the economic base of the aristocracy.

Where the forces promoting governmental organization over larger territories were weak, towns sometimes became fully independent. Besides creating a tradition of political independence that served as a brake on absolutism, the free-city zone also fostered the consolidation as an independent social stratum of the alternative leadership group to the aristocracies, the bourgeoisie.[47] Its economic basis lay not in land ownership but

---

45. Maitland, *op. cit.*

46. Bloch, *op. cit.*

47. Henri Pirenne, *Early Democracies in the Low Countries.*

in commerce and finance. Although craft guilds existed in the urban structure, merchant guilds tended to be more important, especially in the leading towns. On both sides of the Alps, towns came to be the centers of the emerging market economy; their independence from the newly consolidated monarchies in England and France and from domination by the Empire was probably an essential condition of modernization. In the larger system, the independent position of the Rhenish urban groups could not but strengthen the position of their confreres in England and France. Indeed, in certain circumstances, alliances between kings and the bourgeoisie of the capital cities constituted counters to the landed aristocracies, especially as postfeudal conditions emerged. With relative isolation and a period of strong government that followed the Norman conquest, England achieved a higher degree of political centralization than existed on the Continent. At the same time, it turned away from royal absolutism, thanks to the solidarity of the new aristocracy recruited from the followers of William the Conqueror. Within a century and a half, the barons proved capable of integrated corporate action sufficient to impose Magna Carta on their king.[48] This corporate solidarity was related to the conditions that gave rise to Parliament. Under these conditions, the English aristocracy moved farther from feudal anchorage than did any other aristocracy, thus winning a position of power in the emerging state. England was economically backward compared to Flanders and some other areas of the Continent. The English political structure, however, provided favorable soil for future economic developments; the strength of the landed aristocracy vis-à-vis the crown placed the merchant classes in a strategic position. In a tentative way England developed the ingredients for a synthesis of movements toward differentiation.

RENAISSANCE AND REFORMATION

The Renaissance gave rise to a secular culture differentiated from the religious matrix. Originating in Italy, it laid the foundations of the modern arts and intellectual disciplines, including the borderline category of legal culture. Indeed, theology itself was affected through feedback from the new elements of secular culture that later crystallized in philosophy. The cultural components that went into the Renaissance extended not only back into the Middle Ages but into antiquity. Ancient culture itself had not attained the same order of differentiation, for it remained religious in a sense not true of Western culture after the Middle Ages. An important component of rationalized medieval culture, Scholastic

48. Maitland, op. cit.

philosophy, was bound to the theological system and lacked the cultural autonomy of post-Renaissance thought.[49]

From the beginning, the Church had incorporated and developed further elements of classical culture. What the Renaissance meant was an enormous development of this heritage, mainly on the secular side. It was a process of *differentiation*, but insofar as it made possible the reception of elements that had been indigestible by the less differentiated previous cultural system, it was also a process of *inclusion*. Differentiation and inclusion took place *within* the religious framework.[50] The Church and the aristocracies were thus the patrons of the new fine arts, which portrayed religious subjects for the embellishment of churches, monasteries, and other religious edifices. Artists and later scientists were increasingly drawn from laymen rather than clerics, and they went beyond the builders of the medieval cathedrals in developing corporate identities as experts in their work.[51] The universities were not conspicuously involved except in a few areas, such as law. Nevertheless, strides were taken during this period in extending outside the Church the role of the professional specialist in cultural matters. Although some of the later phases of the Renaissance penetrated into Protestant areas only after the Reformation, these phases were not directly antireligious either but were conceived within the religious framework.

The Renaissance originated in the revival of the literary styles of Latin antiquity, especially in the secular writings of the Humanists.[52] The revived themes stimulated visual and plastic arts: architecture, painting, and sculpture. Only later did *science* attain a comparable level of sophistication, through processes of internal differentiation as well as through general differentiation of secular culture from the social matrix. For example, Leonardo was a master of both artistic and scientific elements whereas Raphael was not a scientist or Galileo an artist. This differentiation was basic to modern culture because the new science, which culminated in the seventeenth century with Newton, formed the reference point for the first wave of modern philosophy. And modern philosophy underlay the development of the complexes of secular knowledge, the intellectual disciplines.

Renaissance art turned to secular subjects, often scenes taken from classical mythology (as in many of Botticelli's paintings), or landscapes

49. Troeltsch, *op. cit.*, vol. II; and McIlwain, *op. cit.*

50. Troeltsch, *op. cit.*, vol. II.

51. See Joseph Ben-David, *The Sociology of Science* (Englewood Cliffs, N.J.: Prentice-Hall, 1971), for a discussion of Renaissance science.

52. Paul Oskar Kristeller, *Renaissance Thought: The Classic, Scholastic and Humanist Strains* (New York: Harper, 1961).

and portraits. But even when subjects were religious, new secular concerns may be discerned. The symbolic focus of Italian Renaissance art was the Madonna and child. In religious terms, this focus represented a shift away from the Crucifixion and the martyrdom of saints. It emphasized, indeed glorified, the *human* family, particularly the mother-child relationship. Motherhood was made universally appealing by the portrayal of Mary as an attractive young woman who loves her child. Does this symbolism not reflect the shift of Christian orientation toward positive sanctioning of the right kind of secular order?

The Renaissance was not mainly a movement of synthesis; rather it was a period of cultural innovation. Such changes could hardly have occurred without both philosophical and theological involvement. The dynamic character of Scholastic philosophy should alert us to this principle. Thomism was the central formulation of the late-medieval synthesis, but other movements, such as Nominalism, were stimulated by classical thought and by themes drawn from Islamic philosophy and became the most advanced branch of Scholasticism. These movements were more open to empirical considerations and less inclined to close the Christian world view than was Thomism.[53]

In a variety of other cultural spheres, the Renaissance was concerned not only with differentiating the religious and the secular but also with integrating them. Much as the Madonna symbol indicated concern with "things of this world," newer monastic movements, such as the Franciscan and Dominican orders, were interested in charity and intellectual matters and wielded great influence. Renaissance humanistic and legal studies had philosophical and theological overtones, many of which attracted attention along with the first achievements of the new science. In condemning Galileo, the Church did not indicate indifference to his work. Not unrelated to the problems raised by Galileo was the earlier contribution of Machiavelli, the first European social thinker to be more interested in understanding how secular society actually worked than in justifying a specific religio-ethical point of view. The Renaissance attained its highest development in Italy. Very early, however, a similar movement, most visible in painting, began north of the Alps, also overlapping with medieval culture. Although it never developed as far in Germany as in Italy, it produced artists like Cranach, Dürer, and Holbein. It attained full development in Flanders and later in Holland where it continued into the Protestant era before culminating in the seventeenth century. Not only did this cultural development originate in a social setting comprised of city-states in Italy, but also its northern extension followed the band of free urban communities centering in the Rhine Valley. No com-

---

53. McIlwain, *op cit.;* and Kristeller, *op. cit.*

parable development of the visual arts arose in the predominantly feudal areas that led in forming the large territorial states.

The Reformation was an even more radical movement of cultural change and further differentiated the relations between cultural systems and society. Its cultural innovation was theological, the doctrine that salvation comes, in the Lutheran version, "by Faith alone," or, in the Calvinist predestinarian version, through the direct communion of the individual human soul with a sovereign God without *any* human intervention. This innovation deprived any Protestant church and its clergy of the "power of the keys," the capacity to mediate salvation through the sacraments. Furthermore, the visible church, the concrete collectivity of human believers and their clerical leaders, was conceived as a human association. The attribute of divinity, the status of the church as the "mystical Body of Christ," belonged only to the invisible church, the company of *souls* in Christ.[54] On this basis, human society could not consist, as Thomism had held, of two layers with different religious statuses: the Church, *both* divine and human, and purely human secular society. Rather, it was believed to consist of one society, all members of which were bodies as secular beings and also souls in their relations to God. This view represented more radical institutionalization of the individualistic components of Christianity than had Roman Catholicism.[55] It also had egalitarian implications, which took long to develop.

A further consequence of the elimination of the priesthood's sacramental powers was to undermine the special sphere that Roman Catholic tradition called "faith and morals," in which the visible Church held guardianship over all persons. Although many Protestant movements have attempted to continue ecclesiastical enforcement in this sphere, the tendency in Protestantism has been to define it as ultimately the individual's own responsibility. Similarly, the form of stratification *within* the medieval Church, the differentiation between laity and members of the religious orders, lost its legitimation in Protestantism. On the level of a way of life, all callings had the same religious status; the highest religious merit could be attained in secular callings.[56] This attitude included marriage—Luther himself left his monastery and married a former nun, symbolizing the change. This change in the relations between church and secular society has often been interpreted as a loss of religious rigor in favor of worldly indulgence. I consider this view a misinterpretation, for the Reformation was a movement to upgrade secular society to the highest

54. *Ibid.*

55. Max Weber, *The Protestant Ethic and the Spirit of Capitalism* (New York: Scribner, 1958).

56. *Ibid.*

religious level. Every man was obligated to behave like a monk in his religious devotion, although not in his daily life; that is, he was to be guided by religious considerations. A turn in the process, which dated from early phases of Christianity, was to permeate the things of this world with religious values and to create a City of Man in the image of God.[57]

The institutionalization of the conception of a religiously based human society implied the possibility of establishing a societal community with a corporate character something like that of the Church itself, particularly the Protestant conception of a church that dispensed with the stratification in the Roman Catholic conception. For the larger types of secular society, this effort required a mode of political integration surpassing those of the medieval and Renaissance period. The Reformation legitimated some of the new territorial monarchies such as the German principalities with whom Luther formed alliances.[58] These alliances were essential to the survival of the movement itself, but they also initiated a type of church-state organization that could develop further certain ingredients of modern society. In England the Reformation was precipitated somewhat differently when Henry VIII converted to Protestantism, opening the way for changes in the Church and in its relations with secular society. Where Protestant *state churches* were formed, the tendency (except in England) was toward both religious and political conservatism, especially in Lutherism, which allied itself with territorial monarchical regimes. The Calvinist branch has been more involved in movements stressing the independence of religious groups from political authority,[59] notably in the United States. Developments within American Protestantism made an early separation of church and state religiously, as well as politically, acceptable.

CONCLUSION

This chapter has been concerned with pre-modern roots of modern societies and especially with the cultural innovations contained in Christianity. For example, the early Christian Church was an *associational* religious group independent of an ethnic or territorial community. It was not quite as voluntaristic as a denomination is in the contemporary

57. *Ibid.*; Troeltsch, *op. cit.*, vol. II; Ernst Troeltsch, *Protestantism and Progress* (Boston: Beacon, 1953); and Talcott Parsons, "Christianity" in *International Encyclopedia of the Social Sciences* (New York: Macmillan, 1968).

58. G. R. Elton, *Reformation Europe* (Cleveland: Meridian, 1965).

59. Important exceptions are discussed in J. J. Loubser, "Calvinism, Equality, and Inclusion," in S. N. Eisenstadt (ed.), *op. cit.*

United States, but it had departed from the ascribed religiosity of Judaism. During the Renaissance a secular culture was differentiated from the religious matrix and laid the foundations for the arts and the intellectual disciplines. Thus, a process of cultural differentiation led to a clearer distinction than had previously existed between society (and its organizational requirements) and the cultural system. But the differentiation of secular society was accomplished by a new integration of culture and society, not by each going its separate way.

I shall try to make clearer how and why this new integration occurred as society moved toward modernity by discussing the implications of my four-function scheme for action evolution. In accordance with that scheme a society is analytically divisible into four subsystems (as shown in Table 1). Thus, the pattern-maintenance subsystem is concerned with the relations of the society to the cultural system and, through it, to ultimate reality; the goal-attainment subsystem (the polity) to the personalities of individual members; the adaptive subsystem (the economy) to the behavioral organism and, through it, to the physical world. These divisions are clearest for societies advanced on the scale of modernity.

Within this framework, the core of a society is the fourth com-

Table 1   Society (more generally, social system)

SUBSYSTEMS	STRUCTURAL COMPONENTS	ASPECTS OF DEVELOP-MENTAL PROCESS	PRIMARY FUNCTION
Societal Community	Norms	Inclusion	Integration (solidarity)
Pattern Maintenance or Fiduciary	Values	Value Generalization	Pattern Maintenance (integrity of institutionalization of its value commitments)
Polity	Collectivities	Differentiation	Goal Attainment (political effectiveness)
Economy	Roles	Adaptive Upgrading	Adaptation (economic productivity)

This table attempts to spell out a four-function paradigm for the *society* conceived as the integrative subsystem of a general system of action. The societal community, which is the subsystem of reference for the present analysis, is placed in the left hand column; the other three follow it. Corresponding to this set is a classification in the second column, by the same functional criteria, of four main structural components of societies. In the third column follows a classification of aspects of process of developmental change in societies. Finally, the fourth column repeats the designation of four primary functional categories.

ponent, its integrative subsystem. Because the social system is integrative for action systems generally, special attention must be paid to the ways it achieves—or fails to achieve—internal integration. I have been calling the integrative subsystem of a society the *societal community*. A function of the societal community is to articulate a *system* of norms with a collective organization that has cohesiveness. Following Weber, I call the normative aspect *the system of legitimate order*;[60] the collective aspect is the societal community as a *functional unity*. Societal order requires integration in the sense of normative coherence and of societal coordination. Moreover, normatively-defined obligations must be accepted while, conversely, collectivities must have normative sanction in performing their functions and promoting their legitimate interests. Thus, normative order at the societal level contains a solution to the problem posed by Hobbes—of preventing human relations from degenerating into a "war of all against all." A structure of societal norms should not be treated as a monolithic entity. Hence I distinguish four kinds of societal norms even though they overlap in specific content. The distinctions concern the grounds of obligations and rights as well as the nature of punishing noncompliance and rewarding compliance or unusual levels of performance. There are norms concerned with *loyalty* to the societal community, norms concerned with the social *implementation* of cultural values, norms concerned with the *enforcement* of collective obligations, and norms concerned with economic *practicality*.

The core category, the societal community, is generally discussed in religious and political rather than social terms. The function of this integrative subsystem is to define the obligations of *loyalty* to the societal collectivity for the membership as a whole and for various categories of differentiated status and role within the society. Thus in most modern societies willingness to perform military service is a test of loyalty for men but not for women. Loyalty is a readiness to respond to properly justified appeals in the name of the public interest. The normative problem is the definition of occasions when such a response constitutes an obligation. In principle, loyalty is required in any collectivity, but it has special importance for the societal community. Organs of government are generally the agents of appeals to societal loyalty as well as agents of implementation of the associated norms. However, there are instances in which government and justified community agency do not directly coincide.

The societal community involves relations between subgroups' and individuals' loyalties to the societal collectivity and to other collectivities of which they are members. *Role pluralism,* the involvement of the same persons in several collectivities, is a feature of all human societies. On

60. Max Weber, *The Theory of Social and Economic Organization* (New York: Oxford University Press, 1947).

the whole, an increase in role pluralism is a feature of the differentiation processes leading toward modern types of society. Therefore, the regulation of loyalties to the community itself and to various other collectivities is a problem of integration for a societal community. Individualistic social theory has exaggerated the significance of individual self-interest in a psychological sense as an obstacle to the integration of social systems. The self-interested motives of individuals are channeled into the social system through a variety of memberships in and loyalties to collectivities. The immediate problem for most individuals is the adjustment of obligations among competing loyalties in cases of conflict. For example, the normal adult male in modern societies is both an employee and a member of a family household. Although the demands of these two roles conflict, most men have a stake in fulfilling loyalties to *both*.

A societal community is a network of interpenetrating collectivities and collective loyalties. Thus kinship-household units, business firms, churches, governmental units, and educational collectivities are differentiated from each other. Moreover, there are a number of each type of collective unit—for example, a large number of households, each comprised of only a few persons, and many local communities. Loyalty to the societal community must have a high priority in any stable hierarchy of loyalties. However, it does not occupy the highest place in the hierarchy. The cultural legitimation of a society's normative order occupies a superordinate position. It operates through the institutionalization of a value-system, which is part of both the societal and the cultural systems. Then its subvalues, which are specifications of general value patterns, become parts of every concrete norm integrated into the legitimate order. The system of norms governing loyalties must integrate the rights and obligations of various collectivities and their members not only with each other, but also with the bases of legitimation of the order as a whole.[61]

In its hierarchical aspect, the normative ordering of the societal community in terms of memberships comprises its *stratification* scale, the scale of the accepted—and, so far as values and norms are integrated, legitimized—*prestige* of subcollectivities, of statuses, of roles, and of persons as societal members. It must be coordinated with universal norms governing the status of membership and with the elements of differentiation among the functions of subcollectivities, statuses, and roles, but these functions do not as such imply a hierarchy. The concrete stratification system is a result of the interplay of all these components.

Role-pluralism complicates the problem of the status of individuals in a stratification system. Stratification mechanisms treat individuals as diffusely integrated in large collective systems membership in which

---

61. On these matters, see Robert N. Bellah, "Epilogue," in *Religion and Progress in Modern Asia* (New York: Free Press, 1965).

defines their status. Lineages, ethnic groups, estates, and social classes have operated in this way. However, modern society requires a differentiation of individual statuses from diffuse background solidarities, giving modern systems of stratification a distinctive character.[62]

The position of a subcollectivity or individual in the stratification system is measured by the level of its or his *prestige* (capacity to exercise *influence*). Influence is a generalized symbolic medium of societal interchange in the same general class as money and power. It consists in capacity to bring about desired decisions on the part of other social units without offering them a valued *quid pro quo* as an inducement or threatening them with deleterious consequences. Influence must operate through persuasion in that its object must be *convinced* that to decide as the influencer suggests is to act in the interest of a collective system with which both are solidary. Its appeal is to the collective interest on the assumption that the parties involved are concerned to promote the collective interest and their mutual solidarity. Typical uses of influence are persuasion to enter into a contractual relation in good faith or to vote for a specific political candidate. Influence may be exchanged for *ad hoc* benefits or for other forms of influence in a sense parallel to that in which monetary resources may either be used to obtain goods or pooled or exchanged. Influence may also be exchanged for other generalized media such as money or power.[63]

The bases of cultural legitimation transcend direct contingencies of influence, interests, and solidarity, being grounded at the societal level in *value commitments*. By contrast with loyalty to collectivities, the hallmark of a value commitment is greater independence from considerations of cost, relative advantage or disadvantage, and environmental exigency in the meeting of obligations. The violation of a commitment is defined as illegitimate: its fulfillment is a matter of conscience, which may not be compromised without dishonor and/or guilt. Although this may sound restrictive, as indeed such commitments often are, the degree of restrictiveness depends on a variety of factors. Commitment to values implies the assumption of an obligation to help implement them in concrete action. Especially where the value system is activistic, as it often is in modern societies, this implies acceptance of certain realistic conditions of collective action. Thus, value *systems* contain a category of commitments to valued association, solidarity in legitimate collective relationships and enterprises. What associations are valued is a matter that varies among societies. It is difficult to ensure the legitimacy of association by restricting

62. Talcott Parsons, "Equality and Inequality in Modern Society, or Social Stratification Revisited," *Sociological Inquiry*, 40/2 (spring 1970).

63. Talcott Parsons, "On the Concept of Influence," *Politics and Social Structure* (New York: Free Press, 1969).

legitimation to specifically defined acts, however, because actors need scope for considerable discretion if they are to implement their values under varying circumstances. One factor in setting the breadth of this scope is the level of generality of the legitimating values. For example, an injunction not to exploit others in economic transactions is different from a specific prohibition of lending money at interest. The *generalization* of value systems, so that they can effectively regulate social action without relying upon particularistic prohibitions, has been a factor in the modernization process.

At the cultural level, the relevant aspect of values concerns the evaluation of the objects of experience in the context of social relationships. A moral act implements a cultural value in a social situation involving interaction with other actors. As a matter of interaction, it must involve standards which bind the interactors reciprocally. Moral values comprise only one component of the value-content of a cultural system, others being aesthetic, cognitive, or religious values. Cultures also become differentiated on bases other than the moral, so that religion, art as expressive symbolization, empirical knowledge (eventually science), also become independent, differentiated cultural systems. A differentiated cultural system is a characteristic of modern societies.[64]

In addition to the aspects of a societal normative order centering about membership and loyalty and about cultural legitimation, there is a third. Influence and value commitments operate voluntarily, through persuasion and appeal to conscience. However, no large social system can endure unless compliance with large parts of its normative order is *binding;* that is, negative situational sanctions attach to noncompliance. Such sanctions deter noncompliance—by reminding the good citizen of his obligations—and punish infraction if, as, and when it occurs. The socially organized exercise of negative sanctions, including threats of using them when intentions of noncompliance are suspected, is *enforcement.* The more highly differentiated a society, the more likely enforcement is performed by specialized agencies such as police forces and military establishments.[65]

Regulated enforcement requires some mode of determining the actual circumstances of the infraction of norms. Among the specialized agencies that perform this function are courts of law and the legal profession. A complex normative order requires not only enforcement but also authoritative interpretation. Court systems combine the determination of obligations, and penalties for specific cases with interpretation of

64. Talcott Parsons, "Introduction" to "Culture and the Social System" in *Theories of Society.*

65. Talcott Parsons, "Some Reflections on the Place of Force in Social Process" in *Sociological Theory and Modern Society* (New York: Free Press, 1967).

the meaning of norms.[66] Less developed societies tend to reserve the latter function to religious agencies, but modern societies entrust it increasingly to secular courts. These problems raise questions about the relation between a societal community and the polity. The concept *political* includes not only the functions of government in its relation to a societal community but corresponding aspects of any collectivity.[67] A phenomenon is political in so far as it involves the organization and mobilization of resources for the attainment of the goals of a particular collectivity. Thus business firms, universities, and churches have political aspects. In the development of modern societies, government has increasingly become differentiated from the societal community as a specialized organ of the society at the core of the polity.

As it has become differentiated, government has tended to center on two functions. The first concerns responsibility for maintaining the integrity of the societal community against generalized threats, with special reference to its legitimate normative order. This includes the function of enforcement and a share in the function of interpretation. Moreover, the process of governmental differentiation creates spheres within which it becomes admissible to formulate and promulgate new norms, making legislation part of this function also. The second function, the executive, concerns collective action in whatever situations indicate that specific measures should be undertaken in the public interest. This responsibility ranges from inherently essential matters, such as defense of territorial control and maintenance of public order, to almost any issue deemed to be "affected with a public interest."[68]

The relations between government and the societal community may be ascribed. Even early modern societies defined the common people as subjects of a monarch, ascriptively obligated to obey his authority. Fully modern levels of differentiation have tended to make the power of political leadership contingent on the support of extensive proportions of the population. In so far as this is true, roles of *political* leadership must be distinguished from positions of authority more generally. Differentiation between leadership and authority necessitates generalization of the symbolic medium, power.[69] Power is capacity to make—and make stick—

66. Suggestive in this regard is Lon Fuller, *The Morality of Law* (New Haven: Yale University Press, 1964).

67. Talcott Parsons, "The Political Aspect of Social Structure and Process" in David Easton (ed.), *Varieties of Political Theory* (Englewood Cliffs, N.J.: Prentice-Hall, 1966). (Reprinted in *Politics and Social Structure*.)

68. *Ibid;* see also Gabriel A. Almond and G. Bingham Powell, *Comparative Politics; A Developmental* Approach (Boston: Little, Brown, 1966).

69. Talcott Parsons "On the Concept of Political Power," in *Politics and Social Structure.*

decisions *binding* on the collectivity of reference and on its members in so far as their *statuses* carry obligations under the decisions. Power must be distinguished from influence, for the promulgation of binding decisions differs from attempts to persuade. By my definition, a citizen exercises power when he casts his vote because the aggregate of votes bindingly determines the electoral outcome. Only a little power still is power, just as one dollar, though only a little money, is money.

A fourth component of the normative order concerns matters of *practicality.* Its obvious fields of application are the economic and technological; its governing principle is the desirability of efficient management of resources. Even where issues of collective loyalty, binding obligations, and morality are not involved, the action of an individual or collectivity will be disapproved if it is unnecessarily wasteful. In modern societies, the normative aspect of these considerations clearly regulates the use of labor as a factor of production in the economic sense. Commitment to the labor force involves an obligation to work effectively within the legitimate conditions of employment.[70] As Weber noted, there is a moral element in this obligation. But short of the moral emphasis, rational economic and technological action is generally approved, while deviation from standards of rationality is disapproved.

The differentiation of autonomous structures necessitates the development of a generalized monetary medium in association with a market system. Money and markets operate where there is a sufficiently complex division of labor and where spheres of action are sufficiently differentiated from political, communal, or moral imperatives.[71] Of the generalized mechanisms of societal interchange, money and markets is the least directly involved with the normative order centering in the societal community. Hence, practical rationality is regulated mainly by institutional norms, such as the institutions of property and contract, which have other bases of sanction.[72]

In the next chapter we shall see how normative order was maintained in all four subsystems as modern societies crystallized, including the emergence of national identities that transcended religious particularisms.

70. Neil J. Smelser, *The Sociology of Economic Life* (Englewood Cliffs, N.J.: Prentice-Hall, 1963).

71. *Ibid;* see also Talcott Parsons and Neil J. Smelser, *Economy and Society* (New York: Free Press, 1956).

72. The classic analysis of the significance of property and contract for social systems was developed by Emile Durkheim in *The Division of Labor in Society* (New York: Macmillan, 1933).

CHAPTER 7
THE EMERGENCE OF NATIONAL COMMUNITIES

I attribute the beginning of the system of modern societies to seventeenth-century developments in the societal community, especially the bearing of religion on the legitimation of society, rather than to the eighteenth-century evolution toward democracy and industrialization.

After the Reformation shattered the religious unity of Western Christendom, a division arose, roughly along the north-south axis. All Europe south of the Alps remained Roman Catholic; a Roman Catholic peninsula thrust into northern Europe with France as its main component. Protestantism in Switzerland enjoyed the protection guaranteed by Swiss independence. Although Vienna was predominantly Protestant at the start of the seventeenth century, the Hapsburgs were able to recatholicize Austria, aided by the Turkish occupation of Hungary where Protestantism was strong. As religious struggle intensified, the southern tier of political units consolidated. In the sixteenth century this consolidation involved a union of Austria and Spain under the rule of the Hapsburg Emperor, Charles V. The middle of this empire was protected by the Kingdom of Naples and Sicily adjacent to the Papal States. The presence of the papacy in Italy and the extent of Hapsburg power made effective independence of the Italian city-states impossible. The Counter-Reformation enforced an alliance between Church and state, exemplified by the Spanish Inquisition. In comparison to the liberal trends within late medieval and Renaissance Roman Catholicism, the Counter-Reformation Church stressed orthodoxy and authoritarianism in its organization. Civil alliance with the Church in enforcing religious conformity fostered the expansion of centralized government authority. Such enforcement was undertaken in the name of the Holy Roman Empire, with its religious legitimation and divinely ordained Emperor.[1] By that time the political structure of the Empire was more integrated than it had been in the Middle Ages.

Nevertheless, the Empire was vulnerable; it centered in the loosely organized German nation—Austria's population was only partly German by that time, and the Hapsburgs had assumed the crowns of Hungary and Bohemia through personal unions. The Treaty of Westphalia, which ended the Thirty Years' War, had made Holland and Switzerland independent of the Empire but had also drawn the religious line through the remaining parts; many of the German princes had chosen Protestantism for their domains under the formula *cuius regio, eius religio* (the religion of the king determined the religion of his subjects). More than the defection from Rome of Henry VIII, this choice undermined the legitimation of the old secular structure of Christendom because the Empire had been conceived as the secular arm of a unified Roman Catholic *system*. The settlement was an uneasy compromise, acceptable only as an alternative to the indefinite continuation of a destructive war. Nevertheless, it ended any expectation that a Roman Catholic European system could be restored.[2] For more than three centuries the heartland of the Counter-Reformation remained resistant to modernizing processes, citadels of monarchial legitimism, aristocracy, and semibureaucratic states of the older type.

Although the Protestants dreamed of prevailing throughout Western Christendom, they soon splintered into different branches and never developed a conception of unity like that of medieval Roman Catholicism.[3] This fragmentation furthered the development of independent monarchies based on unstable integration of absolutist political regimes and national churches.[4] It also contained the seeds of the internal religious pluralism that was to advance rapidly in England and Holland. The outcome of the struggle between Reformation and Counter-Reformation was a double step toward pluralization and differentiation. The English-Dutch wing was more advanced, a harbinger for the future. Yet development within the Empire posed the problem of integration *across* the Protestant–Roman Catholic line. Many historians of modern Europe have perceived only stalemated conflict. Yet religious toleration was subsequently extended to Roman Catholics in Protestant polities and even to

1. James Bryce, *The Holy Roman Empire*, rev. ed. (London: Macmillan, 1904).

2. *Ibid.*

3. Ernst Troeltsch, *The Social Teachings of the Christian Churches*, vol. II (New York: Harper, 1960).

4. G. R. Elton, *Reformation Europe, 1517–1559* (Cleveland, Ohio: Meridian, 1963).

Protestants in Roman Catholic polities, though generally without sacrifice of the establishment principle.

Religious pluralization was part of a process of differentiation between the cultural and societal systems that reduced the diffuseness of their interpenetration. Religious legitimation of secular society was retained without committing governmental authority to the implementation of religious goals. The differentiation of modern secular culture from society as a whole has contributed to the interpenetration of religion and society. The focus of this development shifted northward in the seventeenth century to England and Holland but also to France and parts of Germany. *Relative* cultural decline in the heartland of the Counter-Reformation began after Galileo. The cultural vitality of France indicated the equivocal nature, by Counter-Reformation standards, of its Roman Catholicism. Yet politically reactionary powers could be receptive to secular culture, as was Prussia under Frederick the Great. In general, secular culture found Protestantism more congenial than Roman Catholicism throughout this period.

The emergence of sovereign territorial states divided the Holy Roman Empire. They were first successfully established in France and England, which had been only nominally part of the Empire, and next Spain, also on the geographical fringe. Then Prussia and Austria developed on the border of the German area, shifting the Empire's center of gravity toward the eastern frontier. In the central areas of the old Empire, territorial principalities proliferated largely through adherence of the princes to the Reformation.[5] These developments showed the cohesion of the European system, as all four of the leading political-territorial states were frontier units of the system. Both the northwest triangle and the Iberian peninsula faced the open sea and participated in the maritime expansion of Europe. The Iberian peninsula also was partially occupied by the Moors, whose occupation of much of the peninsula through the fifteenth century nurtured the authoritarianism of Hispanic Catholicism.[6]

Imperial gravitation toward the east was also associated with frontier conditions. The boundary between the Germanic and Slavic peoples had been unstable for many centuries—and was complicated even before the Reformation by relations between the Roman and Orthodox branches of Christianity. Hungary, Bohemia, and Poland were ethnically non-German but had become Roman Catholic. Especially after the fall of Byzantium, the Orthodox power was Russia, still peripheral to the Western system. The Germanic drive to organize and protect—and on occasion to domi-

5. Geoffrey Barraclough, *The Origins of Modern Germany* (New York: Capricorn, 1963).

6. Americo Castro, *The Structure of Spanish History* (Princeton: Princeton University Press, 1954).

nate—the western Slavs eventuated in Hapsburg involvement with Hungary and Bohemia in an unstable multi- or non-national state. Incorporation of the non-German frontier peoples was complicated by Ottoman expansion, which remained a threat until the late seventeenth century; Austria thus served as a defender of all *Christian* Europe.[7]

These developments at the borders of the European system hollowed out its center, especially in the Germany of *Kleinstaaterei*. The center failed to develop major territorial units, although a few like Saxony and Bavaria approached such status; numerous other states were very small. These principalities swallowed up the free cities of the Empire, however. The independence of the urban bourgeois classes was undermined by monarchy, aristocracy, and officialdom and by the devastation of wars. This part of Europe fell behind the Northwest in economic development and became a power vacuum before the ambitions of the stronger powers.[8] I have been speaking of the territorial state rather than of the national state. Only in England, France, and perhaps Scandinavia were ethnic community and governmental organization coextensive. In Spain, diverse local elements gradually developed a common language, at least among the upper classes. Prussia became German, partly through Germanizing of large Slavic elements. Austria was multiethnic, including large German, Slavic, and Hungarian elements. Switzerland achieved a limited form of multiethnic political integration and religious pluralism. The small German states divided the ethnic German nation into numerous political units, leaving "Germany" even more disunited than "Italy."

Except in the northwest, the lack of coincidence between ethnic group and territorial organization hindered the development of liberalizing societies based on independent, solidary societal communities, which occurred in the northwest area. The territorial units either lacked the ethnic solidarity that can focus such communities or included segments of larger ethnic communities for which their governments could not presume to speak. For political authorities in this precarious situation, some form of religious legitimation was necessary. Their insecurity also contributed to political authoritarianism and fear of concessions to popular participation in government. Their people were subjects rather than citizens.

The religious fission of European society and the emergence of sovereign states precipitated crises that erupted in the seventeenth century. No functional equivalent of the old Empire appeared, and lack of religious legitimation remained a weakness of the international system;

---

7. Oscar Halecki, *The Limits and Divisions of European History* (Notre Dame, Ind.: University of Notre Dame Press, 1962).

8. Bryce, *op. cit.*, and Barraclough, *op. cit.*

its power relations lacked adequate normative regulation.[9] This situation favored chronic war and inhibited the constructive use of political power that could have emerged in a better-integrated collective system.

THE NORTHWEST

England, France, and Holland, each in a different way, took the lead in the power system of the seventeenth century. Dutch independence represented a defeat for Spain. As the Austrians were engaged against the Turks, Continental hegemony fell to the French. Though not yet a paramount force in Continental affairs, England did become the dominant maritime power during this century. These three nations were the spearhead of early modernity. Important developments occurred in their societal communities. Despite variations among the forms of the three societal communities, each contributed innovations relative to national solidarity. Thus the English conception of national identity provided a basis for a clearly differentiated societal community.[10] This differentiation proceeded on three fronts—religious, political, and economic—each involving normative considerations. Legal innovations favored associational rather than bureaucratic potentials of the structure of national community. They were related to the emergence of parliamentarianism and more developed market economies.

Religion and the Societal Community

The Reformation deprived the visible church of its sacramental character. Supsequently, under the formula *cuius regio, eius religio,* the tendency was to bring the church under secular control, as there was no international Protestant church capable of reinforcing ecclesiastical independence. The Protestant churches tended to become national churches, and conformity was enforced through political authority.

A Puritan phase, based on Calvinism in England and Holland, led to religious pluralism *within* Protestantism, which contrasted with the religious character of Prussia, several other Protestant German principalities, and Scandinavia. In seventeenth-century England, differentiation of the religious system from the societal community required political changes. The Long Parliament, the Civil War, the establishment of the Commonwealth, the Restoration, and the Revolution of 1688 involved not only political issues but the religious future of England. English religious development involved the conversion of the crown to Prot-

9.   Bryce, *op. cit.,* and Troeltsch, *op. cit.*

10.   See Hans Kohn, *The Idea of Nationalism* (New York: Macmillan, 1961).

estantism and a broadening of Elizabethan religious toleration.[11] The *political* legitimacy of the Nonconformists became firmly established, preventing a return to a politically established church with a monopoly of religious legitimacy. Furthermore, through Nonconformism, the Church of England was exposed to influences from the religious left, which might have been repressed in a purely state-church system. Indeed, the evangelical wing of the Church of England fostered subsequent English development.

Interestingly, the repression of Roman Catholicism in England[12] contributed to this outcome. Greater tolerance for Roman Catholicism during the eighteenth century might have led to a second Stuart restoration and an attempt at a Roman Catholic reestablishment. The solidarity of a Protestant societal community and the relative absence of religious tension facilitated such developments as extension of the franchise. Had English rightists been obliged to uphold the "true Church" as well as monarchy and aristocracy, the strains would have been more severe than they were, especially under the impact of the American and French Revolutions.[13] Seventeenth-century Holland went farther than England did in religious toleration. Over the long run, however, its religious constitution proved less stable. A nineteenth-century Roman Catholic revival created a columnar structure among religious groups of approximately equal strength, thus introducing a religious rift into the societal community.[14]

France also failed to solve its religious problem. The outcome of the Reformation struggle was a Roman Catholic victory and suppression of the Protestant movement. Since then, Protestantism in France has never involved more than small minorities. This weakness did not, however, secure the position of the Roman Catholic Church. *Secular* anticlericalism, based on the Enlightenment of the eighteenth century became a political theme of the Revolution.[15] The French pattern has influenced the definitions of religious legitimacy in other modern societies too, particularly in the Latin Catholic countries (including those of Latin America) but also in Germany and Eastern Europe. It has also contributed to the antireligious element in modern socialist movements, especially communism.

11. W. K. Jordan, *The Development of Religious Toleration in England*, 3 vols. (Cambridge, Mass.: Harvard University Press, 1932–1940).

12. The Catholic Emancipation Act was not passed until 1830.

13. See R. R. Palmer, *The Age of the Democratic Revolution*, 2 vols. (Princeton: Princeton University Press, 1959 and 1964).

14. S. M. Lipset and Stein Rokkan, "Introduction," in Lipset and Rokkan (eds.), *Cleavage Structures, Party Systems and Voter Alignment* (New York: Free Press, 1968).

15. See Palmer, *op. cit.*

These European developments constitute a type of differentiation of the societal community and the religious system quite different from the pattern that emerged in seventeenth-century England and reached full development in the United States. The Anglo-Saxon pattern builds on religious traditions of Western society while accommodating societal solidarities that cut across the historic religious particularisms. Indeed, the range of religious solidarities compatible with societal membership has broadened. Secular anticlericalism, especially in its Communist version, remains closer to the formula of *cuius regio, eius religio* with the implication that nonconformists must be excluded from the societal community.

The Polity and the Societal Community

The societal community, as the zone of integration between a normative structure and a collectivity structure in which role loyalties of individuals are centered, involves reliance on religious legitimation under political authority. Absolutism represented a solution of the political aspects of the solidarity problems that arose from post-Reformation developments.[16] It required that government—usually a monarchy—provide a central symbol on which loyalty could focus; such a symbol was enhanced by religious and ethnic unity. Indeed, religion and ethnic affiliation were the bases on which European society divided into territorial political units in early modern times,[17] with the result that government and societal community were relatively undifferentiated. Nevertheless, in Western societies, there has been a tendency, under special conditions, to differentiate the two. England made an early start in this direction, in contrast to France, an absolutist state in which government was identified with the societal community.

Ethnically, England, like France, had the problem of a Celtic fringe, but only in Ireland was religion a complicating factor. Ireland, where among the mass of the people Celtic ethnic affiliation coincided with Roman Catholicism and with class and geographical separation from England, was where integration failed. In the seventeenth century Cromwell fought bitter wars against the Irish, but the Roman Catholic Irish were never integrated into a United Kingdom as part of a unified societal community. Wales, though mainly Celtic, had a geographic disadvantage in maintaining its independence. It became predominantly Protestant, though more Nonconformist than most of England, and posed no threat of religious schism. The Scots developed an ethnic consciousness but fluctuated between Roman Catholicism and a more radical Protestantism

16. See Max Beloff, *The Age of Absolutism, 1660–1815* (New York: Harper, 1962).

17. Kohn, *op. cit.*

than that of the English. The Scottish Stuarts fostered the Roman Catholic threat to the English religious constitution. Once the Protestant alternative had been consolidated, however, Scottish Presbyterianism became an element in British Protestant denominational pluralism. Despite Ireland, therefore, Britian became relatively united ethnically, which contributed to its ability to achieve religious pluralism within the bounds of Protestantism.[18]

Within a societal community, regional and ethnic differences are cut across by vertical axes of differentiation on the bases of power, prestige, and wealth. The geographical location of the center of societal organization—in Britain, London—is a point of intersection. A complex society requires substantial stratification, especially in times of innovation. Because contributing to the innovative process depends on the *kind* of stratification, changes in stratification were to be expected in the seventeenth century. Indeed, both the landed aristocracies that had developed from the feudal order and the urban patriciates were being transformed, and their relations with each other and with other groups were changing. The landed aristocracies were the upper class, providing the support in prestige for the development of modern territorial monarchies.[19] The monarch was not only the chief of state but also the first gentleman of his society, the apex of a structured hierarchy of social prestige. The aristocracy was a seamless web of lineages, an affinal collectivity bound by intermarriage and eligibility for intermarriage.[20] Aristocratic lineages have tended to be anchored in local interest structures, especially in land. Historically, landed proprietorship was also a diffuse superiority status, including not only ownership but also elements of political control and social ascendance.

The rise of the early modern state reduced the political power of particularistically defined aristocratic subgroups, especially their autonomous territorial and military jurisdiction in favor of a prestige position that supported the monarchy.[21] Adequate economic support for those prestige positions rested on land ownership. In predominantly rural areas, therefore, economic elements were not radically different from a more diffuse social matrix, the apex of which was local aristocracy.[22] Under feudal conditions the aristocracy of Europe was, in principle, a seam-

---

18. *Ibid.*

19. See Palmer, *op. cit.*, and Beloff, *op. cit.*

20. This conception of "affinal collectivity" has been influenced by the author's discussions with Charles D. Ackerman.

21. Palmer, *op. cit.*, and Beloff, *op. cit.*

22. See Barrington Moore, Jr., *Social Origins of Dictatorship and Democracy: Lord and Peasant in the Making of the Modern World* (Boston: Beacon, 1966).

less web. This unity was incompatible with division into national states. Religious differences resulting from the Reformation created barriers to intermarriage and helped contain the aristocracy supporting a prince within *eius religio,* but it did not eliminate the problem. In England, since the Tudor period, foreign dynasties have been more the rule than the exception: the Scottish Stuarts, the Dutch House of Orange, and the German Hanoverians. Had this cosmopolitanism extended to the aristocracy, it would have impeded the consolidation of ethnic-national identities. England and France, the two leading national states, split on religious and linguistic lines so that their aristocracies became distinct from each other—and from others. Along with the nationalization of the aristocracy, the integration of top political authority with aristocracy was a factor in enabling royal governments to establish their authority over national societal communities.[23] This possibility depended upon the military functions of aristocracies.

The process of differentiation between government and societal community also involved the relations between monarchy and aristocracy, as shown by the conflicts of interest between the two. The political power institutionalized in *specific* aristocratic status was lessened. Yet the new power position of aristocracies varied greatly, as the examples of England and France show. The differentiation occurred in France in such a way as to leave the aristocracy dependent upon its social prestige. It was deprived of the exercise of political power but also of the functions of contributing contingent support to political authority and of exerting major influence over governmental policy.[24] The sign of this deprivation was the brilliant court of Versailles. Centralization at the court loosened the attachment of the aristocracy to their local communities, depriving them of local power, which facilitated the encroachment of the central government on local affairs.[25]

These remarks are most appropriate to the older, more feudal aristocracy, the *noblesse d'épée.* The position of the newer aristocracy of bourgeois origins and equipped with legal training reinforced the integration of aristocracy and crown. The legal profession was associated with the crown through public offices merging administrative and judicial components. As legal officials, the French lawyers stood between the crown and both the older aristocracy and the bourgeosie. There was considerable upward mobility through these intermediate circles, partly through the

23. Beloff, *op. cit.,* and John B. Wolf, *The Emergence of the Great Powers* (New York: Harper, 1962).

24. Franklin L. Ford, *Robe and Sword: The Regrouping of the French Aristocracy After Louis XIV* (Cambridge, Mass.: Harvard University Press, 1953).

25. *Ibid.*

sale of offices. Yet the upwardly mobile elements sought to attain the status of nobility and to make their offices hereditary.[26] Economically the *noblesse de robe* was dependent upon the crown for perquisites of its offices and, to the extent that it held land, for enforcement of feudal dues and obligations upon the peasantry. It lacked an independent economic base comparable to that of the English landed gentry.

The Church was integrated into this system. More than in England, high clerical offices went to members of aristocratic lineages. Furthermore, there was no equivalent of English Protestant Nonconformism. This absence contributed to the militant anticlericalism of the Revolutionary opposition to the *ancien régime*. There was a collegial aspect to the *noblesse* in the form of the *parlements*. In contrast to the British parliamentary system, the *parlements* were more judicial and administrative than legislative. Furthermore, there was no central *parlement* but a series of regional *parlements*. The *parlement* of Paris had only the precedence of first among equals, rather than the exclusive position occupied by the Parliament of Westminster.

The deprivation of political power among the French aristocracy was related to the group's ambivalent role in the eighteenth century. It developed a snobbish exclusiveness vis-à-vis all bourgeois elements, many of whom had surpassed it in political position, wealth, and cultivation.[27] On the other hand, it sponsored modernizing cultural movements, notably in philosophy, and thus contributed to the French Enlightenment.[28] Both these developments rendered problematic the position of the French aristocracy as the legitimate élite of the societal community. The aristocracy's dependence on the monarchy for its *social* prestige was combined with dissociation from the rest of the societal community in terms of both government power and the supposed cultural mediocrity of the common man. The crown, the two *noblesses,* and the Church were pitted against the bourgeoisie and all the other classes,[29] thus fostering the split in French society that erupted in the Revolution.

England developed differently when it departed from the initial symbiosis between government and aristocracy. Instead of disfranchising the aristocracy, the monarchy became its creature. The executive functions of government and the societal community underwent a process of

26.   Palmer, *op. cit.*

27.   Elinor Barber, *The Bourgeoisie in Eighteenth Century France* (Princeton: Princeton University Press, 1955).

28.   Palmer, *op. cit.*

29.   See especially Moore, *op. cit.,* and Ford, *op. cit.*

differentiation focused on the support system,[30] which articulated the two. This system was centered in Parliament. In contrast to France, Parliament had consolidated a position of real power by 1688. This power did not mean government by aristocracy, the obverse of the French solution. The national aristocracy was too diffuse actually to govern—one reason why both the Stuarts and Cromwell successfully advocated strong executive authority. Eventually there developed the system of cabinet government under a constitutional monarch who reigned but did not govern. Another factor was the special character of the British aristocracy. Primogeniture in England, reinforced by entail, tended to keep estates intact over generations and to produce continuous social gradations between the titled nobility and their untitled collaterals, the gentry, who were sometimes closely related to titled families. This system favored upward mobility into the aristocracy and indefinite extension of the status of gentleman downward from the titled nobility.

The status of the gentry became formalized in the House of Commons. As there were too many gentlemen for the Commons to be an assembly of an estate of the realm, as was the House of Lords (to which every peer belonged), it became a *representative* body.[31] As the Commons became increasingly important relative to the Lords, the distinction between those actually exercising political power and their constituencies became important. The gentry became a constituency, not a component of government. During the earlier period, the aristocracy, as a component of the societal community, constituted the active element in the support system of government, yet remained independent of governmental organization. Furthermore, representative participation in government facilitated the emergence of a party system under which the policies of active executive leadership became responsive to constituencies.[32]

The other type of inherited privilege was that of the urban upper class, which rested on commerce. Because the rural sector of the economy was still predominant, territorial consolidation under the monarchies favored rural interests and was less favorable to urban upper groups: a reason why urbanized areas were for a long time not incorporated in

30. Talcott Parsons, "The Political Aspects of Social Structure and Process," in David Easton (ed.), *Varieties of Political Theory* (Englewood Cliffs, N.J.: Prentice-Hall, 1966). Reprinted in *Politics and Social Structure* (New York: Free Press, 1969) Chapter 13.

31. C. H. McIlwain, *The High Court of Parliament* (New Haven: Yale University Press, 1910); and F. W. Maitland, *The Constitutional History of England* (Cambridge: University Press, 1908).

32. See Lewis Namier, *England in the Age of the American Revolution* (2nd ed.; London: Macmillan, 1961).

territorial monarchies but defended the free-city pattern. Holland was an execption. In winning its independence from Spain, it became a federation of urban communities led by merchant groups. It experienced difficulty in integrating its rural areas, however, and lacked the cohesion of its rivals. Yet, in avoiding the social dominance of a landed aristocracy, it set an example for future development.

England's middle position facilitated a synthesis. The representative character of the House of Commons provided machinery for the political involvement of the bourgeois groups, and the line between them and the untitled gentry did not become rigid as in France.[33] This flexibility was facilitated by the pluralistic political system including the crown, the City of London, and the aristocracy, itself divided into nobility and gentry. This pluralism made possible the inclusion of other emerging elements in the societal community. Indeed the constituency of the House of Commons was extended not only to the boroughs but in the nineteenth century to a mass electorate. By the late seventeenth century England had both a firmly integrated national state and a pluralistic support system; these developments favored future democratization in a step-by-step manner, rather than through abrupt revolutionary change.

These political circumstances were reinforced by the English religious constitution and by development of the common law. Universalistic legal principles and the conception of the rule of law, as distinguished from arbitrary authority, were institutionalized in legal systems all over Europe after the Renaissance, building on Roman traditions. Yet the common law was distinctive in three related ways.[34] First was judicial independence from the crown, which came to a head with the successful struggle of Chief Justice Coke against James I.[35] Second was the corporate character of the legal profession, organized about the Inns of Court. Third was the emphasis upon legal embodiment of private rights, sometimes against the privileges of government, sometimes in areas outside the normal range of governmental concern.[36] One aspect of this process involved the "rights of Englishmen," including habeas corpus, fair trial and counsel, the protection of homes against arbitrary search, and ultimately free speech and assembly. Another aspect involved property and contract, foundations of the industrial revolution. Coke's attack on the monopolies

33. See Archibald S. Foord, *His Majesty's Opposition 1714–1830* (Oxford: Oxford University Press, 1964).

34. See Maitland, *op. cit.*, and F. W. Maitland, *English Law and the Renaissance* (Cambridge: Cambridge University Press, 1901).

35. Maitland, *English Law and the Renaissance*, McIlwain, *op. cit.*, and Roscoe Pound, *The Spirit of the Common Law* (Boston: Beacon, 1963).

36. Pound, *op. cit.*

established by royal charter was a legal precursor of Adam Smith's attack on mercantilism.

English legal developments contributed to differentiating government from the societal community. Law became less an instrument of government and more a mediating interface between the two. It had to serve the needs of government but was sufficiently independent to serve pluralistic private needs as well. Government was thus placed in the position of enforcing legally embodied restrictions on its own powers. The legal profession came to occupy an interstitial status. It became tradition that judges, even in the exercise of the judicial powers of the House of Lords, should be professional lawyers. Both judges and barristers, the core of the legal profession, served mainly private clients, which might include government agencies.

Members of the legal profession—including judges—became the guardians of the rights of the general public, especially civil rights[37] and those of property, contract, and torts.[38] The independence of the judiciary and the bar seems also to have been related to the emergence of the second branch of the British legal profession, the solicitors, who lacked the privilege of pleading in court but were the legal advisers to groups of all sorts. Through the solicitors, the legal system penetrated the pluralistic structure of interest groups; through the bar and judiciary, it maintained its delicate relation to government. The Inns of Court were reminiscent of medieval guilds. They resisted the streamlining of law that occurred on the Continent, the formalization of university training, the appointment of influential lawyers as civil servants, and an examination system to guarantee competence.

Although judges were public officials, they were also lawyers trained in an extragovernmental profession and *responsible* to the traditions of the common law. The barristers and solicitors, though private professional practitioners, also had public prerogatives and responsibilities. Furthermore, the adversary system acquired a special status. More than on the Continent, legal actions were conducted between private parties, each represented by counsel, before a judge and often a jury under *procedural* rules. The judge tended to become an umpire rather than a decision maker. Furthermore, the courts themselves shaped law, especially in rendering decisions and setting precedents relatively independently of royal decrees and acts of Parliament. The English system left the boundaries of the legal system open, permitting approaches to consensus before full

37. See T. H. Marshall, *Class, Citizenship, and Social Development* (Garden City, N.Y.: Anchor, 1965).

38. In Durkheim's terms, this development indicated emphasis on "restitutive" over "repressive" law. See Emile Durkheim, *The Division of Labor in Society* (London: Macmillan, 1933).

legalization of a norm and its enforcement by governmental authority were reached. Appeals to collective solidarity, moral standards, and practicality had a place in the system other than through high-level policy determination.

Continental legal systems differed from that of England despite common origins and some common features. The new Continental monarchies tended to maintain the Roman legal tradition and its emphasis on the unitary authority of the state.[39] This tradition tended to make civil law the instrument of government by bringing the dominant group of legally trained people into governmental service, often as the core of the developing civil services.[40] Civil administration was differentiated from the military, which remained largely in the hands of the aristocracies. The Continental legal systems promoted the effectiveness of government more adequately than did the British one,[41] yet the latter made possible greater differentiation and integration between government and the societal community.

The Economy and the Societal Community

Economic developments in England during the sixteenth and seventeenth centuries centered on the enclosure movement and its aftermath: the growth of commercial farming oriented toward markets as distinct from the subsistence farming under which the sale of produce extended only to neighboring towns.[42] The break with the subsistence system was the development of a large export trade with the wool manufacturers of Flanders and Italy. Large-scale sheep raising required displacement of much of the tenant population, for sheep raising was less labor-intensive than was crop raising and was hindered by the traditional open-field system of manorial agriculture. Many of the gentry and even noble landowners actively promoted the change, either becoming commercial farmers themselves or renting their lands to commercial tenants. The secular owners of previously ecclesiastical lands, especially of monasteries that had been dissolved, were less traditional in estate management than the Church had been. Many members of the gentry also engaged, directly or through agents, in nonagricultural economic enterprise, particularly commercial ventures. Commercialization of agriculture was not complete by the end of the seventeenth century, but it already had major consequences.

39. See the discussion in Talcott Parsons, *Societies: Evolutionary and Comparative Perspectives* (Englewood Cliffs, N.J.: Prentice-Hall, 1966).

40. Ford, *op. cit.*

41. This aspect was emphasized by Weber; see Max Rheinstein (ed.), *Max Weber on Law in Economy and Society* (Cambridge, Mass.: Harvard University Press, 1954).

42. Karl Polanyi, *The Great Transformation* (New York: Beacon, 1957).

First, the proportion of peasants who were individual tenants, or even independent proprietors, had diminished. Instead, agricultural laborers appeared,[43] and the surplus rural population tended to leave the countryside and became a laboring class in the towns. A concern with indigence and vagabondage emerged[44] in response to the dislocations and human suffering that they entailed; from then on, the Poor Laws were to be an issue. The peasant class was weakened so that struggles over its rights and position were not as troublesome in England as in France.[45] Second, the land-owning classes tended to become defeudalized. Their economic position came to depend increasingly upon the market success of their farming enterprises rather than upon the enforcement of feudal obligations on a peasant class. This increased the productivity of agriculture, but it also gave the aristocracy more economic flexibility, enabling it to incorporate commercial and then industrial elements.[46] This relaxation created a common interest and a partial fusion with the predominantly urban upper classes, partly at the expense of the peasantry.

The situation in France was quite different. There the aristocracy was economically dependent upon the crown.[47] Because of the independence of the French Church from Rome, the crown had control of ecclesiastical appointments, which, along with military commissions and the sale of civil offices, it used to fortify the loyalty of aristocrats. In addition, the aristocracy was dependent upon privileged exemptions from taxes and upon enforcement of obligations upon the peasantry.[48] French agricultural traditions were thus not conducive to reorganization in the interest of productivity. The peasantry remained intact and in potential conflict with the landowning class, which helped to entrench the *combination* of monarchy, aristocracy, and Church further under the *ancien régime*[49] as well as fostering peasant support for the Revolution, though in some circumstances, as in the Vendée, the peasants did swing to the other side.[50]

43. An interesting reflection of the situation is that the classical economists, particularly Ricardo, generally took commercial agriculture as a paradigmatic case in their analyses. It was the agricultural laborer, the employee of a commercial farmer, who was primarily discussed in connection with wage theory.

44. *Ibid.*

45. Moore, *op. cit.*

46. *Ibid.*

47. Ford, *op. cit.*, and Moore, *op. cit.*

48. Moore, *op. cit.*, see also Georges Lefebvre, *The Coming of the French Revolution* (New York: Vintage, 1960).

49. Palmer, *op. cit.*

50. Moore, *op. cit.*; and Charles Tilly, *The Vendée* (Cambridge, Mass.: Harvard University Press, 1964).

Furthermore, in France there was little reason for urban groups to support the old regime. In Holland aristocracy was weaker, but there were conflicts of interest between the commercial urban groups and the rural society of the hinterland.[51]

The export trade in wool supported the higher level of English commercial activity. It strengthened urban commercial interests centered in London, the seat of government, as well as the commercial and financial center and a major port. The putting-out system[52] between spinners and weavers of wool in the countryside and the wool merchants provided escape from the restrictive rules of the urban guilds. Merchants in the towns staked countryside weavers with yarn, collected the finished cloth, and sent it to London merchants for export. This system provided another bridge of economic interest between the land-owning gentry and the upper groups in the towns.

The differentiation engendered by these economic changes was similar to the differentiation that emerged between governmental organization and societal community. The medieval differentiation between town and country involved only partial economic differentiation. Its basis in the distinction between primary (extractive) production (notably agriculture) and trade and manufacture (mostly handicrafts) extended economic functions through *whole communities*. A rural village was an agricultural unit, and a neighboring town was a unit for the provision of manufactured goods. Other functions, like government, were centralized and could not be spread equally through all the small community units. The squires held much of the local power, and the gentry contributed the social leaders of county society. The employment of tenant farmers by owners, however, differentiated their own functions as social and political leaders in the local community from those of economic production in which their land was a factor of production. When farms became specifically economic enterprises, agricultural laborers and tenant farmers were employed in something closer to modern occupational roles than the hereditary status of villein had been, and the standards of success for enterprise became solvency through market operations. Through the market, land owners established connections with groups outside their own rural communities, especially merchants and putting-out entrepreneurs. Those connections proliferated through economic relations that did not coincide with relations of other sorts, for example, citizenship in local communities. Although the participants in the economic system could thus be divided generally into an agricultural interest, a mercantile interest, and, increasingly, a manufacturing interest, it became more

51. Palmer, *op. cit.*

52. See Edwin F. Gay, "Putting-Out System," in *Encyclopedia of the Social Sciences* (New York: Macmillan, 1934).

difficult to identify these interests with whole communities rather than with differentiated units within communities.

CONCLUSION

My thesis has been that England had become by the end of the seventeenth century the most differentiated society in the European system, having advanced farther in this direction than had any previous society. The societal community became differentiated from religion, government, and the economy.

First, within the Protestant establishment the emergence of religious toleration and of denominational pluralism broke the traditional European fusion of religion and government with the societal community. Not only did English government accord rights to religious nonconformists, citizenship in the societal community was no longer linked to traditional religious conformity. This separation entailed a new mode of integration and greater differentiation; the acceptable societal community was not confined to the coreligionists of the king (*eius religio*) but *included* Protestant nonconformists as well.

These developments involved value generalization in English society. The basis of value consensus had to be morally more general than any one denominational position would be. The Reformation and the splintering of Protestantism had threatened the solidarity of the societal community. In England denominational religious commitment was differentiated from moral consensus at the societal level. For example, there emerged a common commitment to the value of rational knowledge of the world, partly because of its practical utility. Although not without strain, philosophy and science *as such*—not only Anglican philosophy and science—came to be regarded as good things supported across the religious spectrum.

Given the establishment of a national community, two mechanisms of differentiation between the societal community and government developed. One was a government in which influential elements of the societal community were constituents of representative bodies rather than members of government. The second mechanism was the law. More than any other legal system, English law drew a distinction between the status of *member in the* societal community, with rights that the government was obligated to observe, and the status of *subject* of the king as chief of government. This differentiation was reinforced by the trend of relations between aristocracy and government in England. Much of the English aristocracy became an active *constituency* of government instead of remaining part of the undifferentiated structure of government without an opportunity to play a decisive part in it. This pattern permitted later extension so that larger groups could gain inclusion in the political aspect of citizenship.[53]

The consolidation of the common law and the supremacy of Parliament in government were connected with Puritanism and the special religious settlement that emerged in England.[54] Denominational and political pluralism expressed the differentiation of the societal community from religious collectivities and governmental organization. Both aspects involved a process of inclusion associated with that of differentiation. Legitimate status of full membership in the societal community was accorded to religious dissenters and to political opponents of the group currently in office as long as they constituted a loyal opposition. The legal system both in its normative content and in its structural independence was a mechanism regulating the boundary relations among these differentiated elements. There were *legally* institutionalized rights of religious and political dissent. England never resorted to a written constitution that would formally bind the "crown in Parliament" as the theoretical sovereign of the realm; nor were the courts of law ever accorded the power of judicial review in the sense of authorization to declare acts of Parliament unconstitutional. Nevertheless, the record confirms the effectiveness of the legal institutionalization of constitutional limitations upon the powers of government despite the close relation between government and the coercive sanctions of the courts.

The differentiation of societal community and economy was exemplified in the commercialization of agriculture, especially as it affected the landed gentry. Generally, rural communities have undifferentiated ascriptive structures resistant to modernization. The orientation of English agriculture to the market, however, created commercial interests that linked the rural communities horizontally with the towns rather than vertically with a feudal type of aristocratic governmental hierarchy and reduced the severity of the peasant problem. In the towns, a parallel process of differentiation broke down the particularism of the guild system. Because England was less urbanized than were some areas of the Continent, the fact that rural interests favored this differentiating process was helpful. The *institutional* foundations of a differentiated market economy were laid in England before the mechanical inventions of the industrial revolution. The Puritan influence contributed to the orientations of the innovative merchant groups and also among the gentry, many of whom were Puritans.

The economic phase of English development promoted pluralism in the community structure as well. The processes of differentiation, which

---

53. Marshall, *op. cit.*

54. See David Little, *Religion, Law, and Order* (New York: Harper and Row, 1969).

occurred within both rural and urban communities, strengthened a community of economic interests that cut across the old rural-urban distinction. This trend was necessary in view of the political power of the landed classes. Economic differentiation provided a basis on which future urban groups could be included in a single solidary system. Rural-urban conflicts were not as severe in England as elsewhere in subsequent periods; compared with the situation in France, conflict between the bourgeoisie and the landed aristocracy was mild. The process of adaptive upgrading was associated with economic development. Not only in England, but in the entire northwestern triangle, the seventeenth century was a period of substantial economic advance. There were increases in the extent of the market, both internally and externally, for each political unit.

Within societies as social systems, adaptive capacity depends on the economic sphere; nevertheless it is affected by developments in the cultural and personality systems. On the cultural side, the process of upgrading was conspicuous in the development of secular culture with its emphasis upon cognitive rationality in philosophy and science. This was furthered in Holland and England in the seventeenth century by the values of ascetic Protestantism.[55] Although the growth of cognitive culture had no major consequences for the structure of society, it had an impact. After Newton and Locke, cultural leaders could not ignore the implications of the new science and philosophy for many concerns; they were equipped with a new level of adaptive resources. An adaptive aspect of personality development was the emphasis of ascetic Protestantism upon "worldly asceticism." It enhanced motivation to achievement in wordly callings. The meaning of such achievement was culturally defined as this-worldly, rather than as otherworldly, as oriented toward the building of the good society and not only toward the salvation of souls in the afterlife. It was universalistic and innovative; the mandate for achievement was applicable to all men and was to build a new kingdom, not to perpetuate tradition.

Encouragement of this type of personal orientation had effects in different spheres. One effect was to enhance scientific investigation. Another was pressure for a type of individualism in English law.[56] The special connection with the economic sphere through market relations did not develop primarily because the market opened the doors to self-interest. It developed because the market mechanism constituted the first institu-

<hr>

55. Merton's analysis of the relations of Puritanism and science in England has been not refuted but merely qualified by recent research. See Robert K. Merton, "Science, Technology and Society in Seventeenth Century England," *Osiris*, 4 (1938) reprinted in *Social Theory and Social Structure*, chapter 18, rev. ed. (Glencoe, Ill.: Free Press, 1957); see also Joseph Ben-David, *The Sociology of Science* (Englewood Cliffs, N.J.: Prentice-Hall, 1971).

56. Little, *op. cit.*

tional context within which it was possible to isolate individual achievement and contributions from a diffuse matrix of irrelevant ties The market represented a differentiation of the social structure to the point at which differential opportunity, evaluation of individual contributions, and proportional rewards were possible on a wider scale than ever before. This possibility of differential rewards was the main significance of the connection between the Protestant Ethic of individual achievement and its expression in market activity.[57]

57. The connection between Protestant religious orientations and modern economic ethics has long been the subject of academic debate. The classics of the debate are Max Weber, *The Protestant Ethic and the Spirit of Capitalism* (New York: Scribner, 1958); and R. H. Tawney, *Religion and the Rise of Capitalism* (New York: Mentor, *Books,* 1947). See also R. W. Green (ed.), *Protestantism and Capitalism* (Boston: Heath, 1959); and Talcott Parsons, "Richard Henry Tawney," *American Sociological Review* (December 1962).

CHAPTER 8
FURTHER DIFFERENTIATION IN THE AGE OF REVOLUTIONS

NATIONAL DIFFERENTIATION

The Counter-Reformation societies tended to freeze the process of differentiation because of the relations between their political regimes and a defensive Church. Not only Protestantism but also other modernizing trends were opposed, especially those that might foster the independence of universalistically oriented units from the core structure (government, aristocracy, and church). Universalistic units included the business elements, groups advocating more democratic political participation and intellectual groups, which by the eighteenth century were viewed with suspicion by the authorities. The heartland of the Counter-Reformation, the Italian states and the papacy, served a pattern-maintenance function in the general European system. Spain became a militant spokesman for the pre-Reformation order of society, often seeming more Catholic than the Pope. In its secular social structure, Spain offered an example of a society frozen at an early modern level. Its intransigent traditionalism effectively isolated it from the rest of Europe.[1]

Austria, held together by aristocratic intermarriage and Roman Catholic allegiance, contrasted with Spain in its handling of ethnic heterogeneity. Although at first committed to the Counter-Reformation, the Austrian Habsburgs later accepted a limited religious pluralism

1. Americo Castro, *The Structure of Spanish History* (Princeton: Princeton University Press, 1954).

established by the settlement of 1648. They were anachronistic in their lack of concern with political nationality, but they played an integrative role by maintaining a political structure that became ethnically and then religiously pluralistic.[2] Although the Empire eventually disintegrated under the centrifugal forces of nationalism, it was important over a long transitional period. Indeed, as late as the Holy Alliance, Austria was the keystone of conservative integrationism in Europe. Furthermore, Austria played a role in mediating Russia's entry into the European system, a role encouraged by mutual conflict with Napoleonic France.

Germany resembled the Counter-Reformation center despite its religious diversity. Its small states were necessarily on the defensive also, threatened as they were with absorption by their larger neighbors. As in the Italian states, structural innovations were inhibited.[3] The Prussian role in the European system, conditioned by the open eastern frontier, crystallized as a variant of the Protestant pattern. The Hohenzollern rulers had converted to Calvinism, whereas the bulk of the population adhered to Lutheranism. What emerged was a form of the Protestant national church that amalgamated the two elements.[4] Calvinism, within the activist pattern of ascetic Protestantism, postulated the dominance in the community of a religious élite, the predestined elect, setting it above even the faithful Protestant common people. It was also collectivist; it conceived any Calvinist community to be founded upon its religiously ordained mission. This orientation—activist, authoritarian, and collectivist—fitted the Prussian monarchy as a boundary unit seeking to expand at the expense of the Slavs. Furthermore, it dovetailed with the Lutheran emphasis on the legitimacy of duly constituted authority in maintaining a given order and in checking disorder. Calvinism was suited to a forcible governing class, Lutheranism to its subjects. Along with the general flux of any frontier community, this religious situation helps to explain Prussian advances in rationalizing military and civil administration. Like most of Continental Europe, Prussia was organized about a land-owning aristocracy, the Junkers. The Junkers did not become a parliamentary opposition to royal absolutism as had the English gentry; instead they were a support of the monarchy, particularly in a military capacity. As in England, they transformed their traditional estates into commercial farming operations oriented toward the export of grain. The changes incorporated the old class structure, which was strengthened when the agricultural

2. James Bryce, *The Holy Roman Empire*, rev. ed. (London: Macmillan, 1904).

3. Geoffrey Barraclough, *The Origins of Modern Germany* (New York: Capricorn, 1963).

4. Christine Kayser, "Calvinism and German Political Life," doctoral dissertation, Radcliffe College, 1961.

workers who migrated to the new industries were replaced by Polish laborers.[5]

Before the nineteenth century, Prussia's advances were in governmental effectiveness; in both military and civic bureaucratic administration it set new standards for Europe.[6] Prussia's military record made it the Sparta of modern Europe. All classes in its hierarchically organized population accepted a stringent conception of duty like the one formulated by Kant but duty specifically to the state. The state managed to combine an amenable lower group, a traditionally military landed gentry, and a not large but urban-oriented upper *Bürgertum* in an effective operating organization.[7] Gradually, it took advantage of the liberal-national movements in the German world rather than being threatened by them, a trend culminating in the career of Bismarck. Prussia's effectiveness as a sovereign state facilitated its political domination over other territories; it gained control of practically all northern Germany, foreshadowing the exclusion of Austria from leadership in the unification of Germany. When the German Empire was constituted in 1871, it included a large Roman Catholic minority (nearly one-third of the population), the reverse of the settlement of 1648, which had included a Protestant minority in the old Roman Catholic Empire.[8] Prussia's expansion into other parts of Germany produced strains in the societal community, the religious diversity of which was not yet integrated in a pluralistic structure.

Coincidentally with Prussia's expansion, the new Germany became the site of the second phase of the Industrial Revolution. The economic buildup that established the political position of imperial Germany did not generally include any advance beyond that of early modern Europe. The change came slowly[9] considering how long the British example had been available. It centered not in the areas of Prussian efficiency but in the territories about the Rhineland, which were more Roman Catholic than Protestant.[10] Until the spread of the industrial revolution to the Continent, Britain, Prussia, and France had been in the forefront of change. In the differentiation of the European system as a whole, primacy

5. See the account of Weber's early researches in Reinhard Bendix, *Max Weber: An Intellectual Portrait* (Garden City, N.Y.: Anchor, 1962); see also Reinhard Bendix, *Nation-Building and Citizenship* (New York: Wiley, 1964), chapters 4, 6.

6. Hans Rosenberg, *Bureaucracy, Aristocracy, and Autocracy: The Prussian Experience, 1660–1815* (Cambridge, Mass.: Harvard University Press, 1958).

7. *Ibid.*

8. Barraclough, *op. cit.*

9. See David Landes, *The Rise of Capitalism* (New York: Macmillan, 1966).

10. See Rainer Baum, "Values and Uneven Political Development in Imperial Germany," doctoral dissertation, Harvard University, 1967.

of goal-attaining functions characterized the Northwest; new institutional developments and structural differentiation were emerging there. These processes increased the adaptive capacity of England, and to a lesser extent the other societies, particularly in economic terms.

For this same period, primacy of the more general adaptive function characterized Prussia. It had become the stabilizer of Europe's open eastern frontier. Furthermore, it had pioneered in the development of instrumentally effective collective organization, a generalized resource that has since been diffused throughout all functional sectors of modern societies.

THE INDUSTRIAL REVOLUTION

The late eighteenth century saw the beginning of two developments marking the transition from the early phase of Western modernity to the one that crystallized in the mid-twentieth century. These changes were the industrial revolution and the democratic revolution. The former began in Great Britain; the latter erupted in France in 1789. These developments in the northwest sector of Europe capped the developmental trends of the earlier period. They occasioned strains where they emerged and more severe strains when they spread into areas less prepared for them.

The developmental trend after the Reformation stressed, under an activist value system, the adaptive and integrative capacities of societies, which involved new differentiation and increased organic solidarity in Durkheim's sense. The industrial revolution was part of this trend, in that increases in economic productivity entailed extension of the division of labor. Such extensions in differentiation produce a need for new integrative mechanisms. The democratic revolution involved the integrative aspect of the societies; it focused on the political meaning of membership in the societal community and thus on the justification of inequalities in wealth, political authority, and social privilege. My interest in the industrial revolution is not in its technological and economic aspects but in associated changes in social structure. Nevertheless, the technological changes had revolutionary economic effects, making possible large cost savings, lower prices, and the development of many new products.[11] In England the process began in the cotton-textile industry and spread to heavier industries, whereas on the Continent and in the United States the main development coincided with the spread of the railroads.[12]

11. There is an enormous literature on these problems. Landes, *op. cit.*, is a thorough and particularly illuminating survey.

12. J. H. Clapham, *Economic Development of France and Germany, 1815–1914* (Cambridge: Cambridge University Press, 1963).

The key to the industrial revolution is the extension of the market system and of the attendant differentiation in the economic sector of the social structure. The market system itself did not undergo a revolution but a long, continuous evolution. The prosperity of England and Holland especially, but also of France, preceded the new inventions. Prosperity resulted from the development of market systems, which depended upon legal and political security and legal frameworks based on property and contract that favored the extension of commercial enterprise. English and Dutch prosperity was also a function of light governmental pressures on economic resources, especially the absence of large standing armies and of aristocratic objections to trade that prevailed in most Continental countries. Before the industrial revolution, the most developed sector of the market system was finished commodities, generally luxury goods.[13] The exception in England was the production for export first of wool, then of woolen cloth. In some areas, grain was a major market commodity, but most foodstuffs and articles of general consumption entered the market system only within local limits, if at all. Typical was the exchange of foodstuffs grown in the locality for handicraft products of a market town.[14]

From this origin the market system could spread in several directions. From the consumer product, it could extend back into earlier stages of the production processes and eventually to the production of factors of production. There were also intermediate products like the gray cloth that putting-out merchants bought from weavers. Transportation and commercial-mediation services between spatially separated producers and consumers became necessary. Raw materials, primary production, and the land itself became increasingly involved in the market nexus. Sociologists have a special interest in two other factor markets: those for capital and for labor. The capital market entered a new stage of development in the Renaissance, a symptom of which was the religious controversy over the morality of usury.[15] Long before the industrial revolution, money lending had existed on a substantial scale, organized in money markets of various sorts, some already international. Companies also existed in which individuals could invest free of the contingent liabilities of partnerships. By the end of the seventeenth century, England possessed the beginnings of a central bank, a sign of its economic advancement.

The industrial revolution saw a proliferation of financial markets at a new level of organization. These developments culminated ultimately

---

13. See Max Weber, General Economic History (New York: Adelphi, 1927) op. cit., and his Theory of Social and Economic Organization (Glencoe, Ill.: Free Press, 1947).

14. Karl Polanyi, The Great Transformation (Boston: Beacon, 1957).

15. Benjamin Nelson, The Idea of Usury: From Tribal Brotherhood to Universal Otherhood, 2nd ed. (Chicago: University of Chicago Press, 1969).

in the middle of the nineteenth century when general incorporation acts were adopted in England and in most of the American states[16] and organized securities markets were established. One advantage of German industry, when it surpassed British industry in the late nineteenth century, was the superior organization and spirit of enterprise of its investment banking system.[17] Expanded financial markets provided flexible mechanisms of adjustment for the expanding economic system. More and more, money went beyond its functions as a medium of exchange and measure of value to become the control mechanism of the economic process. Control of money was used to influence the allocation of resources through the market. The new dependence of credit creation upon large-scale financial institutions provided a type of built-in mechanism of economic growth.

A trend has been the development of *generalized* physical facilities. Transportation facilities like railways would not be economically viable if limited to the transportation of one product. Once lines existed between given centers, however, they could be used for many purposes. Similar considerations applied to provision of mechanical power. The steam engine was one of the innovations of the early industrial revolution; electric power and the internal-combustion engine came later. Sources of energy, transmission of energy and fuel, and modes of using power were thus enhanced. Finally, the development of tools to make tools, the machine-tool industry, also contributed to the technology of many different industries.[18] These technological developments were interdependent with changes in the social organization of the productive process, especially the differentiation of labor (of services) from the diffuse matrix in which it had been embedded. This differentiation distinguished the work-role complex from the family household and also increased the mobility of labor—the readiness of households to respond to employment opportunities by changing residences or learning new skills. These changes affected family systems and local communities profoundly. Features of the modern nuclear-family kinship structure emerged during the nineteenth century. And industrial society became urbanized to a degree never known before.

These processes established the *occupational role,* specifically contingent upon status in an employing organization structurally distinct from the household.[19] Usually the employing organization has only one

---

16. For an analysis of these legal developments and their importance, see J. Willard Hurst, *Law and the Conditions of Freedom* (Madison: University of Wisconsin Press, 1956).

17. Landes, *op. cit.*

18. *Ibid.*

19. Neil J. Smelser, *Social Change in the Industrial Revolution* (Chicago: University of Chicago Press, 1959).

member in common with the household; it also has premises, disciplines, authority systems, and property distinct from those of the household. Typically the employed person receives (according to his employment status and role performance) a money income that is the main source of his household's access to the market for consumer goods. The employing organization markets its product and pays the employee wages or a salary, whereas the typical peasant or artisan sold his own products. The organization thus comes between the worker and the consumer market. The spread of occupational roles extended the range of consumer markets because of consumers' increased dependence upon money incomes in meeting their wants. Adam Smith's dictum "The division of labor depends on the extent of the market," pointed out that the increasing division of labor made possible increasing productivity and a rise in the standard of living among the general population.

In the factories, roles were occupationalized from the bottom up. The first to become employees were propertyless wage workers, the mill hands of the textile industry. Management was based upon proprietorship. The owner, usually a kinship group, organized production, raised capital, set up factories, employed and supervised workers, and marketed the products. The early capitalistic industrial firm was thus a two-class system, consisting of the proprietary lineage on one side and the employees on the other.[20] This system was the structural basis for the Marxist conception of class conflict in capitalistic society, in which ownership and organizational authority are assumed to operate together.

The industrial revolution emerged under a free enterprise system and very likely could not have *originated* under a different one. Furthermore, a free-enterprise economy, rather than socialism in the sense of governmental operation of the economy, remains in the mainstream of evolution. Private economic enterprise and government organization of economic matters are not, however, related in a zero-sum manner: An increase in one does not require a corresponding decrease in the other. As Durkheim demonstrated,[21] a developed free-enterprise economy, compared to a primitive form of economic organization, requires a stronger governmental structure, not a more restricted one.

A universalistic legal system, a feature of any industrial society, cannot exist without strong government. Furthermore, complex regulatory functions are necessary to the economy, for example, in the control of the cyclical disturbances that upset early industrial economies. Government and economy are interdependent. Government requires taxable sources, which are increased by increments in productivity and by the mobility

20. See Reinhard Bendix, *Work and Authority in Industry* (New York: Wiley, 1956).

21. Emile Durkheim, *The Division of Labor in Society* (New York: Macmillan, 1933).

of resources in a developed market system. Similarly, government, in its own participation in the labor markets, benefits from the mobility of manpower. This interdependence involves the interchange of money and power between the market system and the system of formal organization. Not only government but also such private organizations as firms participate in the power system; conversely, government participates in the market system. The power of private units is dependent upon that of government in two respects beside the institutionalization of property and contract. First, the corporation as a legal entity is in part a delegation of public authority on the basis of a publicly granted and revocable charter. The use of authority within corporate organizations is *legitimated* by this authorization.[22] Second, modern economies depend upon the credit mechanism for capitalization. Extension of credit involves the use of power by credit agencies, especially banks; they make funds available to borrowers, funds that they themselves do not own, and bind themselves with legally enforceable contracts. This enforceability provides the basis of confidence in the time-extendability of loan relations, which have the inherent risk of investments that cannot pay off except over a considerable period.

In a modern society, underdevelopment of the power system is thus deleterious to the economy, and underdevelopment of the monetary and market systems is deleterious to the polity.

THE DEMOCRATIC REVOLUTION

The democratic revolution was part of the process of differentiating the polity from the societal community. As in all processes of differentiation, it produced integration problems and, where it was successful, new types of integration. In European societies, political differentiation required popular support for government in the societal community. The starting point was the conception of ordinary people as subjects of their monarch, with ascriptive obligations to obey his authority, often claimed to be divinely ordained.[23] Although the English crown's monopoly of governmental authority had fallen in the seventeenth century, as it had in a different way in Holland, even the English regime was far from democratic; it was aristocratic.

Intellectual discussion during the Enlightenment revealed the internal tensions in the Continental territorial monarchies, exacerbated by the visibility of the British and Dutch examples.[24] This strain was acute

---

22. Hurst, *op. cit.*

23. J. W. Allen, *A History of Political Thought in the Sixteenth Century* (New York: Barnes & Noble, 1960).

24. R. R. Palmer, *The Age of Democratic Revolution*, 2 vols. (Princeton: Princeton University Press, 1959 and 1964).

in France, which had gone farthest in developing the national-ethnic basis of community while at the same time retaining an old-regime absolutism. The common people, including some high in the bourgeoisie, were still subjects, whereas the aristocracy, allied to the crown, had consolidated its privileges. These developments identified those who counted in the societal community with positions in government, while relegating subjects not participating in government and its aristocratic penumbra to a status of dubious inclusion in the national community. As everywhere on the Continent, the central government, reinforced by the Counter-Reformation, pressed its diffuse claims to authority. The tradition of legally protected rights was weaker on the Continent than in England. Within the framework of national consciousness, the French Revolution demanded a community that included *all* Frenchmen and abrogated the special status of the *privilegiés*. The central concept was *citizenship*, the claim of the *whole* population to inclusion.[25]

The slogan of the Revolution, *Liberté, Égalité, Fraternité*, embodied the new conception of community. *Liberté* and *Égalité* symbolized dissatisfaction with political authoritarianism and privilege. *Fraternité* referred to the context of belonging, brotherhood being a primordial symbol of community. In the late eighteenth and nineteenth centuries the symbol of liberty had two references.[26] One was paramount in England, where Adam Smith stressed *economic* liberty, in contrast with the governmental control associated with mercantilism. The other was paramount in France, where Rousseau was influential. It emphasized the liberty of the *societal community*, of the people vis-à-vis government. The problems of liberty of the people and liberty of the individual were not clearly distinguished, especially in the political sphere. It was the tyranny of the regime that had to be eliminated. The dictatorial tendencies of the Revolution emerged only after the power of the old regime had been broken.

The problem of equality is even more difficult. Whereas one can think of liberty in terms of casting off restraints, equality inherently involves relations among units that are *positively* valued. Units that claim a right to equality cannot legitimately oppose recognition of the equality of others. Whereas in the context of liberty, the evil is illegitimate constraint, in the context of equality it is illegitimate *discrimination*. The ideology of equality often suggests that all differences of status or function are illegitimate, particularly if they are hierarchical. Social systems require varying kinds of social differentiation: a qualitative division of labor (in the Durkheimian sense) and a hierarchy.

25. *Ibid.;* see also Bendix, *Nation-Building and Citizenship.*

26. See Bernard Bailyn, *The Ideological Origins of the American Revolution* (Cambridge, Mass.: Harvard University Press, 1967).

The French Revolution, stressing both liberty and equality, rebelled not only against political authority but also against the system of privilege for the aristocracy. Tensions had been exacerbated by the association of the *noblesse de robe* with the monarchy and the older aristocracy under the *ancien régime* so that the people stood against the *privileged*, who were identified with the government. There has been ideological distortion of the European aristocracies' social irresponsibility at the expense of the people. The issue of privilege hinged on hereditary ascription of status, which conflicted with standards of achievement or equality or both. The Revolution raised the question of whether privilege can be a meaningful *reward* or even legitimated on instrumental grounds—unless no other way of institutionalizing responsible leadership is possible. The French Revolution's attack on the principle of privilege was led by the higher bourgeoisie, many of whose members were richer than were most aristocrats and, if not more powerful in the formal sense, more influential in governmental affairs. In England, aristocracy, which included the gentry, was more private and less identified with the regime. Reform movements were often led by members of the aristocracy; the French question of aristocracy versus bourgeoisie was not explicitly raised.

The Revolutionary concept of equality, in relation to differential instrumental qualifications and the hierarchical dimension of social status, emphasized *equality of opportunity*. To the extent that this emerging value was institutionalized, achievement and achievement capacity became the criteria of eligibility for differentially valued statuses. The attainment of a status or its retention under competitive pressure could then be evaluated as a reward for significant contribution to the society. This complex gave support to a normative component of the industrial revolution. The French Revolution was against *inherited* aristocratic privilege and toward equality of membership status, not precisely equality of opportunity, even though the two are interdependent. The pattern of privilege under the *ancien régime* had divided the societal community into two status classes. The common man was a second-class citizen, who was denied by his hereditary status access to privileges enjoyed by the aristocracy, especially tax exemptions.[27]

Marshall has analyzed equality of membership as possessing three components: civil, political, and social.[28] The French Revolution involved the first and second, whereas the third became an issue only in the mid-nineteenth century. The *civil* component of citizenship includes guarantees of "natural rights"—in Locke's formulation, "life, liberty, and property." They were specified by the French Declaration of the Rights

27. *Ibid.*

28. T. H. Marshall, *Class, Citizenship, and Social Development* (Garden City, N.Y.: Anchor, 1965).

of Man and the American Bill of Rights. The revolutionary movement in France was encouraged by the fact that English and American law had already institutionalized many of these rights. The concept of "equality before the law" characterizes the civil component of equality of membership if it is taken to include both procedural and substantive protections. Here law means not only rules enforceable through the courts but also the general patterning of the society's normative order.

The *political* component of citizenship concentrates upon the democratic franchise. Although the principle of equality among citizens in the final voice of government dates from the ancient Greek polis, the French Revolution applied it to the government of a large-scale society and to all the people. Of course modern governments cannot give equal direct participation to all citizens. Developments have therefore been in the direction of *representative* institutions, in which political equality is focused upon the selection of top governmental leadership, generally through participation in an electoral system. The forms of these institutions vary, especially between the presidential and parliamentary types and between republics and constitutional monarchies.[29] Despite such variations, European political systems, except the Communist ones but including overseas societies of European origin such as the United States and some members of the British Commonwealth, have evolved toward a common pattern.[30] This pattern includes two components and two contextual features of equality.

The first component of equality is universality of the franchise. The trend has been toward universal adult suffrage; women's suffrage was adopted early in the twentieth century in most Western nations. Only minors, aliens, and small classes of disqualified persons are now excluded. The other component of equality has been elimination of the *weighting* of votes. Historically, various systems have weighted votes unequally, either explicitly as in the Prussian class system of voting or implicitly as in discriminatory apportionment in the United States. The trend is toward the principle of one citizen, one vote, both in access to the polls and in the weight of each vote in determining electoral outcomes. The first contextual feature of equality is the formal electoral procedure, including rules of eligibility for voting and rules by which votes are counted. The latter aspect establishes a *binding* relation between the individual voter's choice and the effects of many such choices on the outcome. The second contextual feature is secrecy of the ballot, which further differentiates government and societal community by protecting the individual's inde-

29. See S. M. Lipset and Stein Rokkan, "Introduction," in Lipset and Rokkan, *Cleavage Structures, Party Systems, and Voter Alignment* (New York: Free Press, 1965).

30. Stein Rokkan, "Mass Suffrage, Secret Voting, and Political Participation," in *European Journal of Sociology* (1961), 132–52.

pendent participation in each. It guards the voter from pressures from status superiors (for example, employers) and also from status peers (for example, fellow union members)[31] This safeguard favors political pluralization relative to the rest of the society and discourages unanimous bloc voting (for example, *all* trade-union members voting for socialist or other left parties) and encourages minorities within each interest group (or religious, ethnic, or local group) to vote differently from the majority. This enhances community flexibility; mobilizing government as an agency of change responsible to the community becomes possible.

The *social* component of citizenship is the most fundamental of the three.[32] Some form of equality of social conditions as an aspect of social justice has been a primary theme of Western history since the French Revolution but one that did not become institutionally salient until later. The full emergence of this theme had to await reduction in the inequalities of governmental absolutism and aristocracy; this reduction raised new tensions between the imperatives of equality of opportunity and equality of membership. Members of the society must have realistic, not merely formal, opportunities to compete with reasonable prospects of success, but the community may not accord full membership to those inherently excluded from the opportunity complex. Allowance is thus made for those, like children, who are inherently unable to compete; those, like the unskilled poor, who are severely handicapped through no fault of their own and must be helped to compete; and those, like the aged, who must be supported. Furthermore, there should be a floor under the competitive system that defines a standard of welfare to which all members are *entitled* as a matter of right, not as a matter of charity.

The third Revolutionary catchword, *Fraternité,* suggested a synthesis of liberty and equality at a more general normative level. It was the embodiment of the implications for secular society of the Reformation. The solidary societal community that it proclaimed could not be a two-class system in any of the medieval senses—Church and state, clergy and laity, or aristocracy and commons—but had to be a *unitary* community. Its members were to be considered not only free and equal but also bound together in a national autonomous solidarity. This societal community was to be differentiated from government as its superior, legitimately entitled to control government. Yet the degree of its differentiation was not completely modern, particularly in regard to its incomplete pluralization. French society during the nineteenth century institutionalized the democratic pattern of societal community only partially and unstably.[33]

31.   *Ibid.*

32.   See Marshall, *op. cit.*

33.   See Stanley Hoffmann, "Paradoxes of the French Political Community," in Hoffmann *et al., In Research of France* (Cambridge, Mass.: Harvard University Press, 1963).

The French right held to the patterns of the old régime down into the present century. It led several experiments in monarchical restoration and maintained a de facto ascendance in social prestige for the aristocracy and a strong position for the established Roman Catholic Church. This conflict within France was exacerbated by the survival of the older system in most of the Continent, despite the spread of revolutionary patterns through Napoleon's conquests. Although England went farther in the process of pluralization, a fact connected with its leadership in the industrial revolution, radical pressures toward democratization were absent, and the franchise was extended only gradually from 1832 on. Aristocracy remained strong in British society throughout the nineteenth century, although it was less rigid than in most Continental countries and less of an impediment to pluralistic differentiation and gradual democratization.[34]

The struggle over democratization was a component of European social conflict during the nineteenth century. Napoleon was the heir of the Revolution. The restored legitimism of the Holy Alliance was directed not only against French imperialism but also against Revolutionary ideas. Its breakdown in 1848 started in France but then became intense on the eastern fringe of the European system. Through the nineteenth century, leadership of the European system remained in the northwest sector, where a conflict emerged between the British and French attitudes. Both were essential to the emerging synthesis; one emphasized economic productivity and pluralization of the social structure, the other democratization of the nation-state, nationalism, and a new kind of societal community.

There were also developments in the less advanced areas. Imperial Germany represented a disturbance to the European system. It exploited the potentials of both the industrial revolution and the undemocratic authoritarian state while France and Britain were still insufficiently strong to cope with the new power by genuinely *synthesizing* the components of modern society. At the same time, the shadow of the colossi of the East and the West fell over the European system. Russia had emerged to assume a major role in the European system by contributing to Napoleon's defeat and had become a participant in the settlement of Vienna and a guarantor of the Metternich system. By the time of World War I the United States had also emerged as part of the system.

CONCLUSION

What this chapter has shown is the increasing differentiation of modern societies. The industrial revolution further differentiated the economy and the democratic revolution further differentiated the polity

34. Marshall, *op. cit.*

from the societal community. Unless modern societies were to be torn apart by these differentiating tendencies, integrative processes were necessary. The next chapter will consider how these integrative processes worked out in practice, particularly in the "lead" society of the modern world, the United States. The rest of this chapter will undertake to set forth the kinds of factors capable of integrating modern societies: the legal system, the extension of citizenship, market systems, bureaucratic organizations, and associational organizations.

The Legal System

The societal normative order comes close to the concept of law. Much discussion of law stresses the criteria of bindingness and enforceability, associating law with government and the state. The consensual elements in the normative validity of law is another theme, one that places emphasis on its moral legitimation. I treat law as the general normative code regulating action of, and defining the situation for the members of a society.[35] The societal normative code is an integrated system of rules governing loyalty, cultural legitimation, the wielding of influence, and economic-technological matters.

Modern legal systems usually contain constitutional components, whether written as in the United States or unwritten as in Britain. In the zone of interpenetration between the pattern-maintenance system and the societal community, the constitutional element defines the main outline of the normative framework governing societal relationships in general— as in the American Bill of Rights. On modern levels of differentiation, such content is not religious; its normative validity is framed for the societal system, not the full range of action in general. There has been a modern tendency to dissociate specific religious commitment from the constitutional rights and obligations of citizenship. Because religious affiliation generally involves the formation of collectivities, it must have a place in the societal community. However, the two need not be coextensive.

Neither is the constitutional element purely moral, for moral considerations extend over a wider range than do societal values. Constitutional norms articulate with the societal community and involve the component of societal loyalty in the form of valued association; law concerns the morality of citizenship, but not all morality. Furthermore, the moral element can provide grounds for legitimized revolts against a societal normative order, varying from minor civil disobedience to revolution.

Although the constitutional element is presumptively enforceable, enforcement raises a question of whether the organs of government are

---

35. Cf. Fuller, op. cit.; also his Anatomy of the Law (New York: Praeger, 1968).

acting legitimately: in a constitutional—and back of that a moral—sense. Hence, a second aspect of the constitutional element is the normative definition of the functions of government, including limitations on powers of the various governmental agencies. Constitutional law becomes more important as the societal community comes to be differentiated from its government. The powers of government then need specific justification, for the societal community would not be adequately protected from arbitrary uses of power if it were to grant blanket legitimacy to its rulers to act upon their own interpretations of the public interest.[36]

Executive authority gets differentiated from the governmental functions that have direct constitutional relevance. In premodern societies, explicit legislation as a differentiated function is minimal because the normative order is *given* in a tradition or founding revelation. The legitimation of a continuing legislative function is a modern development. With qualifying complications, it requires that the legislative process should actively involve the societal community through a system of representation. The power to legislate becomes contingent upon the legislators' interaction with the interested elements of the community, ultimately the total electorate in most modern societies.[37] Indeed, a similar contingency applies to occupants of executive authority. The changeability of the law, which has resulted from these developments, has made it necessary to have provision for concern with the constitutionality of law. Although the American system of judicial review is special in some respects, modern constitutions usually establish some agency that is not purely governmental in the executive sense to pass judgment on constitutional issues.

Under this constitutional framework the lower-order functioning of the legal system consists in the making of binding decisions, for the most part by officially authorized agencies (usually courts of law), and in their implementation by administrative procedures. The extraconstitutional content of law is not confined to specific acts of legislation, nor to publicly binding decisions of executive agencies. It also includes elements of the legal tradition generated in court decisions that stand as precedents and the administrative law (of generalized rulings rather than particular case decisions) promulgated by administrative agencies.

Normative order involves a political dimension in *any* society system, although the relation is clearer between government and the societal community especially. Only government is authorized to use socially organized physical force as an instrument of compulsion. Indeed an effec-

36. On our usage of the concept of legitimation, compare Weber, *The Theory of Social and Economic Organization*.

37. Cf. Parsons, "The Political Aspect of Social Structure and Process" in *Varieties of Political Theory*.

tive governmental monopoly of force is a criterion of integration in a differentiated society.[38] Moreover, only government is entitled to act for the societal collectivity as a whole in contexts of collective goal-attainment. Any other agency that presumes to do so commits a revolutionay act *ipso facto*.

Membership in the Societal Community: Citizenship

In discussing the *legitimate order* of society, I have frequently referred to the *collective aspect* of the societal community. My multiple criteria of a society indicate that the relation between these two aspects must be complex because the jurisdiction of the norms cannot neatly coincide with community membership. The discrepancy derives from the territorial basis of societies. Territorial jurisdiction requires that normative control is to some extent independent of actual membership in the societal community. For example, temporary visitors and long term resident aliens, as well as the property holdings of foreign interests, must be regulated.

These considerations indicate that part of the relation between the normative and collective aspects of a societal community concerns their mutual relations to government. Government cannot simply rule but must be legitimized in governing a relatively bounded community by taking responsibility for the maintenance of its normative order. At one extreme, the principal content of the normative order may be considered universal to all men. However, this raises problems of how far such universalistic norms can be effectively institutionalized in the operations of so extensive a community. At the other extreme, both government and the normative order may apply only to a particular small community. Within the range of variation between these extremes, modern societal communities have taken a nationalistic form. The development of this form has involved a process of differentiation between societal community and government as well as reform in the nature of societal community with respect to membership.

The point of departure was absolute monarchy, in which the individual was considered to be a subject of his king. This direct relation of subject to sovereign replaced the tangle of particularistic solidarities that characterized feudal society. Then the subject pattern of societal membership was replaced by a citizenship pattern. The first phase in the development of modern citizenship was the creation of a legal framework that redefined the boundary-relations between the societal community and the government.[39] The new boundaries defined rights of the citizen, the pro-

---

38. Weber, *The Theory of Social and Economic Organization.*

39. Our discussion of citizenship is in debt to T. H. Marshall's *Class, Citizenship, and Social Development* (Garden City, N.Y.: Anchor Books, 1965).

tection of which became an obligation of government. In the early phase, the protection of rights went farthest in English Common Law of the 17th century. However, it was a pan-European development that also produced the German conception of the *Rechtsstaat*. The process was simplified in Protestant areas because the citizens had to deal with one main focus, the political authority, which organizationally controlled the church as well as the state.[40] In England the first phases of religious toleration within Protestantism comprised part of the broader process of establishing citizen rights.

The second phase in the development of citizenship concerned participation in public affairs. Although the legal rights of the first phase did protect attempts to influence government, especially through rights of assembly and freedom of the press, the next phase institutionalized positive rights to participate in the selection of governmental leadership through the franchise. The spread of the franchise downward in the class structure has been gradual, yet there has been a trend toward universal adult suffrage, the principle of one citizen, one vote, and secrecy of the ballot.[41]

A third component of citizenship is social concern with the welfare of citizens, treated as a public responsibility.[42] Whereas legal rights and the franchise support capacities to act autonomously in the status of citizenship, the social component concerns the provision of realistic opportunities to make good use of such rights. Hence, it attempts to ensure that adequate minimum standards of living, health care, and education are available to the masses of the population. The spread of education to wider circles of the population, as well as an upgrading of the levels of education, has been connected with the development of the citizenship complex.

The development of modern institutions of citizenship has made possible changes in the pattern of nationality as a basis of the solidarity of the societal community. In early modern society, the strongest foundation of solidarity was found where the three factors of religion, ethnicity, and territoriality coincided with nationality. In fully modern societies there can be diversity on each basis, religious, ethnic, and territorial, because the common status of citizenship provides a sufficient foundation for national solidarity, e.g., Switzerland. The institutions of citizenship and nationality can nevertheless render the societal community vulnerable if

40. C. Seymour Martin Lipset and Stein Rokkan, "Introduction" to *Party Systems and Voter Alignment* (New York: Free Press, 1968).

41. Stein Rokkan, "Mass Suffrage, Secret Voting, and Political Participation" in *European Journal of Sociology*, II (1961): 132–52.

42. Marshall, *op. cit.*

the bases of pluralism are exacerbated into sharply structured cleavages. Since the typical modern community unifies a large population over a large territory, its solidarity may be strained by regional cleavages, particularly where the regional cleavages coincide with ethnic and/or religious divisions. Many modern societies have disintegrated before varying combinations of these bases of cleavage.

Bureaucratic Organizations, Market Systems, and Voluntary Associations

Where societal solidarity is emancipated from the more primordial bases of religion, ethnicity, and territoriality, it tends to foster other types of internal differentiation and pluralization based on economic, political, and associational (or integrative) functions. The economic category refers to the development of markets and the monetary instruments essential to these functions, which presuppose the institutionalization in new forms of contract and property relations. Thus, they rest on the rights component of citizenship, for an economy that is purely administered by agencies of central government would violate the freedoms of private groups to engage in market transactions autonomously. Once the market system of an economy is highly developed, it becomes important to government as a channel for the mobilization of resources.

In the earlier phases of modernization, markets are commercial, involving trade in physical commodities, and financial, involving operations of lending and borrowing. The large-scale entrance of the primary factors of production into the market system is the hallmark of the industrial phase of economic development. In addition to the advances in technology, this centers on the social *organization* of the productive process, involving new forms of the utilization of manpower in bureaucratic contexts.[43]

In discussing the political aspect of societies, I dealt primarily with the relation of government to the societal community, stressing the articulation between them in the support system. This system concerns the interaction of leadership elements, both within and aspiring to governmental positions, and elements of the social structure that are not directly involved in the governmental system. The processes of interaction comprise the interchange of political support and leadership initiative and the interchange of governmental decisions and demands from various interest groups. These interchanges constitute a system requiring equilibration if the polity is to be stably integrated with the societal community. The other operative structure of government is the administrative organiza-

43. Smelser, *op. cit.*

tion, including the military establishment, through which policy decisions are implemented. Bureaucratization developed primarily in governments. Among its features is the institutionalization of roles as *offices* that have well-defined spheres of official function, authority, and power separated from the incumbent's private affairs. Offices are differentiated on two bases: function performed for the organization and position in the hierarchy (line authority).[44]

The development of bureaucratic organization necessitates that the relevant form of office be an *occupational* role, an incumbent being appointed through some kind of contract of employment. His family's subsistence depends on his salary or wage remuneration. This requires a labor market for the allocation of human services in terms of negotiations over employment opportunities and conditions. A feature of an industrial economy is the bureaucratic organization of production and the mobilization of manpower through labor markets. By a progression through a number of phases, the economy has produced a proliferation of bureaucratic organization outside the governmental sphere. One stage was based upon the family firm of early industrial capitalism, which was bureaucratized at the labor but not the managerial level. Bureaucratic organization is primarily political because it is oriented to collective goal-attainment. In the case of the business firm, the collectivity is a private group within the societal community; in the case of government it is the community organized for collective goal-attainment. I treat employment as a form of membership in a collectivity, leaving aside the problem of its relations to membership through other modes of participation in economic enterprise. Private bureaucracy is not confined to economic production, but is found in churches, universities, and many other types of collectivity.

Market systems are involved in interchanges between the economy and the pattern-maintenance system and between the economy and the polity. They do not directly involve the societal community since its functions vis-à-vis these subsystems are regulative through the normative order more than directly constitutive. Let me also emphasize the distinction between the commercial markets, dealing with physical commodities, and the labor markets, dealing with human services, including those at high levels of competence and responsibility. From a sociological point of view, I find confusing the economists' common practice of treating goods and services together as *the* primary output of the economy.

A third type of structuring that modern societal collectivities make possible is associational. The prototype of an association is the societal collectivity itself, considered as a corporate body of citizens holding

44. Talcott Parsons, *Structures and Process in Modern Societies* (New York: Free Press, 1960), chaps. 1–5.

primarily consensual relations to its normative order and to the authority of its leadership. A trend of modern associations has been toward egalitarianism, manifested in the three aspects of citizenship that we have discussed. Another trend of associational structure is toward voluntariness. This principle cannot be applied to compliance with a normative order or collective decisions, for an element of bindingness is essential to all collectivities. However, it often applies to decisions to accept and retain membership, an alternative to compliance being resignation. The relationship between the societal community and government, however, is special. Other associations exist under a general governmental and societal protection, but the basis of security rests on the combination. Hence, elements of compulsion and coercion are present in the enforcement of the societal normative order that are absent in other cases. The equivalent of resignation, emigration, entails a heavier cost than does the relinquishment of other associational memberships. It also entails accepting another societal-government order, whereas in the case of divorce, one need not remarry.

A characteristic of associational organization, which applies to the societal collectivity and to governmental agencies, is procedural institutions.[45] Although particularly significant in the legal system, procedural institutions also permeate the processes of associational decision making, both at the level of representative bodies and at that of membership participation. Procedural systems consist of two levels, each governed by a code of rules. The first level regulates the discussions by which interested parties may attempt to persuade the participants in the making of binding decisions. Generally meetings are conducted according to rules of order, which a presiding officer is responsible for implementing. Discussion within associations is a sphere of the operation of influence as a medium for facilitating social process. From the viewpoint of an interested party, discussion serves to improve the chances of having his or her view prevail; from the viewpoint of the collectivity, it facilitates an approach to consensus.

The second level concerns the actual process of deciding. In courts of law, the deciding agency is a jury, judge, or panel of judges. However, the common practice—within juries and judicial panels as elsewhere—is voting, with its tendencies toward the principles of one member, one vote, and the equal weighting of votes, the logical consequence of which is majority rule. Decision by voting must follow rules fixed in advance, including the expectation that decisions arrived at by correct observance of the procedural rules will be accepted by defeated elements. In such cases as the election of governmental leadership, this may be a focus

45. Compare Weber's concept of formal rationality in *Max Weber on Law and Society*, Max Rheinstein (ed.), (Cambridge, Mass.: Harvard University Press, 1954).

of strain; implementing this requirement is a test of the institutionalization of democratic solidarity. Concurrent with the development of associationalism in government has been a proliferation of associations in other sectors of society. Political parties articulate with governmental process but also with many sorts of associated interest groups, most of which represent operative collectivities. There are also associations organized about innumerable causes, as well as interests of diverse sorts, for example, recreational, artistic, etc.

Two operative functions of modern societies are performed almost entirely by associational structures. The first is the involvement of fiduciary boards in the larger-scale sectors of business enterprise and in many other types of corporate organizations. In relation to executive management, they parallel the relations of the legislature to the executive organs of a modern government. Sometimes the members of such boards are elected, e.g., by stockholders, but often not. They have largely replaced the kinship element as the nonbureaucratic top of the predominantly bureaucratic structures of business.[46] In the private nonprofit sector, too, ultimate control, especially in regard to financial responsibility, tends to be held by fiduciary boards. Another associational development concerns the professions.[47] Though much professional function has traditionally been performed in the framework of individual private practice, professionals have long tended to associate in order to advance their common interests, including the maintenance of professional standards of competence and integrity. Higher education has gained prominence in this complex, not least in the training of practicing professionals. Hence, the profession of higher education and of scholarly research has also been acquiring greater relative importance. The core structure of the academic profession, the faculty, is basically associational.

All three types of operative organizations (markets, bureaucracy, and associational structures) have been growing more salient in the course of differentiation and pluralization of modern societal communities.

46.   In *The Theory of Social and Economic Organization* Weber emphasizes that all bureaucracies must be headed nonbureaucratically.

47.   Talcott Parsons, "Professions," in the *International Encyclopedia of the Social Sciences.*

CHAPTER 9
THE CENTRAL PROBLEM OF MODERN SOCIETIES
INTEGRATION

The industrial and democratic revolutions were transformations by which the institutional bulwarks of the early modern system were weakened. European monarchies survived only where they have become constitutional. Aristocracy still twitches but mostly in the informal aspects of stratification systems—nowhere is it structurally central. There are still established churches, but only on the less modern peripheries like Spain and Portugal is there restriction on religious freedom. The trend is toward the separation of church and state and denominational pluralism (except for the Communist countries). The industrial revolution shifted economic organization from agriculture and the commerce and handicrafts of small urban communities; it also extended markets.

The emergence of full modernity thus weakened the ascriptive framework of monarchy, aristocracy, established churches, and an economy circumscribed by kinship and localism to the point where ascription no longer exercises decisive influence. Modern components had already developed by the eighteenth century, particularly a universalistic legal system and secular culture, which had been diffused through Western society by the Enlightenment. Further developments in the political aspects of societal community emphasized the associational principle, nationalism, citizenship, and representative government. In the economy differentiated markets developed for the factors of production, primarily labor. Occupational services were increasingly performed in employing organizations structurally differentiated from households. New patterns of effectively organizing specific functions arose, especially administration (centering in government and the military) and the new economy. The democratic revolution stimulated efficient administration, the industrial revolution the new economy. Weber saw that in a later phase the two tend to fuse in the bureaucratization of the capitalist economy.[1]

The modern structural pattern crystallized in the northwest corner of Europe, and a secondary pattern subsequently emerged in the northeast corner, centering in Prussia. A parallel development took place in the second phase of modernization. The United States, the "first new nation," has come to play a role comparable to that of England in the seventeenth century.[2] America was ripe for the democratic and industrial revolutions and for combining them more intimately than had been possible in Europe. By the time of Tocqueville's visit, a synthesis of the French and English revolutions had been achieved: The United States was as democratic a society as all but the extreme wing of the French Revolution had wished for, and its level of industrialization was to surpass that of England. We shall therefore concentrate in the following discussion upon the United States.

THE STRUCTURE OF
THE SOCIETAL COMMUNITY

Behind the developments outlined in the preceding paragraphs were a special religious constitution and societal community. The United States was in a position to make new departures from the ascriptive institutions of early modern society: monarchy with its subjects rather than citizens; aristocracy; an established church; an economy committed to localism and only a little division of labor; and an ethnically defined societal community or nation. American territory was settled mainly by one distinctive group of migrants. They were nonconformists in search not so much of freedom from persecution as of greater religious independence than they could enjoy at home.[3] They were predominantly Puritans, the prototypes of ascetic Protestantism. In the colonies, however, they were divided into a number of denominations and sects. In the early period, for instance in Congregational Massachusetts, the colonies established their own churches. But a conception of the church as ideally a voluntary association emerged only gradually. It was fairly well accepted

1. Max Weber, *The Theory of Social and Economic Organization* (New York: Oxford University Press, 1947).

2. Seymour M. Lipset, *The First New Nation* (New York: Basic Books, 1963).

3. Perry Miller, *Errand into the Wilderness*, (New York: Harper, 1964).

by the time of independence,[4] though in Massachusetts disestablishment did not occur until more than a generation later. The religious pluralism of the thirteen colonies and the rationalistic, Enlightenment-influenced cultural atmosphere set the stage for the First Amendment, which prescribed a constitutional separation of church and state for the first time since the institutionalization of Christianity in the Roman Empire.[5]

Religious pluralism spread from differences among the original colonies to pluralism within each state, in contrast to the pattern of *cuius regio, cius religio*. This pluarlism formed the basis for toleration and eventually for full inclusion of non-Protestant elements, a large Roman Catholic minority, and a small Jewish minority.[6] This inclusion was clearly symbolized in the 1960s by the election of a Roman Catholic, John F. Kennedy, to the presidency. American society thus went beyond England and Holland in differentiating organized religion from the societal community. One consequence of this differentiation was that publicly supported education developed in the nineteenth century as secular education. There was never, as in France, a major political struggle over that problem. A parallel development occurred in ethnic composition, the other historic basis of nationality. The United States was for a time an Anglo-Saxon society, which tolerated and granted legal rights to members of some other ethnic groups but did not fully include them. This problem grew acute with the arrival of waves of non-Anglo-Saxon immigrants from southern and eastern Europe, predominantly Roman Catholic and Jewish, from about 1890 to the beginning of World War. I.[7] Although the process of inclusion is still incomplete, the societal community has become ethnically pluralistic. Negroes are still in the early stages of the inclusion process. The bulk of the Negro population was until recently concentrated geographically in the rural South, a region insulated from the rest of American society since the Civil War. But the South has been undergoing modernization through inclusion in the society as a whole, and there has been migration of Negroes to the northern and western cities. These developments have stimulated a further process of inclusion

4.   *Ibid.* See J. J. Loubser. "The Development of Religious Liberty in Massachusetts," unpublished doctoral dissertation, Harvard University, 1964; and Alan Heimert, *Religion and the American Mind: From the Great Awakening to the Revolution* (Cambridge, Mass.: Harvard University Press, 1966).

5.   Perry Miller, *The Life of the Mind in America: From the Revolution to the Civil War* (New York: Harcourt, 1965).

6.   Will Herberg, *Protestant, Catholic, Jew,* rev. ed. (Garden City, N.Y.: Anchor, 1960); and Talcott Parsons, "Some Comments on the Pattern of Religious Organization in the United States," in *Structure and Process in Modern Societies* (New York: Free Press, 1960.)

7.   Oscar Handlin, *The Uprooted* (New York: Grosset & Dunlap. 1951).

that is creating tensions. The long-run trend, however, is toward success-ful inclusion.[8]

One reason that the American community has moved toward shed-ding its identity as a white, Anglo-Saxon, Protestant community is that the "WASP" formula was never monolithic. Not only do the Irish speak English, but there are many Anglo-Saxon Roman Catholics and many Protestant Negroes. Pluralism has also been fostered by the socialization of the newer immigrant groups in more general societal values. This trend offers a possible solution to the instability of ethnic nationalism, the problem of securing congruence between the boundaries of the so-cietal community and the state. One difficulty is inherent in ethnically pluralistic systems, however. Because language is a determinant of ethnic membership, the right of each ethnic group in a pluralistic community to use its own language can lead to disruptive internal tensions, as demonstrated by the conflicts between Walloons and Flemish in Belgium and English and French in Canada.[9] Where the language of one ethnic group has become the community language, strains may be imposed upon members of other groups. There are enormous benefits in linguistic uni-formity, however. Its adoption in a multiethnic community depends on the type of priority enjoyed by the ethnic group whose language becomes the national language and on the number of competing languages; a plurality encourages the designation of only one language as official. In both twentieth-century superpowers (the U.S. and the USSR), the societal communities have gone beyond ethnic bases and adopted single languages.

The settlement of American territory was originally by English-speaking colonists from Great Britain. Other language groups were small and geographically limited—the Dutch in New York, the French in back-woods outposts and Louisiana, the Spanish in Florida and the Southwest —and none could seriously claim to provide a second language for Ameri-can society as a whole. The first large ethnically distinctive immigrant group was the Roman Catholic Irish, who spoke English (Gaelic was a romantic revival, not the actual language of Irish immigrants). As non-English-speaking Roman Catholic elements arrived, the Irish pressed for their assimilation into the English-speaking community by opposing foreign-language parochial schools. Indeed, common Roman Catholic interests could not have been promoted had the Roman Catholic popula-tion been split into language groups. The Protestant immigrants (for example, the Scandinavians) were assimilated easily, without language becoming an issue. Jewish groups arrived quite late and did not represent one European language. Furthermore, they never exceeded 5 percent of

8. Talcott Parsons, "Full Citizenship for the Negro American?" in Talcott Parsons and Kenneth Clark (eds.), The Negro American (Boston: Houghton Mifflin, 1966).

9. Hans Kohn, The Idea of Nationalism (New York: Macmillan, 1961).

the total population. The United States has thus retained English as the common language of the total societal community without widespread feeling that it represents the imposition of Anglo-Saxon hegemony.

A relatively well integrated societal community has thus been established in the United States on bases that are not primarily ethnic or religious. Despite diversity within the population, it has largely escaped pressure by ethnic-linguistic or religious communities for political independence or equal rights that would undermine the solidarity of the more inclusive community. Parallel developments occurred in American patterns of ascriptive stratification, especially compared with European patterns of aristocracy. The American population was nonaristocratic in origin and did not develop an indigenous aristocracy.[10] Furthermore, a considerable proportion of upper-class elements left the country during the American Revolution. Granting of titles came to be forbidden by the Constitution, and neither landed proprietorship nor wealth have legal recognition as criteria for government office and authority. Although American society was from the first differentiated internally by class, it never suffered the aftermath of aristocracy and serfdom that persisted in Europe; the nearest approximation appeared in the South. The participation of the wealthier and more educated groups in government has been disproportionate, but there has also been a populist strain and political mobility, advancement coming first through wealth and recently through education.

American society thus abandoned the tradition of aristocracy with only a mild revolutionary disturbance. It also lacked the heritage of Europe's peasant classes. As an industrial working class developed, the European level of class consciousness never emerged, largely because of the absence of aristocratic and peasant elements.[11] American society has also carried differentiation between government and societal community very far. For government and societal community to become differentiated, the right to hold office must be dissociated from ascription to monarchy and aristocracy and associated with achievement. Furthermore, authority must be limited to the legally defined powers of office so that private prerogatives and property interests are separated from those of office. Finally, the elective principle requires that holding office be contingent upon constituent support; loss of office through electoral defeat is an inherent risk. The independence of the legal system from the executive and legislative branches of government has been one mechanism for maintaining this kind of differentiation.

Another mechanism is the connection between the government and community stratification. The newly independent nation opted for a

10.   Clinton Rossiter, *Seedtime of the Republic* (New York: Harcourt, 1953).

11.   Louis Hartz, *The Liberal Tradition in America* (New York: Harcourt, 1955).

republican form of government (with precautions against absolutism)[12] linked with the societal community through the franchise. Although the franchise was originally restricted by property qualifications, it was extended rapidly, and universal manhood suffrage, except for Negroes, was attained early in the nineteenth century. The highest government authority was vested in elected officials: the President and members of the Congress, the state governors and members of state legislatures. The exception has been the appointment of Federal (and increasingly state) judges, with the expectation that they be professional lawyers. A competitive party system based upon the participation in politics of broad segments of the societal community soon emerged.[13] It has been fluid, oriented toward a pluralistic structure of interest groups rather than toward the regional, religious, ethnic, or class solidarities more typical of Europe.

The societal community must articulate not only with the religious and political systems but also with the economy. In the United States the factors of production, including land and labor, have been free of ascriptive ties, and the Federal Constitution has guaranteed their free movement among the different states. This freedom has encouraged division of labor and the development of an extensive market system. Locally oriented and traditionally directed economic activities and the ascriptive community structures in which they were embedded have thus been undermined, which has had consequences for the stratification system; to the extent that stratification was rooted in occupational structure, it was pushed toward universalism and an open class structure but not toward radical egalitarianism. The American societal community that emerged from these developments was primarily *associational*. This characteristic reflected components of the value system. Universalism, which had its purest modern expression in the ethics of ascetic Protestantism, has exerted continuing value pressure toward inclusion—now reaching the whole Judeo-Christian religious community and beginning to extend beyond it. The inclusion component *alone* could lead to a static, universalistic tolerance. It is complemented by an activist commitment to building a good society in accordance with Divine Will that underlies the drive toward mastery of the social environments through expansion in territory, economic productivity, and knowledge. The *combination* of these two components contributes to the associational emphasis in modern social structure—political and social democracy being conspicuously associational.

12. Rossiter, *op. cit.;* and Merrill Jensen, *The Articles of Confederation* (Madison: University of Wisconsin Press, 1940).

13. William N. Chambers, *Political Parties in a New Nation, 1776–1809* (New York: Oxford University Press, 1963); and Richard P. McCormick, *The Second American Party System* (Chapel Hill: University of North Carolina Press, 1966).

The associational emphasis has been enhanced in the United States by the partial elimination of ethnic membership and social class as ascriptively constitutive structures. In the early modern phase, the basis of community in Europe was ethnic-national. Yet the coincidence between ethnic membership and territorial organization throughout Europe was incomplete. Ethnic-centered nationalism was thus not an adequate substitute for religion as a basis of societal solidarity, even though it gained in importance with secularization and the inclusion of religious diversity within the same political jurisdiction. The new basis of inclusion in the societal community has been *citizenship*, developing in association with the democratic revolution.[14] Citizenship can be dissociated from ethnic membership, which leans toward nationalism and even racism; race provides an ascriptive criterion of belonging. The alternative has been to define belonging in universalistic terms, which must include reference to voluntary allegiance, although no societal community can be a purely voluntary association.[15] The institutionalization of access to citizenship through *naturalization*, regardless of the ethnic origins of individuals, represents a break with the imperative of ethnic membership.

The development of the American pattern of citizenship has followed the pattern outlined by Marshall for Great Britain, starting with the civic component and developing the political and social components from there. The social component, though it has lagged behind that of the principal European societies, has been extended through public education, social security, welfare policies, insurance, and union benefits, in the present century. Contemporary concern with problems of poverty marks a new phase in that development. The structural outline of citizenship in the new societal community is complete, though not yet fully institutionalized. There are two stress points: race and poverty. Their salience reflects the need to extend the processes of inclusion and upgrading still farther.

A developed legal system is necessary for a stable societal community that has dispensed with religious and ethnic uniformity as radically as has American society. The Puritan tradition and the Enlightenment fostered a predilection for a written constitution, with its echoes of covenant and social contract.[16] An individualistic fear of authoritarianism fostered the

---

14. T. H. Marshall, *Class, Citizenship and Social Development* (Garden City, N.Y.: Anchor, 1965).

15. See Karl W. Deutsch, *Nationalism and Social Communication* (Cambridge, Mass.: M.I.T. Press, 1953).

16. See Edwin S. Corwin, *The "Higher Law": Background of American Constitutional Law* (Ithaca, N.Y.: Cornell University Press, 1955).

separation of government powers.[17] A federal structure was practically necessitated by the legal separation of the colonies. All three circumstances placed a premium on legal forms and on agencies charged with legal functions. Furthermore, many of the framers of the Constitution had legal training. Even though they provided for only one Supreme Court, without specifying membership qualifications and with little specification of its powers, they did lay the foundations for an emphasis on the *legal* order.

But three developments were not foreseen by the Founding Fathers. First was the effect of judicial review in settling conflicts among the branches of Federal government, among the states, and between the states and the Federal government. The second was the adoption of English common law and the resulting proliferation of judge-made law. Finally, there was the professionalization of legal practice. In contrast to the system in Continental Europe, the legal profession, though participating freely in politics, has not been organized about governmental functions.[18] Because the separation of powers and federalism have decentralized American government, legal institutions have been important in the attenuation of local autonomy. The recent reintegration of the South into the nation is a conspicuous example. The Constitutional framework emphasizes universalistic criteria of citizenship. These criteria have undergone continuous evolution, involving both specification and generalization in interdependence with the evolution of the legal system. One consequence has been pressure toward inclusion, most dramatically of Negroes.

The duality in the civic component of citizenship has become noticeable in the United States because of this nation's reliance on a written constitution. One aspect is the citizen's rights and obligations as they have been formulated in the course of legal history. This component covers a wide range, including principles of equality before the law. Back of it stand more general principles, first embodied in the Bill of Rights and extended both by amendment and by judicial interpretation. The second aspect, increasingly stressed over time, consists of the basic equalities of citizens' rights to protection, freedoms, basic conditions of welfare, and opportunities, especially access to education and occupational development. At least in principle, the new societal community has come to be defined as a company of equals. Departures from the egalitarian

17. Bernard Bailyn, "General Introduction," in *Pamphlets of the American Revolution* (Cambridge, Mass.: Harvard University Press, 1965).

18. See Roscoe Pound, *The Spirit of the Common Law* (Boston: Beacon, 1963); and James Willard Hurst, *Law and the Conditions of Freedom* (Madison: University of Wisconsin Press, 1956).

principle must be justified, either on the basis of incapacity to participate fully—as among small children—or of being qualified for special contributions, as through competence, to the societal welfare.

THE EDUCATIONAL REVOLUTION AND THE CONTEMPORARY PHASE OF MODERNIZATION

The educational revolution is as characteristic of modernity as the industrial and democratic revolutions have been. As a child of the Enlightenment, education consisted of inculcating intellectual disciplines grounded in secular philosophy and organized in the natural sciences, the humanities, and the social sciences. These secular disciplines have become institutionalized in the system of higher education based on the universities. The universities are centers not only of instruction but of the systematic pursuit of new knowledge through research. Compared to its medieval and early modern antecedents, the contemporary university has a new comprehensiveness.[19]

One aspect of this revolution is the spread of basic education. Before the nineteenth century, elementary literacy had not extended beyond a small élite in any large-scale society. To attempt to educate the *whole* population was a radical departure. Formal education has had a long history, but until the educational revolution it was limited to a small proportion of any generation and was generally of short duration. The educational revolution has thus meant an extension of equality of opportunity. A decreasing proportion of each successive generation has been handicapped by lack of access to educational qualifications for statuses, occupational roles, and life styles. The spread of coeducation has also been an egalitarian development. At the same time, the educational system is necessarily selective. Differences in inborn ability to do intellectual work and in family orientations and individual motivations mean that levels of educational attainment and distinction vary. This factor is prominent in meritocracy, which, though compatible with ideals of equality of opportunity, introduces achieved inequality into modern society in place of *ascribed* inequality.

A feature of the educational revolution has been continuous extension of the education of the population beyond literacy. Secondary education has expanded to the point at which the high-school dropout is viewed as lacking full membership in the societal community. Furthermore, increasing numbers of people are involved in higher education. Late nineteenth-century Europe accorded higher education to an élite group, never more than 5 percent of the age group. In the United States the proportion

19. Joseph Ben-David, *The Sociology of Science* (Englewood Cliffs, N.J.: Prentice-Hall, 1971); and Talcott Parsons and Gerald M. Platt, "Some Considerations on the American Academic Profession," *Minerva*, 6, No. 4 (Summer 1968), 497–523.

of youth receiving some higher education is around 50 percent and is edging upward. The creative-innovative aspect of the educational system has increased its momentum. The earlier inventions of the industrial revolution were the work of practical men. Applied science did not have a major impact upon technology until the late nineteenth century. But technology has now become dependent upon research payoffs, involving ever-wider ranges of the natural sciences, from nuclear physics to genetics, and also the behavioral sciences. The social sciences share with the natural sciences the benefits of innovations in the technology of research. For example, mathematical statistics and computer technology facilitate the objective investigation of large populations and extend the range of empirical procedures.[20]

In the United States an *associational* pattern of social development favored early initiation of the educational revolution and its extension farther than in any other society. The educational revolution strengthened the associational trend, primarily through its effects upon the stratification and occupational systems. Ascriptive elements in the system of stratification have generally eroded. The hereditary principle has given way slowly but not completely. As long as kinship and family remain important, the hereditary principle cannot be altogether eliminated. Family solidarity requires that children share the advantages and disadvantages of their parents during their earlier years, and the premium on competence in the larger society is so high that pressures to perpetuate approximate status from generation to generation are unavoidable.[21] But this tendency is different from hereditary privilege as an institutionalized norm.

The twentieth century opened a new phase in the transition from hereditary ascriptive to nonascriptive stratification. Each of the first two revolutions generated an ideology embodying the aspirations for non-ascriptive status of certain groups. In the industrial revolution the ideology extolled pursuit of self-interest by the individual for his own (and implicitly his family's) economic advancement. The ideal participant in this competitive system was the self-made man, who linked his inborn capacity to the opportunities opened up by a competitive market system. Allegedly the most capable succeeded most fully. Associated with the democratic revolution was the ideology of political equality among citizens in contrast to the ascriptive inequalities of the system of privilege, aristocracy, and governmental absolutism. The ideological dilemma of capitalism versus socialism hinged on this pair of conceptions, neither of which considered the aristocratic system acceptable. The capitalist alterna-

20. See Harvey Brooks, "Scientific Concepts and Cultural Change," in Gerald Holton (ed.), *Science and Culture* (Boston: Beacon, 1966).

21. Talcott Parsons, "A Revised Analytical Approach to the Theory of Social Stratification," in Talcott Parsons, *Essays in Sociological Theory* (New York: Free Press, 1954).

tive emphasized freedom from the ascriptive past and protection from governmental interference. The socialist alternative proposed the mobilization of governmental power to institute equality, ignoring the exigencies of economic efficiency and governmental effectiveness. Both failed to develop adequate conceptions of the societal community and of the conditions necessary to maintain its solidarity.[22]

The new phase is the educational revolution, which synthesizes the themes of the industrial and democratic revolutions: equality of opportunity and equality of citizenship. The native ability of the individual to attain a *just* standing through market competition is no longer assumed. Instead, stratification by ability is recognized as mediated through a series of stages in the socialization process. Increasingly, there are opportunities for the disadvantaged to succeed through selection regulated by universalistic norms. The utopianism of political equality is modified by structures intermediate between the absolute individual and the ultimate national collectivity. These structures do not preclude inequalities and even legitimate some forms of it—but they minimize the ascriptive fixity of such inequalities and the arbitrariness of their imposition. People are trained and selected according to *socialized* capacity for the more responsible roles, which require higher levels of competence and carry higher levels of reward, including income, political influence, and power.

Education is a factor in the stratification system in socialist as well as in free-enterprise societies of the modern system.[23] Future changes will have to build on this pattern rather than bypassing it. They cannot be based upon purely economic criteria of selection, the enforcement of flat equality by political authority, or the presumption that equality will arise spontaneously if barriers are removed, which is the eighteenth-century romantic conception of the goodness of natural man. The educational revolution is having growing impact on the occupational structure of society, especially through general occupational upgrading and the increasing importance of the professions. Sociological discussion has tended to consider occupational roles as part of the pattern of bureaucracy, which stresses hierarchical organization and line authority. The professional component, however, is institutionalized in another pattern, the collegial, a form of *association* in which membership involves an occupational role, a job, not casual participation.[24]

22. See Marshall, *op. cit.*

23. See R. Bendix and S. M. Lipset, *Class, Status, and Power*, 2nd ed. (New York: Free Press, 1965).

24. See Talcott Parsons, "Professions," in *International Encyclopedia of the Social Sciences* (New York: Macmillan, 1968).

The professional complex reaches back into classical antiquity and the Middle Ages, including the priesthood and the practice of law and medicine. The new phase began with emphasis on scientific competence, first in law and in the scientific medicine of the later nineteenth century and then in branches of engineering and other applied sciences, as well as in the social-behavioral fields. The competence required in the professions is usually gained through formal training in academic settings. The modern university has thus become the keystone in the professional arch. The profession par excellence is the academic, the profession of seeking and transmitting knowledge. It is surrounded by a ring of professions charged with applying knowledge to social order (law), health (medicine), effectiveness in governmental and private collectivities (administration), efficient use of the nonsocial environment (technology), and so on.[25] The educational revolution, through the development of the academic complex and of channels for applying academic competence, is transforming the structure of modern society. It reduces the importance of the market and bureaucratic organization. The emerging emphasis is on associational organization, especially in its collegial form.

THE INCREASING DIFFERENTIATION OF THE PATTERN-MAINTENANCE SUBSYSTEM FROM THE SOCIETAL COMMUNITY

Pattern maintenance is one of the four functional requirements of any society. We define it, first, as the maintenance of the basic pattern of values institutionalized in the society and, second, as the shaping of the appropriate motivational commitments of individuals in the society. The foregoing religious and educational developments represent a change in the American pattern-maintenance system. The pluralization of the American religious complex, culminating in the inclusion of large non-Protestant groups, has been a process of secularization in contrast to the functioning of the older established church. Because the values of society are rooted in religion, one possible consequence of the pluralization of religion is *reduced* moral consensus. This reduction has not yet occurred in the United States. Value *generalization* has been much more important: The underlying moral consensus has persisted, but is defined at a higher level of generality than in the European societies that have institutionalized internal religious uniformity. These general values are, through specification, made applicable to the numerous structural contexts necessary in modern societies. In short American society and other modern

25. *Ibid.*

societies maintain strong moral commitments that have survived through, and have even been strengthened by, religious pluralism and secularization.

Contemporary social structure is characterized by special integration with the cultural system. Modernity began with the secularization of the medieval integration of society and religion, resulting in both the Renaissance and Reformation. The societal *system* has since undergone a series of declarations of independence from cultural—especially religious—supervision. This independence has involved three foci: legal order, first institutionalized in seventeenth-century England; national-political order, especially in pre-Revolutionary France; and market-economic order, especially in the aftermath of the industrial revolution. The newest phase returns to concern with cultural elements. The focus is not religion but the secular intellectual disciplines and, in a special sense, the arts. Whereas philosophy was in the ascendance in the early modern phase, science has become so in the twentieth century through extending its scope to the social and behavioral fields and even to the humanities. The educational revolution has introduced mechanisms by which the new cultural standards, especially those embodied in the intellectual disciplines, are institutionalized in ways that partly replace traditional religion.

This new pattern is not without strains, Unlike a century ago, when the religious implications of Darwinism stimulated bitter controversies, there has been little recent ideological agitation about science. There has been much concern with culture, however, especially the arts and some aspects of philosophy, one theme being an aristocratic disdain of mass culture expressed by such figures as T. S. Eliot, Dwight MacDonald, and Ortega y Gasset. Even religious concern has a different flavor from the nineteenth-century conflict between religion and science. One aspect of this concern is ecumenism, heralded by liberals, including the Roman Catholic shift away from rigid dogma since the papacy of John XXIII and Vatican II. Another is the skepticism about traditional organized religion, as in the atheist branch of existentialism (Sartre)[26] and the "God is dead" movement within Protestantism.

Intellectual alienation is one manifestation of strains involved in value generalization. The value specificity of older symbolic systems hindered the establishment of a *moral* consensus that, at the level of societal values, could have more integrative than divisive effects. Resistance to value generalization ("fundamentalism") occurred in religious contexts, often linked with societal conservatism, as among the Dutch Calvinists in South Africa. The Fascist movements of the twentieth century have been

---

26. See Michael Crozier, "The Cultural Revolution: Notes on the Changes in the Intellectual Climate in France," in Stephen R. Graubard (ed.), *A New Europe?* (Boston: Beacon, 1966).

fundamentalist in this sense. There has been also a fundamentalism of the extreme left, from certain phases of various Communist parties to the current New Left.

Changes have also occurred in the mechanisms by which appropriate motivational patterns are created and sustained among members of the society, the second focus of the pattern-maintenance function. Some of these changes involve the family.[27] The differentiation between employing organizations and households removes most economically productive activity from the home. This shift creates pressures toward isolating the nuclear family: the married couple and its dependent children. The breadwinner of the household—usually the adult male—is involved in an occupational world in which he is evaluated by performance. This evaluation is incompatible with a status system that emphasizes ascribed positions, for either individuals or households, in a kinship or ethnic system. Isolation does not imply breaking ties to extended kin, especially members of the spouses' families of orientation. The nuclear family has, however, become increasingly independent with respect to property, community status, and religious and ethnic commitment. An index of this independence is the decline of arranged marriages, which contrasts with the solidarity of lineages in both peasant and aristocratic statuses.

The dependence of the family, both in status and income terms, on occupational earnings places a premium on residential mobility. The favored residence is for a single family, rented or purchased. Geographic mobility has tended to weaken not only kinship ties but also community ties of a *Gemeinschaft* character. There are emphases on privacy and little presumption of intimacy with one's neighbors. These developments enhance the significance of the family as provider of an emotional base for its members' participation in society. Not only have other diffuse emotional relationships been undermined, but family members are under increasing stress outside the home because of obligations placed upon them at work and school. The general process has thus been one of differentiation in which the nuclear family focuses on pattern maintenance connected with its members' personalities to the exclusion of other functions. These developments have placed strain upon the housewife, who must be increasingly self-reliant in fulfilling her obligations to her husband and children. Furthermore, the women's role has expanded; this expansion is symbolized by women's suffrage and participation in education and the labor force.

The educational revolution has had consequences in the family context, also. Increasingly, socialization with respect to achievement in non-familial roles is left to educational institutions, which are differentiated

27. Talcott Parsons, "The Kinship System of the Contemporary United States," in *Essays in Sociological Theory* (New York: Free Press, 1954).

from the family. The educational system, not the family, increasingly serves as the source of labor for the economy. Consequently, the educational system, not kinship, increasingly determines the distribution of individuals within the stratification system. We venture to make a more general interpretation of the educational revolution than has usually been advanced. Two revolutions shaped early modernity: the industrial, which differentiated the economy and the polity from each other and developed new links between them, and the democratic, which involved analogous changes between the polity and the societal community. The educational revolution is the climax of similar changes between the societal community and the pattern-maintenance system—and through it the cultural system. We have traced the differentiation of the societal community and the pattern-maintenance system through many steps, including the development of a normative order and the definition of a societal community not grounded directly in religion. The educational revolution is a further step in this secularization. It involves integrative mechanisms, among them a means for institutionalizing secular culture. Furthermore, it reflects an emphasis upon socialized capacity as a criterion of full membership in the societal community as well as of distributing new members through the stratification system.[28]

THE INCREASING DIFFERENTIATION OF THE POLITY FROM THE SOCIETAL COMMUNITY

The differentiation between societal community and the political system is fundamental to government but should be understood in the broader analytical setting of the political factor of corporate goal attainment, regardless of the particular referent collectivity.[29] Political function is focused on the specific role type called "office," elective and appointive, in two types of collectivities, the associational and bureaucratic and in the institution of citizenship. When elective office is a component of citizenship, government is differentiated from the societal community, and community members become *constituents* of the government of the societal community. Through the franchise constituents are the source of its formal power—within a constitutional framework—and the ultimate beneficiaries, individually, in groups, and as a community, of government

28. Talcott Parsons and Gerald M. Platt, "Higher Education, Changing Socialization, and Contemporary Student Dissent," in Matilda Riley *et al.* (eds.), *Aging and Society* (New York: Russell Sage, 1971).

29. See Talcott Parsons, "The Political Aspect of Social Structure and Process," in David Easton (ed.), *Varieties of Political Theory* (Englewood Cliffs, N.J.: Prentice-Hall, 1966), reprinted in Talcott Parsons, *Politics and Social Structure* (New York: Free Press, 1969). Several other essays in the latter volume are also relevant.

contributions to societal functioning.[30] Elective office, with power to make and implement collectively binding decisions, is thus at the heart of the leadership function. In large-scale societies support for election and for decision making tends to be mobilized through political parties that mediate between the government leadership and the numerous interest groups in the constituency.[31]

As an elective office is not usually a permanent job, it seldom approaches an occupational role type. Stable democracies, however, develop professional politicians whose concern is to occupy elective office or to assist those aspiring to it, party organizers, for example. In the United States, federalism and the decentralization of local governmental units have enlarged this group.[32] Anchorage in appointive office and in the private sector (for example, in legal practice) in order to obtain occupational security and personal property are essential to those who commit themselves to political leadership. Democracies need a functional equivalent to aristocracy as the security base for leadership. The size and complexity of American society has fostered an extensive system of governmental administrative agencies but without upsetting the balance between the political (elective) and the bureaucratic components of government.

What is true of the democratic polity as an associational collectivity is true of other associations that proliferate in modern societies. The problems of associations vary according to size, complexity, interest, and internal conflicts. Securing a sufficiently independent position for leadership *across* these partisan divisions is always a problem. The choice between centralization, which enhances collective effectiveness, and decentralization, freedom of expression, and the pursuits of interest by groups, is a dilemma for democratic associations.[33] The institutionalization of associational patterns is correlated with intracommunity pluralization. When a collectivity has associative functions but the exercise of authority is dictatorial, obstacles probably exist to full institutionalization. Another index of incomplete institutionalization is the insistence by individuals and groups on recognition of their particular rights by means of techniques ranging from assertion through organized protest to obstruction. When basic interests are at stake, the optional functioning of

30. *Ibid.*

31. Talcott Parsons, " 'Voting' and the Equilibrium of the American Political System" and "On the Concept of Political Power," in Parsons, *Politics and Social Structure* (New York: Free Press, 1969), and of course an immense literature.

32. See V. O. Key, *Politics, Parties, and Pressure Groups*, 5th ed. (New York: Crowell, 1964).

33. See S. M. Lipset and Stein Rokkan (eds.), *Party Systems and Voter Alignments* (New York: Free Press, 1967), especially the Introduction.

democratic associations involves a delicate balancing of many factors. Although representative democracy has proved to be workable at the government level under some circumstances and in some private associations, it cannot be extended to all organizational contexts. In representative democracy, the elected component is the "nonbureaucratic top" of the bureaucratic organization.[34] Another device for filling this role is the fiduciary board prominent in nonprofit sectors; the fiduciary board is also becoming the governing agency of the large private business corporation. Bureaucratic organization is characterized by appointive office, emphasis on effective goal attainment, use of authority to coordinate implementation of centrally adopted plans, and a hierarchical structure. Criteria connected with elective office, like subordination to universalistic norms and the separation of the private and official spheres, apply also to the business corporations.[35] The spread of bureaucracy, both public and private, has been a hallmark of later modernization. In nineteenth-century Europe, the civil service expanded but had difficulty in remaining independent of aristocratic connections in France, in England, and (somewhat less) in Prussia. In the United States, this tendency was counteracted by the spoils system and democratic populism.[36]

Bureaucratic elements began to emerge close to the top of government. In industry, they emerged at the bottom, with the employment of laborers, whereas managerial and technical functions (along with ownership), were mainly in the hands of ascriptive proprietors. This situation has changed, especially through the separation of ownership from control (active management) in the large corporation during the last half-century.[37] Although owners still exercise some authority in a fiduciary sense, for example, in the selection of managers and in setting policy, management is organized predominantly in occupational roles, which depend little upon personal property rights or lineage structures in which property rights are institutionalized. Higher management has become increasingly professionalized as technical qualifications and formal training increase in importance. Competence is no longer a matter of horse sense and a diploma from the school of hard knocks.

The combination of the spreading democratic revolution and the differentiation of modern societies has been a source of new freedoms

---

34. See Max Weber, Theory of Social and Economic Organization (Glencoe, Ill.: Free Press, 1947), pp. 324 ff.

35. Weber, The Theory of Social and Economic Organization.

36. The classic discussion is M. Ostrogorski, Democracy and the Party System in the United States (New York: Macmillan, 1912).

37. A. A. Berle and Gardiner C. Means, The Modern Corporation and Private Property (New York: Commerce Clearing House, 1952).

and adaptive capacities, on one hand, and of new integrative strains, on the other. The phase discussed in this chapter has involved, in the United States and in most modern societies, the completion of the universalization of the franchise within the constituency. There has also been a spread of this pattern of equal membership and power within a variety of private associations, though what the limits of this process will turn out to be in such organizations as universities remain unclear.

The increase in the scale and the burden of collective responsibility of associational systems has intensified the need for responsible leadership, which presumably cannot be provided without considerable concentration of power. Administrative bureaucracy is one way of meeting this need; accountability within such organizations presents problems, and the modern solution has been to make bureaucracy ultimately responsible to electorates but more immediately to elective officers of the political system: in the American government to the executive and legislative branches. This solution involves giving immense power to elected officials—presidents and governors of states as well as members of Congress and of state legislatures. They are held accountable through the electoral process, which may be regarded as a device for handling the inevitable tension between the egalitarian basis of citizens' rights of participation and the functional exigencies of effective collective action.

The professions also have been increasingly involved in business, other areas of the private sector, and government. Professional competence is not usually organized in line authority patterns, even in a rational-legal framework. Consequently, professionalization has modified both public and private bureaucratic organizations, reducing the importance of line authority so that the organizations have become more associational; the cooperation of specialists must be secured without asserting coercive authority.[38] Much of modern bureaucracy thus verges on the collegial pattern.[39] This collegial pattern, modifying bureaucracy in an associational direction, involves membership roles, that are occupational; participation is a full-time job. Collegial responsibilities cannot be specified in the fashion that line authority ordains for bureaucratic organizations. Nor are they peripheral and segmental as are membership responsibilities in associations generally, including the political component of citizenship; a full-time voter would be peculiar in a pluralistic polity, though such a concept perhaps describes the Communist party member.

The collegial pattern is also institutionalized in the academic world and is not giving way to bureaucratization,[40] even though higher edu-

38. Parsons, *Structure and Process in Modern Societies*, chapters 1, 2.

39. The issue of collegiality, as distinct from papal monarchy, has become prominent in the Roman Catholic Church under the stimulus of Vatican II.

40. Parsons and Platt, *op. cit.*

cation recently experienced unprecedented expansion. The equality of colleagues in a faculty or department sharply contrasts with bureaucratic hierarchy. A second feature of collegial structure is election, as distinguished from appointment from above. Most modern academic appointment systems involve a complex balance: Fiduciary agencies (for example, boards of trustees) usually have final authority, whereas professional peers have control at earlier stages in staff selection. The imposition of an appointee unacceptable to his prospective colleagues is rare in the higher-level academic institutions. Professors elect their colleagues, indirectly, if not directly.[41]

Many organizations stereotyped as bureaucracies have become collegialized in many ways. Modern government is not predominantly bureaucratic, not only because it has been democratized through elective office and responsiveness to the public but also because its internal structure, especially its executive branch, is collegialized to a considerable degree. Furthermore, the attenuation of owners' control of economic organizations has not only resulted in bureaucratization. With the salience of scientific technology, academically trained professionals have become more necessary in industry because of their substantive contributions and also because of their impact on organizational structure. A recent development is large-scale industrial employment of research scientists, as well as engineers, with corresponding developments in fields like health and educational services.

THE INCREASING DIFFERENTIATION OF THE ECONOMY FROM THE SOCIETAL COMMUNITY

As it has evolved into the contemporary phase, the economy has departed from the classical pattern delineated in nineteenth-century capitalist ideology. It is subject not only to *institutional* control, especially legal regulation based on laws of contract and property, but also to a complex system of constraints through government price policies, oligopolistic business practices, and collective bargaining. There is also substantial redistribution of resources, through the use of tax revenues to subsidize many activities beyond the primary functions of government, ranging from relief of the indigent to subsidies for scientific research. Nevertheless, the market system is still an autonomous, differentiated

---

41. For some purposes a third process of achieving occupational membership must be considered: hiring. It suggests the naked economic nexus, treatment of the incumbent's service as a commodity. Modern occupational systems, partly influenced by union organization, have been developing away from such economic casualness for all but a decreasing minority.

subsystem of American society.[42] The stark contrast between a free enterprise system with minimal social and governmental controls and socialism
with government ownership and control of *all* the principal means of
production is unrealistic. The emerging pattern in all modern societies
is to a general trend toward structural differentiation and pluralization.
In societies identified as having free enterprise economies, only the rear
guard of the political Right (that opposes all modification of nineteenth-
century laissez-faire) would challenge this judgment. Indeed, the instability inherent in approximations of the pure capitalist system, as formulated by both its proponents and its socialist opponents, is a reason for
treating the nineteenth-century phase of modern society as transitional.

Around the turn of the century, the United States surpassed England
and then Germany in quantitative economic growth. This rapid growth
resulted from a variety of conditions. At Independence, the United States
had fewer than 4 million people, concentrated along the Atlantic coast,
with room for westward expansion. Partly because of British control
of the seas, the imperialist energies of France and Spain ebbed in the
Americas. It was therefore possible for the United States peacefully to
purchase Florida and the Louisiana Territory; somewhat later Mexico
put up weak resistance to further territorial expansion, which made room
for population growth and provided immense economic resources. Such
expansion also predisposed the nation to a liberal immigration policy,
which, among its many consequences, guaranteed the labor force for
industrialization. The development of monetary, banking, and credit
institutions grounded in commercial banking was rapid. (Thanks to the
banking system, the circulating medium now consists mainly of bank de-
posits—cash represents a small fraction—and supports many forms of
credit, corporate securities, and the public debt.[43] The credit system
favors continuing economic innovation, just as the contemporary academic system favors cognitive innovation. No other society rivals the
United States in monetarization of economic affairs, especially the use
of banks and credit instruments.)

The American pattern of capitalism has been distinctive in two
respects. The first was the development of mass production, pioneered by
the Ford Motor Company. Because mass production is oriented toward
large consumer markets, mostly domestic, it came to be understood that
profits depend not only upon the share of the market captured by a
particular firm but also upon the total disposable income of consumers.
Henry Ford's high-wage policy, instituted apart from labor-union pressure,

42. Talcott Parsons and Neil J. Smelser, *Economy and Society* (New York: Free
Press, 1956).

43. J. M. Keynes, *The General Theory of Employment, Interest, and Money* (London:
Macmillan, 1936).

marked a turn toward production that was capital-intensive rather than labor-intensive. This shift has resulted in a continuing relative decline in the *manufacturing* labor force despite increases in production. There have been corresponding increases in service and white collar occupations.[44] The second feature originated in Germany but evolved farthest in the United States: the harnessing of scientific knowledge to industrial production. From the chemical and electrical industries it spread to others. Electronics, closely related to cybernetics and information processing, is the farthest-reaching development so far.

The American legal system has also favored economic growth. The Constitution prohibited tariffs and restrictions on the movement of people among the states at a time when Europe was more fragmented by interstate tariffs. The legal framework regulating property and contract was adopted from England but then was developed substantially farther, mostly through judicial decisions.[45] Later American lawyers pioneered in developing the private corporation, laying the legal groundwork for differentiation of ownership from managerial control.

A system of occupational roles based on employment rather than on proprietorship was institutionalized in American society early and spread with industrialization and urbanization. It involves differentiation between households and employing organizations, mainly business firms, though it also applies to employment in government and the private nonprofit sector. Occupationalizing of work in the early phases of modernization was generally restricted to employed laborers at the bottom of the occupational hierarchy. Later, employment—and thereafter the labor market—spread upward; it now includes executives (managerial or administrative) and professionals, elements that were previously considered proprietary. This structural transformation is overlooked in most comparisons of capitalism and socialism.[46] In the fully modern phase, with the decline in the proportion of the labor force in agriculture, the contributions of adult males to larger functional interests of the society are made in occupational jobs. Furthermore, the participation of women, particularly married women, in employment has also increased sharply.

Certain functions resist occupationalizing. They reflect diffuse interests that would be threatened by the specialization inherent in occupational roles. Their diffuseness may take in several systems. The family and household are central both to personality and organic concerns. Culture has been historically conspicuous in religious functions, but in

---

44. Neil J. Smelser, *The Sociology of Economic Life* (Englewood Cliffs, N.J.: Prentice-Hall, 1964).

45. Hurst, *Law and the Conditions of Freedom.*

46. Talcott Parsons, *Structure and Process in Modern Societies.*

the modern world it is also expressed by artists, who resist professionalizing. Aside from the role of the politician, there are many government
and private fiduciary roles, like trustees of organizations that are not
exclusively profit making. For the individual citizen, however, fiduciary
responsibility for the public interest becomes segmented; it involves his
roles as voter and optional participant in communication processes and
in associations that further his views. Many categories of people are under
pressure to become engaged to the point of giving political causes priority
over their jobs or their families. These pressures are intensified in modern
society by continuous change and attendant conflicts. Furthermore, the
attainment of such limited goals as economic security and a fairly high
standard of living opens possibilities for further improvements, to which
emotions become attached. In social-psychological terms, our times are
an age of relative deprivation.

A labor-union movement exists in every modern society. Structurally
it is rooted in the gap between household and job that has been created by
the spread of occupations. Its leaders have been not the most disadvantaged workers but those with higher levels of skills and social status,
so that in some respects it is a successor to the craft guilds. Its strength
has been among manual workers, and its orientation has been toward the
protection and improvement of their economic interests and status. It has
spread unevenly both among the most unskilled and among white-collar
workers. In the United States, especially since the New Deal, the union
movement has acquired strength in industry without providing a base for
a political socialist movement as it has in most of Europe since the late
nineteenth century. This anomaly reflects the extent to which American
society was already democratized, including opportunities for economic
and social mobility.

There has been continuous upgrading within the occupational
world. The proportion of the modern labor force that is composed of unskilled laborers has been shrinking. Historians of the industrial revolution
treated growth in physical volume of output, investment of money capital,
and numbers employed in an industry as alternative measures of productive growth, presuming that they were closely correlated. But they have
ceased to be so. Since the 1920s, the total output of manufacturing industry in the United States has increased greatly, whereas the number employed in it has remained almost constant, and the proportion of the labor
force employed in it has declined. This decline is a result of mechaniza-
tion, now merging into automation, and to improvements in organization,
which have occasioned technological unemployment, as in the case of
the early nineteenth-century hand-loom weavers. There has been a restriction of employment opportunities for those without specific qualifications.
This restriction has produced not a rising unemployment rate but a
rise in the competence of the labor force resulting from educational up-

grading. In the middle third of the present century the early phase of mass production placed a premium on semiskilled labor, often to the detriment of older skilled craftsmen. Now, levels of competence, which presume secondary-school education rather than particular skills, are increasingly required.

The development of occupational roles and the attendant emphasis upon performance have undermined the significance of ascriptive background conditions. Although discrimination by lineage membership, social class, ethnic origin, religion, race, and so on continue, there is steady pressure for evaluation—and thus admission to membership and achievement opportunities—on predominantly universalistic grounds.[47]

Distribution of income among households is complex. The major factor is the labor market, which reflects differential demand for different services. Independent proprietorship has steadily declined, especially in agriculture. Wages and salaries, along with such forms of income as commissions, are a function of competence and responsibility required in occupational roles, which are increasingly influenced by education. Because of increasing financial aid to higher education, the latter is no longer available mainly to children of the well-to-do.

Modification in the pay scale determined by demand for occupational services—some of the demand, as for academic professionals, is subsidized—occurs at both ends. In all modern societies massive transfer payments (as economists call them) subsidize the living standards of the lower-income groups through relief, old-age security, unemployment benefits, health services, low-rent housing, and many other measures. A floor—below which it is felt no major category of people should fall—defines the minimum content of the social component of modern citizenship.[48] The pattern is uneven, as indicated by present concern over poverty in the United States. Nevertheless, the adoption of such a floor is characteristic of industrial societies in the twentieth century. Furthermore, transfer subsidies merge with measures to help otherwise handicapped individuals to help themselves, for instance, through universal public education. Furthermore, under pressure from trade unions, increased wages and growing fringe benefits have improved the economic position of the working class.

The market is historically the location of competitive individualism, institutionalized in the expectation that market participation would lead to differential success. Most capitalist theory has focused only upon guaranteeing the fairness of competitive conditions, the pattern of equality of opportunity. There are many facets of the balance between equality and differential success as it has been worked out since the eighteenth

47. Parsons, "A Revised Analytical Approach to the Theory of Social Stratification," and "Equality and Inequality in Modern Society," 40/2 (Spring 1970).

48. Marshall, op. cit.

century. One phenomenon has been the increasing differentiation between the success status of the firm and the occupational status of the individual participating in the firm's productive activities.

Socialism has tended to set up an alternative to the free enterprise market economy for the poor, advocating concentration of control of major factors of production in central government. This alternative to the pure market is not the only one; the establishment in all industrial societies of some kind of floor of income and welfare open to *all* participants in the economy demonstrates this. I shall remark on mechanisms that tend to counteract extreme tendencies to inequality in the other direction. Here again there is an integrative problem of balancing the egalitarian component in modern values and those components of the achievement complex that engender differences of hierarchical status within the societal community. I shall comment briefly on the general problem at the end of this chapter.

At the high end of the income scale, there is appreciable *property* income. This income is dissociated from proprietorship. Rural landed proprietorship, the politico-economic base of early modern aristocracies, has lost its importance. In the most recent phase, the significance of business proprietorship has also declined, though less drastically. Property has come to be fluid, marketable assets; corporate and government securities are the prototypes. In the United States property income is estimated at something over 20 percent of personal income, a proportion that seems not to have varied greatly for a generation or more.[49] Much of such property is in forms outside currently disposable income, for example, investments in private insurance. Another development is the extent to which property income goes to institutional rather than to individual holders such as foundations, colleges and universities, hospitals, charitable organizations, and other endowment funds.

Although property income is concentrated among the well-to-do, there is wider participation in its nonproprietary forms than there was in the earlier phase of free-enterprise societies, extending especially to the upper middle class. The accumulation of wealth by the rich is checked by progressive taxation of incomes and estates. Income distribution is more nearly equal in the later phases of modern societies than it was in the earlier phases or is in most contemporary underdeveloped societies. What is true of income is true also of opportunity, especially since the opening of higher education to increased proportions of recent age cohorts. Although the long-run stability of the current pattern is uncertain, the trend is toward still greater equality.

A curious counterpoint to these developments exists in criticisms of

---

49. William Haber (ed.), *Labor in a Changing America* (New York: Basic Books, 1966).

the high-prestige classes of modern society. They are accused of having "gone soft"; they are also accused of being too absorbed in the narrow interests of their work. Although such accusations invite suspicion, the preoccupation with work sounds realistic. Occupationalizing and professionalizing management entailed upgrading of educational standards, expectations, and average attainment, requiring high motivation to achieve among participants. The motivational commitment necessary probably did not exist during earlier phases of social development. Despite reductions in the hours of formal work and a slackening of effort in some types of work, commitment to occupational performance remains high. It has probably been increasing, particularly at the highest occupational levels. The upper occupational groups in modern society, far from constituting a leisure class, are among the hardest working groups in human history. Paradoxically, the allegedly exploited working class has moved closer to becoming the leisure class of modern society. The hard work of the upper groups does not consist of muscular exertion or adherence to supervisory discipline; it involves solving difficult problems and taking responsibility for solutions.

There has been a raising of standards of nutrition, clothing, housing, and other components of the standard of living. Only in the lowest brackets of the modern poor is there *drastic* deprivation—to the point of near starvation, lower life expectancy, ragged clothing, and the like— as characterizes much of the underdeveloped world today. This problem is not the same as that of the incidence of such social pathologies as drug addiction. There has also been upgrading in expressive standards, as demonstrated by rising consumption of cultural goods and by levels of aesthetic taste in household furnishings, food, and the like (including participation in public recreation). Even though previously disadvantaged or isolated groups have fostered aesthetic monstrosities that later upper groups have not been slow to ridicule, sophisticated tastes are shared by a larger proportion of the population in modern societies than ever before. This development is difficult to evaluate. Increased consumption is apt to be disapproved by puritans, who regard it as evidence that the current generation is "going soft." From another perspective, *Gemeinschaft* romantics allege that the taste of simple people has been corrupted by modernization.

Another theme in the discussion of standards of living in affluent societies is competition for status through conspicuous consumption, extending from the ostentatious entertainment and palaces of the old aristocracies to contemporary keeping up with the Joneses. Some such competitiveness is unavoidable when standards of universalism and achievement are institutionalized. Yet the decline of the aristocracy has reduced invidious consumption differences. For example, the White House, though hardly a log cabin, is far from another Palace of Versailles. The

Gilded Age mansions of New York's Fifth Avenue and Newport are either disappearing or being turned over to public use; similar trends are apparent in Europe. In most modern countries bourgeois ostentation is now less extreme than it was in the eighteenth or the nineteenth centuries, though there is broader enjoyment of some kinds of luxuries. Since conspicuous consumption is not new and has declined among élites, it is difficult to see in modern luxury consumption a symptom of the decadence of contemporary society.[50]

An associated development is investment in consumers' durable goods, including the dwelling as well as such equipment as central heating, appliances, and furniture. Privacy is also part of the modern standard of living—a room of one's own for the married couple and for all but young children is now taken for granted. These developments are partly a consequence, partly a determinant, of the reduction in the servant class. Early in the present century the typical middle-class home had one domestic servant living in, whereas to be upper-middle-class required a considerable staff. Today only the rich have a staff of servants, a large proportion by virtue of some institutional position. The upper-middle-class household generally operates with a cleaning woman one or two days a week and baby-sitters.

There are other reasons for the scarcity of servants. Modern industry has become increasingly capital-intensive, making labor the increasingly expensive factor of production—the reciprocal of the general rise in the standard of living. Furthermore, increasing egalitarianism has stigmatized the status of servant,[51] making employment in factories or stores preferable to domestc service. These developments have not been without cost to the middle-class married woman. Deprived of household help and subject to increasing demands in the emotional management of family relations, in the broader range of citizenship, and in occuptions as well, she relies upon an array of modern household appliances that is not sheer extravagance.

CONCLUSION

The United States' new type of *societal community,* more than any other factor, justifies assigning it the lead in the latest phase of modernization. It attains fairly successfully the equality of opportunity stressed in socialism. It presupposes a market system, a legal order relatively inde-

---

50. Perry Miller shows that Americans had much the same concern with decadent affluence in the seventeenth and eighteenth centuries as they have now. See *Nature's Nation* (Cambridge, Mass.: Harvard University Press, 1967).

51. Vilhelm Aubert, "The Housemaid: an Occupational Role in Crisis," in S. M. Lipset and N. J. Smelser (eds.), *Sociology: The Progress of a Decade* (Englewood Cliffs, N.J.: Prentice-Hall, 1961).

pendent of government, and a nation-state emancipated from religious and ethnic control. The educational revolution was a crucial innovation with its emphasis on the associational pattern as well as on openness of opportunity. American society has gone farther than any comparable large-scale society in its dissociation from the older ascriptive inequalities and the institutionalization of an egalitarian pattern. Contrary to the opinion among many intellectuals, American society—and most modern societies without dictatorial regimes—has institutionalized a broader range of freedoms than had previous societies. This range is not greater than that enjoyed by small privileged groups as eighteenth-century European aristocracy, but it is broader than ever before for large masses of people.

Such freedoms begin with freedom from some of the exigencies of physical life: ill health, short life, and geographical circumscription. They include reduced exposure to violence for most of the population most of the time. Higher incomes and extensive markets enhance freedom of choice in consumption. There is also general access to services like education and public accommodations. There is freedom of marital choice, of occupation, of religious adherence, of political allegiance, of thought, of speech and expression. From a comparative and evolutionary perspective, the more privileged societies of the later twentieth century have successfully institutionalized the liberal values of a century ago.

There are flaws. One, surely, is war and the danger of war. Because we are dealing here with the nature of the societal community, however, we shall postpone discussion of intersocietal relations to the concluding chapter. The deficiencies of the new societal community type do not lie mainly in the older grievances against the tyranny of authoritarian regimes, especially of the monarchical variety, or the privileges of aristocracies. Nor do they lie in class antagonism and exploitation in the Marxian sense. The problems of inequality and social justice remain, but framing these problems in terms of bourgeoisie versus proletariat is no longer justified.

There is one context in which equality-justice complaints are justified in the United States: the existence of substantial poverty in combination with the large Negro minority that has suffered a long history of discrimination originating in slavery. Poverty is not exclusively a Negro problem. By most criteria the majority of the American poor is white, and a substantial nonwhite population is not poor. There is, however, a coincidence of the two aspects of the problem among ghetto blacks in the central cities. The older view of these problems stresses absolute deprivation, malnutrition, and disease. The conviction that *relative* deprivation is more important, that what hurts most is the sense of *exclusion* from full participation in the societal community has been growing among social scientists.[52] In our paradigm of social change we have stressed the connection between inclusion and adaptive upgrading—through rising income—but they are not identical. The connection does help to explain why, considering the recent reduction of legal and political discrimination, tensions over the race problem have intensified, not subsided. That mitigation of feelings of relative deprivation through inclusion is in a sense symbolic does not make it the less urgent.

In a second context, the problem of equality and social justice is more difficult to assess. The old grievances of tyranny, privilege, and class in the Marxian sense are less central than they once were. But there remains a sense that advantaged groups use their positions illegitimately to promote their interests at the expense of the common interest. In an earlier generation these grievances were defined in economic terms, as in Franklin D. Roosevelt's reference to "malefactors of great wealth." The tendency now is to invoke the symbol of power—in C. W. Mills' phrase, a "power élite" is now held responsible for our social ills. Members of the power élite are less likely to be defined as office holders than as sinister wire-pullers behind the scenes. Ideological complexes with paranoid themes are old, but the question of what lies behind this one nevertheless arises.

Indignation over the economic privileges of the rich does not seem to be a major source of the moral malaise in modern society; indeed, indignation seems less than at the turn of the century. There is consensus that those elements below the poverty line should be brought above it. Beyond that consensus, the problem of economic inequality becomes complicated. The trend has been one of reduction in conspicuous consumption among élite groups. Though not much has happened for a generation, the future trend will be toward greater equality.

In terms of power and authority, society has become more decentralized and associational rather than more concentrated. This trend again suggests an explanation of discontent in terms of relative rather than absolute deprivation. Bureaucracy has become a negative symbol, implying centralized control through rigid rules and authority. The trend is actually not toward increased bureaucracy, even if bureaucracy were not in process of transformation, but toward associationism. But many sensitive groups *feel* that bureaucracy has been increasing. This sense is also related to accusations against the "military-industrial complex" in the United States, which is associated with a pervasive sense of limitation on freedom; in extreme groups, recent gains in freedoms are denied.

52. See Lee Rainwater and William Yancey, *The Moynihan Report and the Politics of Controversy* (Cambridge, Mass.: M.I.T. Press, 1967); and Talcott Parsons and Kenneth Clark (eds.), *The Negro American* (Boston: Houghton Mifflin, 1966).

In the expression of relative deprivation two symbols are prominent. One is community, widely alleged to have deteriorated in the course of modern developments.[53] The residential community has allegedly been privatized and many relationships have been shifted to the context of large formal organizations. However, bureaucratization is not actually sweeping all before it. Furthermore, the system of mass communications is a functional equivalent of features of *Gemeinschaft* society; it enables an individual selectively to participate according to his own standards and desires.[54] A second symbol is "participation," especially in the formula of "participatory democracy." Demands for it are stated as if power were the main desideratum, but the diffuseness of these demands casts doubt on this conclusion. The demands are actually another manifestation of the desire for inclusion, for full acceptance as members of solidary groups. Similar considerations seem applicable to the fear of *illegitimate* power. What form participation can take compatible with the exigencies of effective organization is a difficult problem.

This interpretation is compatible with the recent prominence throughout modern societies of student unrest associated with the development of mass higher education. The themes stressed by student radicals have resonance in society at large. Both negatively and positively power is a potent symbol; the wrong kind of power allegedly explains what is wrong in society, and "student power" is among the remedies advocated. Bureaucracy and related themes are associated with the wrong kind of power. A new concept of community, with respect to which participation is urged, is endowed with magical virtues.[55]

I have stressed the importance in modern society of three revolutions. Each has been a center of tension, producing radical groups that opposed features of the existing social structure as well as revolutionary changes. The French Revolution, a phase of the early democratic revolution, spawned the Jacobins, the absolutists of Rousseauean democracy. The industrial revolution generated conflicts about which I have had a good deal to say; the socialists were the radicals of this phase. The student

---

53. One form is the nostalgia for *Gemeinschaft,* which has been a prominent feature of the ˈsociological tradition, especially as portrayed by Robert Nisbet, *The Sociological Tradition* (New York: Basic Books, 1967).

54. The orientation of sociology is not toward restoring the societies that preceded the industrial and democratic revolutions, or even the educational revolution. Rather it has been toward a search for components of social systems that have accounted for the positive features of earlier societies with a view toward understanding how they can be reshaped to meet the functional exigencies of emerging modern societies. See Edward A. Shils, "Mass Society and Its Culture," *Daedalus* (Spring 1960); and Winston White, *Beyond Conformity* (New York: Free Press, 1961).

55. Parsons and Platt, *op. cit.,* p. 26.

radicals of the New Left have begun to play an analogous role in the educational revolution.

We face a paradox. Revolutionaries resent hearing that they share any values with those whose immoral systems they seek to overthrow. As I have used the concept of values in analysis, however, it is legitimate to raise the question whether or not the basic value *patterns* of modern society, and especially of the United States, are being fundamentally challenged. Are the institutional achievements associated with the progressive values of the nineteenth century no longer relevant? Have they been repudiated by the new generation? In my opinion these values are taken for granted, not repudiated.[56] Modern society is indicted for not living up to its professed values, as demonstrated by the existence of poverty and racial discrimination and the persistence of war and imperialism. On the other hand, there is insistence that society should not be content with these value implementations but should introduce new ones.

Egalitarian themes suggest what the next phases may be; the two symbols of community and participation point a direction. The modern system, particularly in the United States, completed one phase of institutional consolidation, but it is also undergoing the ferment that accompanies the emergence of new phases. The strategic significance of the societal community to new phases seems clear. The emergence of important features of this community is recent. Furthermore, the United States has led the change, but its features will spread through all modern societies. A description of these features is therefore in order.

The principle of equality is being applied more pervasively than ever before. A societal community *basically* composed of equals seems to be the final development in the process of undermining the legitimacy of older, more particularistic and ascriptive bases of membership, such as religion (in pluralistic society), ethnic affiliation, region or locality, and hereditary in social status (in the aristocracy but also in more recent versions of class status). This theme of equality has many antecedents but

56. One objection to this statement is obvious: The extreme student radicals of the 1960s resorted to the revolutionary tactic of confrontation, including the use of violence and deliberate disruption of academic discussions to deny what liberals consider a fair hearing for those whose positions they opposed. This behavior is a repudiation in practice of the procedural values of liberal society; it is often defended as necessary because of the repressive character of the Establishment. At the same time people who engage in such tactics repeatedly invoke *their* rights in a way that precludes their having repudiated these liberal values. Furthermore, this trait is common to *all* extreme radicals and not only to current ones. The Terror under the Jacobins was hardly democratic, yet it was perpetrated in the name of democracy. Communist tactics have been similar. This conflict between supposed ultimate values like equality and freedom and the tactics of radicalism is built into extreme radical movements.

first crystallized in conceptions of natural rights under the Enlightenment and found expression in the Bill of Rights of the American Constitution. The Bill of Rights has proved to be a time bomb; some of its consequences emerged long after its official adoption, dramatically through Supreme Court action but also more generally. Concern over poverty and race problems in the United States reflects the moral repugnance that the conception of an inherently lower class or an inferior race arouses in modern societies.

Some radical ideologies claim that genuine equality requires abolition of all hierarchical status distinctions. This version of community has been a persistently recurrring ideal for many centuries. Such approximations to realistic institutionalization as have occurred, however, have always been on a small scale and of short duration. Too intensive a drive in this direction would disrupt larger-scale institutions of modern societies as law, markets, effective government, and competent creation and use of advanced knowledge. It would shatter society into primitive small communities. The direction of modern societal development is toward a new pattern of stratification. The historical bases of legitimate inequality have been ascriptive. The value base of the new egalitarianism requires a different basis of legitimation. In general terms, this basis must be *functional* to society conceived of as a system. Differential outcomes of the competitive education process must be legitimatized in terms of societal interest in the contributions of especially competent people; special competence is a function of both native ability and good training. A societal interest in economic productivity (with no presumption that every individual or collective unit that participates will be equally productive) implies special rewards for the economically more productive units. Similarly, effective organization is a functional necessity of complex collectivities and one of the factors in such effectiveness is the institutionalization of power, which has an inherently differential aspect.

Two modes of reconciliation exist between the value imperative of basic equality and the functional needs for competence, productivity, and collective effectiveness—all of which intersect in concrete areas of the social structure. The first is the institutionalization of *accountability*, one example of which is the accountability of elected officials to their constituencies. Economic markets perform analogous functions, though imperfectly, as do mechanisms for certifying competence in the academic world, the professions, and other fiduciary bodies. The second mode is the institutionalization of equality of opportunity so that no citizen shall for ascriptive reasons (race, social class, religion, ethnic affiliation), be barred from equal access to opportunities for performance, as in employment, or to opportunities for making effective performance possible, like health and education. This ideal is far from full realization, but the view, so prevalent today, that equality of opportunity is sheer mockery suggests that the ideal actually is being taken seriously. In earlier times the lower classes, or individuals disadvantaged on other ascriptive bases, took for granted that opportunities open to their betters were not for them, and they did not protest. The volume of protest is not a simple function of the magnitude of the evil.

Balancing value-commitments to equality against inequalities implied in functional effectiveness presents integrative problems to modern societies because many of the historic bases of hierarchical legitimation are no longer available. This difficulty is compounded by the appearance of the problem not in one overarching sphere but in many different spheres. There are many bases for functional inequality; the classification competence–economic efficiency–collective effectiveness constitutes only an elementary framework. There must be integration not only between claims to special prerogatives and the principles of equality but also among different kinds of claims to special prerogatives in a pluralistic social system.

This integration is the focus of emerging institutions of stratification. None of the inherited formulas purporting to describe modern stratification is satisfactory. The basis is not, except in special instances, national or ethnic membership. It is neither aristocracy in the older sense nor class in the Marxian sense. It is still incompletely developed and essentially new. The integration of such a societal community must depend upon mechanisms that center around the attachment of generalized prestige to specific groups and to the statuses that they occupy, including the office of bearers of authority in collectivities. The prestige of such groups and statuses must be rooted in combinations of factors rather than in any one, like wealth, political power, or even moral authority. *Prestige* is the communication node through which factors essential to the integration of the societal community can be evaluated, balanced, and integrated in an output, *influence*. The exercise of influence by one unit or set of units can help to bring other units into consensus by justifying allocations of rights and obligations, expected performances, and rewards in terms of their contributions to a common interest. The common interest is that of the society conceived as a community.

The concentration on the societal community that has characterized this book as a whole and the present chapter in particular should be balanced by a recognition that values potentially transcend any particular community. That is why this book has been concerned with the *system* of modern societies rather with any one society. The processes that transformed the societal community of the United States and promise to continue to transform it are not peculiar to this society but permeate the modern—and modernizing—system. Only on such an assumption of commonality is it understandable that European societies with no racial problems of their own can feel justified in taunting Americans about their callousness in the treatment of blacks or small independent countries in raising outcries of imperialism. From the vantage point of common membership in the modern system, the *intersocietal* institutionalization of a new value system, including its relevance to stratification, is worth studying.

The foci of conflict and thus of creative innovation in the modern system are not mainly economic in the sense of the nineteenth-century controversy over capitalism and socialism, nor do they seem political in the sense of the problem of the justice of the distribution of power, though both these conflicts are present. A cultural focus, especially in the wake of the educational revolution, is nearer the mark. The indications are that the storm center is the societal community. There is the relative obsolescence of many older values like hereditary privilege, ethnicity, and class. There are also unsolved problems of integrating the normative structure of community with the motivational basis of solidarity, which remains more problematic. The new societal community, conceived as an integrative institution, must operate at a level different from those familiar in our intellectual traditions; it must go beyond command of political power and wealth and of the factors that generate them to value commitments and mechanisms of influence.

CHAPTER 10
THE
DIFFERENTIATED
SYSTEM
OF MODERN
SOCIETIES

The system of modern societies, though originally European, has been extended to the entire world. What does it mean to say that the many different countries of the contemporary world constitute one *system* of societies? It means (1) that, increasingly, all contemporary societies share the same general ideas and values but (2) that, even in an interdependent world, societies are not carbon copies of one another; they play different roles in the world community.

In connection with Point (1), the previous chapter paid special attention to the United States, not out of my own parochial loyalties, but because I believe that the United States is a model for other countries in structural innovations central to modern societal development. The United States is extending the organization of social life in individualistic, decentralized, and associational directions (the historic roots of which can be traced to the feudal period in Europe). Comparable patterns of individualism, decentralization, and associational pluralism also characterize closely related societies, Canada and Australia.[1] Other societies will necessarily adopt these features as they move toward modernity. This perspective on the United States is congruent with the picture of American society first presented by Tocqueville in the 1830s and is an alternative interpretation to recent portrayals of the United States as the prototype of bureaucratization and the concentration of power.

In connection with Point (2), the United States has specialized

---

1. See S. M. Lipset, *The First New Nation* (New York: Basic Books, 1963).

also in a different kind of world leadership: in attempting to influence through political and economic intervention the way life is lived on this planet. This kind of leadership—an explicit promoting of goals for the world to attain—has led to American involvement in two world wars, in post-war reconstruction, and in a variety of alliances and smaller military conflicts. Like the United States, the Soviet Union has also sought to promote goals for the world to attain. Since the goals of these two societies are different, their societal emphasis on goal attainment has inevitably brought them into conflict—but so far not direct nuclear confrontation. Other societal emphases (in a differentiated world system) are possible. Unlike the United States and the Soviet Union, the role of France and Germany has emphasized maintaining the cultural traditions of the world community rather than leading it toward new goals.[2] Still another emphasis is the integrative one: attempting to mediate differences among fellow members of the community of nations and thereby fostering solidarity. Japan, Sweden, Switzerland, many Third World countries have sought alternatives to aligning themselves either with the United States or the Soviet Union. This is what I mean when I speak of a *system* of modern societies: extension of a common culture to all societies, yet different societies playing differentiated roles within the world community. In what follows in the rest of this chapter, I shall discuss the place of the Soviet Union, the New Europe, and modernizing non-Western societies in the system of modern societies.

THE SOVIET UNION

As the Russian Revolution took shape after the chaos created by collapse of the 1914–17 war effort, by civil war, and by international intervention, political control took the form of dictatorship of the proletariat, the Communist variant of socialism. The party and the government became agencies of modernization as much as of revolutionary conquest. Although industrialization had begun in Russia before the Revolution of 1917—some authorities argue that the Revolution slowed its pace[3] —efforts at massive development were launched by the Soviet regime. As between the two revolutions of the early modernizing period (the indus-

2. I do assume a *general* continuity in the Western world in the pattern of value orientation since the Renaissance and the Reformation—despite the innumerable conflicts over the specific applications of these values. See Talcott Parsons, "Christianity," in *International Encyclopedia of the Social Sciences* (New York: Macmillan, 1968).

3. See Alexander Gerschenkron, "Problems and Patterns of Russian Economic Development," in C. E. Black (ed.), *The Transformation of Russian Society* (Cambridge, Mass.: Harvard University Press, 1960).

trial and the democratic), the Soviet Union's success has been greater in industrialization; in a short time it has attained second position in the world.

The Soviet regime has also introduced features of the democratic revolution despite its dictatorial character. Many ascriptive components of the older society have been eliminated: The monarchy was abolished; the aristocracy, which had been more tightly linked to the throne than in France, was wiped out as a status group; for a time the children of bourgeois and aristocrats were so discriminated against that there is now a predominantly new upper class.[4] The identification of the Russian Church with czarist regime was closer than any church-state relationship in Western Europe. The Communist movement followed the French Revolution in its anticlericalism and carried it farther than had any non-Communist nation. The older position of the Church has been destroyed, and organized religion enjoys limited toleration. Marxism-Leninism has attained semireligious status, which obstructs religious pluralism. Industrialization has reduced traditional localism and particularism. Urbanization, education, geographical mobility, and status mobility have all increased even though freedom of movement and employment are restricted.[5]

These processes indicate a shift toward citizenship within the societal community. The Soviet system stresses universalistic standards and strives to qualify all its citizenry for full inclusion through both general education and indoctrination in established beliefs. Yet even more than the French Revolution, Soviet policy confronts a dilemma between control by party and government and maximization of freedom, the expressed ideal of the "withering away of the state." Institutions intermediate between the central authority and the masses of the people reflect this dilemma. Some of these institutions, formerly opposed by the Communist party, have regained acceptability. One is inequality of occupational income, reflecting, as in other societies, differential competence and responsibility. Another is the family. After a period when divorce was available upon request, it became more difficult to secure than in most capitalist societies.[6] Related to both is permission for individuals and families to hold some private financial resources in the form of savings accounts.[7] Adjudication independent of administrative authority, though

4. Merle Fainsod, *How Russia Is Ruled,* rev. ed. (Cambridge, Mass.: Harvard University Press, 1963).

5. Alex Inkeles and Raymond A. Bauer, *The Soviet Citizen* (Cambridge, Mass.: Harvard University Press, 1959).

6. See Kent Geiger, *The Family in Soviet Russia* (Cambridge, Mass.: Harvard University Press, 1969).

7. See Inkeles and Bauer, *op. cit.*

restricted, has become significant.[8] Although such institutions are now accepted, there is uneasiness about their scope and autonomy, as, for example, in parents' control over their children.

The government's administration of the economy has been an issue. In the Stalinist phase of five-year plans, military insecurity, and war, concentration of authority was extreme. It was the era of political totalitarianism and the command economy.[9] Economic development was extraordinary, but, as the Great Purge of the late 1930s demonstrated, it was accompanied by political strains of which the de-Stalinization crisis of the middle 1950s was an aftermath. The command economy suppressed many of the mechanisms of other industrial economies, most obviously money and markets.[10] A system of hierarchical decisions was substituted for the market. Plant managers implemented the instruction of the central planning authority, using the materials and manpower allocated to them from other centrally controlled units.[11] Many difficulties resulted from such centralization, and the Soviets are still attempting to reduce it without compromising socialist principles. The allocation of manpower is a sensitive issue because a policy of assignment restricts individual freedom. The same problem appears in consumption. Although Soviet planners deride capitalist consumer sovereignity, they have had to tailor production plans to what consumers find acceptable, especially since recent increases in consumer income[12] have initiated the phase of "mass consumption."[13]

The most serious problem remains the demarcation between the rights of government and of the citizen. From the Western point of view, the totalitarian phase, symbolized by terror and the secret police, denied the rights of the citizen enforceable *against* government.[14] Since Stalin's death, its rigor has been relaxed, although how firmly rooted civil rights are remains uncertain. Ideologically, individual freedoms are supposed to

8. See Harold J. Berman, *Justice in the U.S.S.R.*, rev. ed. (Cambridge, Mass.: Harvard University Press, 1963).

9. See Gregory Grossman, "The Structure and Organization of the Soviet Economy," *Slavic Review*, 21 (June 1962), 203–22.

10. See Gregory Grossman, *Economic Systems* (Englewood Cliffs, N.J.: Prentice-Hall, 1967).

11. Joseph S. Berliner, *Factory and Manager in the U.S.S.R.* (Cambridge, Mass.: Harvard University Press, 1957).

12. Marshall I. Goldman, *The Soviet Economy* (Englewood Cliffs, N.J.: Prentice-Hall, 1968).

13. Walt W. Rostow, *The Stages of Economic Growth* (Cambridge, Mass.: Harvard University Press, 1960).

14. Barrington Moore, Jr., *Terror and Progress: U.S.S.R.* (Cambridge, Mass.: Harvard University Press, 1954).

become nearly absolute with the advent of communism, but practically it is not clear how they are to become so. The Soviet Union has institutionalized the franchise, but it applies to "yes-no" choices, permitting no organized opposition to the incumbent leadership. Although it fails to present the average citizen with genuine choice about the general direction of governmental policy, it nevertheless does differ from the older European pattern that treated individuals as the subjects of their monarchs.[15] From these beginnings, political citizenship of the general Western pattern may develop. A Stalinist type of dictatorship is no longer possible. The leadership requires endorsement by the Central Committee of the Communist party, which can no longer be manipulated as it was by Stalin. This system may evolve toward an approximate equivalent of the British parliamentary system of the eighteenth century.

There are instabilities inherent in the dictatorship of the Communist party. The party and therefore its leadership is *self*-appointed. The nearest parallel seems to be the saints of Calvinist polities, including early New England. In each instance, the legitimating cultural tradition has given no universal criterion defining *who* is qualified for the élite. The Soviet system does not recognize legitimation by birth, the classic stabilizer of aristocratic systems. To the degree that the party succeeds in educating the population as good socialists, there may emerge democratizing pressures parallel to those that developed in Western polities and in Protestantism for eliminating the status of an elect. The processes of the democratic revolution have not yet reached an equilibrium in the Soviet Union. Further developments *may* well run in the direction of Western types of democratic government with responsibility to an electorate rather than to a self-appointed party.

The social component of Soviet citizenship has developed. Although it is embedded in more hierarchical, bureaucratic, and authoritarian structures than exist in Western societies, it shows how far the Soviet Union has evolved from seventeenth-century absolutism.[16]

Although formal education at all levels had been available to a minority before the Revolution, one of the first Soviet efforts was to advance mass education. The result has been that the Soviet people are now among the most educated in the modern world. They have also extended the levels of education upward faster than has almost any society except the United States and Canada. Physical science and technology have been emphasized because of the goal of rapid industrialization and because of

15.   See Alex Inkeles, *Public Opinion in Soviet Russia* (Cambridge, Mass.: Harvard University Press, 1950).

16.   Inkeles and Bauer, *op. cit.*

military considerations as well as because these fields were safe in ideological terms. Ideological indoctrination has been conspicuous in higher education and has shaped the humanities and social sciences to a considerable extent. Literary intellectuals and artists, who suffer from repressive measures, are among the disaffectd elements. Soviet research is concentrated in academies of science separate from the universities. A related organizational feature is control of training in the professions by the respective ministries rather than by universities. For example, medical schools are under the Ministry of Health rather than the Ministry of Education. The reasons for this organizational pattern are probably political. The academy system insulates research from public sectors of the society, giving research personnel greater freedom than they could have if the social repercussions of their work were to be more directly controlled.

The establishment of new Communist regimes in Eastern Europe after World War II and then in China ended "socialism in one country." The European socialist societies have not constituted an "iron curtain" but a permeable boundary vis-à-vis Western non-Communist influences. This boundary, along with such channels as broadcasting, publications, and visits in both directions, has affected the Soviet system. Before World War II the boundary countries were more European than was Russia. Not surprisingly, they have shown stronger liberalizing trends in the Western sense, though sporadically and unevenly. Whereas the Soviets have occasionally taken measures to repress movements toward autonomy in Eastern Europe—as in Hungary in 1956 and in Czechoslovakia in 1968—the long-run impact on the Soviet system itself will probably favor liberalization. In some ways, the cost to the Soviet Union of maintaining its empire parallels the cost to capitalist powers of coping with independence movements in their former colonies.

Communist China has raised a challenge to Soviet leadership of world communism, engendering tensions that few would have anticipated several years ago. This challenge may push the Soviet Union toward accommodations with the West. In the first post-Stalin phase of Soviet communism, Khrushchev introduced the formula of peaceful coexistence, a parallel to *cuius regio, eius religio*, the formula that ended the wars of religion. It also represented negative toleration: The foreign ideological adversary was no longer to be fought with force, but no concessions on the legitimacy of its ideological position were to be allowed. Despite American involvement in Vietnam, the hot phase of the cold war is coming to an end. If the parallel with the earlier religious situation is valid, however, peaceful coexistence is not a stable stopping place. The development will probably continue through many vicissitudes toward an ideologically more ecumenical situation.

THE NEW EUROPE[17]

There have been turbulent developments at the European core of the modern system: two world wars, the first spawning the Russian Revolution and the Fascist movements, the second ending the imperial status of the European powers and shifting leadership to the United States and the Soviet Union. Europe's main line of development is Americanization, a term used pejoratively by European intellectuals. I disregard this negative evaluation and also the question of how much the changes result from American influence and how much from indigenous developments. The ideological reaction to Americanization is analogous to the Counter-Reformation or the conservative alliance against the effects of the French Revolution. The Reformation, the democratic revolution, and Americanization have all been processes of irreversible change in Western society.

The Continental center of gravity moved to France and the new Germany after 1870. Despite conflicts between them, together they constitute the main pattern-maintenance base of the emerging New Europe and of the modern system as a whole, although this base has since World War II extended to include northern Italy. The new north-cental base was of mixed religious composition. Despite conflicts like the *Kulturkampf* in Germany and that between clericals and anticlericals in France, this composition has favored religious pluralism, as has the weakening of the papacy by the largely secular state in Italy.

France, the inspiration of the democratic revolution, lagged behind in the industrial revolution; a large proportion of its labor force remained in agriculture and small proprietary enterprise. Aristocracy, regionalism, peasantry, and other ascriptive components of society remained prominent. The nonascriptive integration of the societal community, which went very far in the United States, did not go far in France.[18] The system of higher education and secondary education (the *lycées*) was until recently geared to the humanistic education of a small élite drawn mainly from the upper bourgeoisie. Gaullism served as a mild equivalent of the Nazi movement. It emphasized nationalism, partly in compensation for the humiliation of 1940 and the loss of the French colonial empire, and has been economically conservative, especially in its concern with the

---

17. For a general discussion, see Stephen R. Graubard (ed.), *A New Europe?* (Boston: Houghton Mifflin, 1964).

18. See Stanley Hoffman *et al.*, *In Search of France* (Cambridge, Mass.: Harvard University Press, 1963).

international monetary position of France. But the processes of economic revival after a generation of inflation have brought new inequalities. The working classes have not shared equally in the growing national income.

Compared to France, Germany industrialized rapidly before World War I. This rapidity put strains on its poorly integrated societal community, which was split religiously, regionally, and in other ways.[19] Although Germany pioneered in social security and was the seat of active trade-union and socialist movements, its democratic revolution was delayed, and its opportunities for higher education were restricted. The system of social stratification preserved many elements of ascriptive inequality. These factors, combined with the defeat of World War I, unstable political democratization, and the rise of Soviet communism, provided the background for the Nazi eruption. The internal structure of the German societal community generated the strains that led to nazism; those strains were reflected in the adoption of the Jew as a negative symbol, the drive to incorporate into the nation all ethnic Germans, and violent nationalism. Anti-Semitism also suggests that the strain centered on the economic and occupational aspects of the societal community; the Jew symbolized a dangerous competitor who could not be trusted because he did not "belong" in the national ethnic community. The emphasis on the virtues of *Gemeinschaft* in German social thought since the nineteenth century has had similar implications.[20] The Nazi movement was a sociopolitical disturbance but not a source of future structural patterns,[21] although it may have contributed to the postwar integration of the German societal community.

Although the political integration of any large-scale, changing society is partial, France and Germany seem to have experienced greater political instability both internally and externally than have others, especially those that are integrative in the modern system. France has had

19. See Rainer Baum, "Values and Uneven Political Development in Imperial Germany," doctoral dissertation, Harvard University, 1967.

20. See Talcott Parsons, "Democracy and Social Structure in Pre-Nazi Germany," in *Essays in Sociological Theory,* rev. ed. (New York: Free Press, 1954). On the relations between anti-Semitism and anticommunism, see "Social Strains in America," in *Structure and Process in Modern Societies* (New York: Free Press, 1960); and "Full Citizenship for the Negro American?" in Talcott Parsons and Kenneth Clark (eds.), *The Negro American* (Boston: Houghton Mifflin, 1966). The latter two essays are reprinted in *Politics and Social Structure* (New York: Free Press, 1969).

21. The contrary interpretation has been presented in many works of social criticism over the past thirty years. A few examples are Erich Fromm, *Escape From Freedom* (New York: Holt, 1941); Hannah Arendt, *The Origins of Totalitarianism,* 2nd ed. (New York: Meridian, 1958); and Erich Voegelin, *The New Science of Politics* (Chicago: University of Chicago Press, 1952). A particularly interesting treatment of this problem is contained in Barrington Moore, Jr., *Social Origins of Dictatorship and Democracy* (Boston: Beacon, 1966).

three monarchical and five republican regimes since the Revolution. Germany's new democratic system, established after World War I, gave way to nazism in only fifteen years. Even aside from its partition, its present stability is somewhat precarious, although a revival of nazism seems unlikely. Franco-German relations gave rise to the international disturbances that set off the two world wars. The European-unification movement, although it has encountered obstacles since De Gaulle's accession to power, may help to stabilize the situation, especially with its economic base in the Common Market. The survival of the United Nations for more than thirty years and the moderate easing of East-West tensions may encourage such stabilization.

Intellectuals enjoy a special status in France[22] but also in Germany and Italy. These countries are the heirs of the European intellectual culture. Historically, this heritage has been associated with both aristocracy and the Church, and the decline of these institutions has contributed to the intellectuals' special status. In contrast to the United States, European intellectuals are a less differentiated group despite their older traditions. The strictly intellectual disciplines are connected with the arts—Bohemian society constitutes a kind of emancipated élite, sharing with the aristocracy a contempt for things bourgeois. Their concern with generalized culture is one reason for treating France and Germany as the core of the pattern-maintenance system of modern European societies despite their political instability.

The old southern tier has become weak. Spain became isolated, involved in internal difficulties, and the first of the colonial powers to lose the bulk of its empire. The rise of Bismarckian Germany weakened the Austrian empire, which collapsed after World War I. Italy was unified a century ago but did not emerge as a first-class power. The northwest corner of the old European system—now comprising Great Britain, Holland, and Scandinavia but not France—is integrative for the modern system. Belgium might also be included, despite its ethnic-linguistic division, as might Switzerland.[23] The integrative societies have relatively stable democratic political institutions and well-organized party systems.[24] The Fascist movements did not make headway in these countries.

22. See Michel Crozier, "The Cultural Revolution: Notes on the Changes in the Intellectual Climate in France," in Graubard, op. cit.

23. Canada and Australia might also be included in the integrative category. See S. M. Lipset on their differences from the United States in The First New Nation (New York: Basic Books, 1965). Today's Austria seems to belong more to the pattern-maintenance group, however.

24. See the relevant contributions in S. M. Lipset and S. Rokkan (eds.), Cleavage Structures, Party Systems, and Voter Alignment (New York: Free Press, 1967); and in Robert Dahl (ed.), Political Opposition in Western Democracies (New Haven: Yale University Press, 1966).

Although the line between the civil-law and common-law traditions runs through this cluster of societies, all have legal systems independent of political pressures. All have traditions of civil liberties, and in none have the laws governing property and contract been undermined by radical socialist policies. All except Belgium enjoy ethnic and linguistic homogeneity. These societies also have welfare states, in which social insurance and other redistributive benefits enhance social security, especially for lower-income groups. This development has been supported by the democratic-socialist parties, which have separated themselves from the communist movement and gained widespread support, often majorities. The impact of socialism has been greater in welfare policies than in socialization of the means of production. Social and cultural developments in these countries reflect comparative affluence and are based on industrial economies in Britain and Sweden and a more commercial one in Holland. Compared with those of Germany and the United States, Britain's economic-growth rate slowed in the late nineteenth century. Since then, its dependence upon foreign trade and the changes in its world political position have caused further difficulties. The British economy is being incorporated into the European Common Market.

The stratification patterns of the integrative societies are of an intermediate type. In terms of *relative* welfare, the integrative societies have aided their lower-income groups more than any but the socialist societies. In contrast to American and Soviet societies, they continue to permit aristocratic elements to share in defining the establishments, especially in Great Britain. Liberalization of opportunities for social mobility —especially the British Education Act of 1944—have taken the place of broad status differentiation and mass educational upgrading conspicuous in the United States.[25] Nevertheless, the stratification pattern has probably begun to shift toward the American pattern. Sweden has also retained some aspects of aristocracy, somewhat resembling those of Germany.

Throughout the modern system, the trend has been for class status to become focused on one central category—which, however, must be reconciled with differential income, various life styles and symbols, and inequalities in political power. The American stratification system is focused on the middle class. The position of an upper class is tenuous. Where it has survived, it has been more as a power élite. Furthermore, there are now few working-class people in the traditional sense, only the poor. In the Soviet Union all respectable people, including industrial managers, scientists, government administrators, and assorted intellectuals (the intelligentsia) are considered members of the working class. The

---

25. See T. H. Marshall, *Class, Citizenship and Social Development* (New York, Anchor, 1965).

other two main sectors of the modern system have preserved more elements of the traditional capitalist two-class system, though in varying guises. Class and status conditions are changing in character practically everywhere in the modern system.

Although the industrial and democratic revolutions are still forces in the new Europe, the important development is the educational revolution. Its ground work was laid in the old Europe, in the cultural tradition and in establishment of universal public education for the first time in large-scale societies, especially in Germany; England lagged in this respect.[26] Compared to the United States and the Soviet Union, the pattern-maintenance and integrative societies have been conservative in regard to the educational revolution but are now moving into it. This trend will promote the growth of meritocracy and pose the problem of balancing technical competence and humanistic cultivation in higher education. The humanistic traditions of the leading European countries will become part of the cultural underpinnings of all modern educated classes. Such infusions will modify the basis of current cultural Americanism.

Student unrest has emerged everywhere in the modern system, in both socialist and capitalist societies.[27] It involves the relations between the democratic and educational revolutions as well as consequences of the industrial revolution—for example, the economic capacity to support mass higher education and sufficient demand for people with higher education in the occupational system. Student status within the academic system is unsettled; parallels exist between the student movements of today and the labor movements of the nineteenth century. Within the academic system, students occupy the lowest positions in prestige and authority. Furthermore, many students' parents have not had higher education,[28] a parallel to industrial workers who migrated from the rural areas. Both movements have been characterized by democratic ideologies with utopian strains; the extreme student position is a demand for fully democratic government of universities so that any student would become the equal of a senior professor. This movement already seems to be splitting into a radical and a moderate wing, as did the labor movement.

26. David Landes, "Technological Change and Development in Western Europe, 1750–1914," in H. J. Habakkuk and M. Postan (eds.), *The Industrial Revolutions and After* (Cambridge: Cambridge University Press, 1965), vol. 6 of *The Cambridge Economic History of Europe*.

27. Student unrest and activism have been conspicuous in modernizing as well as in modern societies. The earliest wave was in Latin America, but other waves have hit the beach, for example, in India and in Indonesia. How the Red Guard movement in China fits into this framework is questionable. My comments point up the generality of this phenomenon in modern societies.

28. Martin Meyerson, "The Ethos of the American College Student," *Daedalus* (Summer 1966), 713–39.

Furthermore, student activism, like labor activism, has two possible focal points: the academic system itself and public policy generally. The parallel has limits. The status of student, unlike that of worker, is temporary. Furthermore, the distinction between workers and capitalists was based on inherited class position, whereas that between faculty and administration on one side and students on the other is not.

MODERNIZATION OF NON-WESTERN SOCIETIES

Both the United States and Soviet Russia have European cultural traditions and have interacted with Europe for centuries. The modern system has extended beyond the Western cultural areas, however.[29] Since the fifteenth and sixteenth centuries, European influence has pervaded the rest of the world through trade, missions, settlements, and acquisition as colonies.

Japan became modernized without European culture or population. Japan's two and one-half centuries of self-imposed isolation from both the West and mainland Asia under the Tokugawa regime was defensive, as were its first steps toward modernization, following the recognition that continued isolation was impossible. The country adopted a modernizing pattern closer to that of the eastern wing of the European system than to that of the British-American wing. Imperial Meiji Japan modeled its constitution after that of imperial Germany,[30] granting special constitutional privileges to the military forces and establishing a centralized national educational system. Also the regime tolerated, though it did not directly further, the concentration of economic power in the *zaibatsu* firms. The selective borrowing of East European institutional patterns fitted Japan neatly. Tokugawa social structure emphasized collective goal attainment.[31] Although it was feudally decentralized, its organization was hierarchical and its human resources easily mobilized, both in the daimyos' territorial domains and in their lineal kinship structure. Japan thus had the potential for an integrated political system, which after the Meiji revolution was able to give central direction to modernization. Comparable institutional resources did not exist in China or India.[32] Furthermore, in relation to an Asian frontier and the exigencies of rapid development, Japan was comparable to Prussia and later the Soviet

29. A general introduction to this question from a point of view similar to that outlined here is S. N. Eisenstadt, *Modernization: Protest and Change* (Englewood Cliffs, N.J.: Prentice-Hall, 1966).

30. See Reinhard Bendix, *Nation-Building and Citizenship* (New York: Wiley, 1964).

31. See Robert N. Bellah, *Tokugawa Religion* (New York: Free Press, 1957).

32. See Talcott Parsons, *Societies: Evolutionary and Comparative Perspectives* (Englewood Cliffs, N. J.: Prentice-Hall, 1966) and references cited there.

Union, where central governmental authority has also been important. The Tokugawa regime seems to have been oriented toward keeping its feudal units in a static balance that rendered internal structures precarious. The Meiji Restoration, oriented toward foreign relations, mobilized these units nationally.

Despite the fit between Japan's indigenous and borrowed elements, modernization occasioned strains, especially in developing formally patrimonial bureaucratic organization in government and business. These strains were the source of Japan's post-World War I tendency toward fascism, which paralleled German developments in that period.[33] Despite differences between the two societies, parliamentarianism and related structures in Japan and their German counterparts were subject to similar pressures. Both nations, encouraged by power vacuums, embarked on militaristic expansion policies. After Japan's alignment with the Axis powers in World War II, its defeat precipitated another turning point. Under American occupation and as an American ally, Japan repudiated its semi-Fascist past and developed a democratic parliamentary regime. Despite a strong internal Socialist-Communist movement, it has supported the democratic nations in the cold war. There has been further industrialization and modernization, including a decline in population growth. Japanese agriculture modernized around a family farm system, making collectivization unnecessary, a feature that Japan shares with the United States, Great Britain, and, increasingly, Western Europe.

Despite Japan's advanced modernization, its patterns are difficult to assess. Indeed, Japan has not yet reached stability. Its early leanings toward the Prussian model were grounded in its indigenous social structure, but they were also nurtured by an international environment in which aggressive defensiveness and then national expansion paid off. Since 1945, Japan has turned toward an adaptive-integrative pattern. Japan's future course, more than that of most industrial societies, will probably depend upon its world position, notably upon whether or not it is drawn into Communist China's orbit.

The pattern of political legitimation symbolized by the imperial institution has inherent instabilities. Unlike the top authority structures of other modern societies, that of Japan is not grounded in one of the historic religions, Christianity, Confucianism, or Buddhism or in one of their derivatives like Marxism. It rests on an historic-ethnic basis with no generalized orientation from which a probable societal tendency can be firmly predicted.[34] The consequences for Japan of the rationalizing

33. Masau Maruyama, *Thought and Behavior in Modern Japanese Politics* (London: Oxford University Press, 1963).

34. See S. N. Eisenstadt, "The McIver Lecture: Transformation of Social, Political, and Cultural Orders in Modernization," *American Sociological Review*, 30 (October 1965), 659–73.

pressures of modernity are uncertain, although it may develop a constitutional monarchy of the British-Scandinavian type. Furthermore, Japan has no strongly institutionalized legal system in the Western sense.[35] Even recently, Japan's legal institutions seem weaker than those of prerevolutionary Russia. The conflicts of interest inherent in rapid modernization must therefore be contained by political processes rather than by formal adjudication and by attendant informal adjustments independent of politics. The political process must carry an unusually heavy burden of integration in Japan.

In short, Japan has less built-in stability than have several other modern societies. Yet the nation has traveled far along the paths of industrial, democratic, and educational revolution and is the first example of modernization of a large non-Western society. Its developmental experience thus raises some questions about the future of the system of modernized and modernizing societies. To the extent that Japan achieves successful modernization and stability as a predominantly integrative society, it may rise to a position of role model for modernizing non-Western societies and as a factor in the balance of international power.

The imperialist phase of Western society's relations with the rest of the world was transitional. The trend toward modernization has now become worldwide. The élites of most nonmodern societies accept aspects of the values of modernity, especially economic development, education, political independence, and some form of democracy. Though the institutionalization of these values is uneven and fraught with conflict, the trend toward modernization in the non-Western world will probably continue. We cannot expect a clear outcome of the contemporary postimperialist ferment for a considerable time. But the burden of proof rests with those who argue that any major part of the world will settle into a *non*modern pattern of society during the next couple of centuries, although the variations within the modern type of society will probably turn out to be great. Furthermore, the decline of the colonial empires, combined with the cold war division within the modern system, has created a climate for the emergence of a third world bloc as a stabilizing factor in the world and in the spread of modernism.

CONCLUSION

A generation ago it seemed a leap of faith when Wendell Wilkie wrote a book entitled *One World*. Today the phrase reflects technological and economic realities. A junior high school student in Nagoya, Japan,

---

35. Richard William Rabinowitz, "The Japanese Lawyer," doctoral dissertation, Harvard University, 1965).

was describing his own experience when he coined the official slogan of the 1964 Olympics: "The World is One." He could watch on his home television screen events taking place anywhere in the world, and he could travel by jet plane to distant places in a few hours. But there is a sociocultural sense—in addition to the technological and the economic ones—in which the world is one. There is a convergence of sociocultural development such that nearly all societies reflect to varying degrees the industrial revolution, the democratic revolution, and the educational revolution. It is therefore only a slight exaggeration to say that all contemporary societies are more or less modern. We should not make too much of the fact that the United States and the Soviet Union have had ideologies varying from older Western European patterns and that some, especially Soviet, are suspiciously viewed by Western European societies. The value content of these ideologies should be regarded as specifications of the more general Western value pattern of instrumental activism rather than as departures from it. The same can be said of the ideologies of social criticism and revolt.

At the same time that the societies of the world have grown similar to one another, have formed one modern culture, they remain differentiated from each other in the roles they play *within* the system. Thus, some societies (the superpowers) attempt to direct the system as a whole toward some goals rather than others, whereas some societies emphasize different functional problems of the world system: pattern maintenance, integration, adaptation to the physico-biological environment.

CHAPTER 11
CONTINUING
EVOLUTION

Societal evolution, this book's dominant perspective, belongs to a movement in contemporary social science which aspires to emulate the Renaissance by doing more than reviving old ideas. I have reconsidered the idea of social evolution in the context of theoretical advances accumulated since the earlier evolutionists wrote. If the idea of evolution is fruitful, the progress of social science in the last two generations has made it *more* fruitful. Furthermore, this progress fits into general developments in modern science. Advances in the biological sciences since Herbert Spencer's day have generated new conceptions of the continuity between organic evolution and sociocultural evolution.[1] Because early evolutionary theory treated society and culture largely by imputing causation to environmental factors[2] within the dichotomous framework of, not just heredity *and* environment, but actually heredity *versus* environment, it conceived of organic and cultural evolution as discontinuous. This perspective is no longer justifiable in the light of modern biology.

THE TREND OF EVOLUTION:
INCREASED ADAPTIVE CAPACITY

To be an evolutionist, one must define a *trend* in evolution—one cannot be a radical cultural relativist who regards the Arunta of

1. See Sol Tax (ed.), *Evolution after Darwin*, 3 vols.: especially vol. II, *The Evolution of Man* (Chicago: The University of Chicago Press, 1960).

2. In this case, both physical and cultural.

Australia and such modern societies as the Soviet Union as equally authentic cultures to be judged as equals in *all* respects. My perspective involves evolutionary judgments—for example, that intermediate societies are more advanced than primitive societies, and modern societies are more advanced than intermediate societies. I have tried to make my criterion congruent with that used in biological theory, calling more advanced the systems that display greater generalized adaptive capacity.

The present analysis differs from older evolutionary theories in that the developmental dimension is compatible with the idea of *branching* among lines of evolution. The evidence indicates that, in the earlier stages of evolution, there have been *multiple* origins of the *basic* societal types. Thus, we need not postulate one primitive origin of all intermediate societies even though independent cultural legitimation and stratification are *necessary* conditions of intermediate societies. At all stages, variability can be adequately treated only by an analytic theory of variable components. The development of such theory since Spencer's time enables us to construct a more sophisticated evolutionary scheme than his.

There are two types of societies besides those which historical evidence links through continuous processes to evolutionary advances. First are those which have been eliminated by the socio-cultural version of natural selection—e.g., no approximation of ancient Israel or Greece has survived as a society in the modern world. Yet, the fact that the kingdom of David and Solomon and the *polis* of Athens were eliminated did not destroy their future *cultural contribution*. Second are those which, though not developing into more advanced types, are established in niches which, despite the existence of more advanced societies, permit them to survive for long periods without undergoing changes of pattern. The many primitive societies studied by anthropologists are of this type. Their characteristics approximate those of our own pre-historical antecedents. The exact extent of such approximation can be detemined only by imperfect theoretical analysis. In dealing with the main patterns of evolutionary development, I have focused mainly on the societies which gave rise to significant evolutionary developments. It has not been possible to give equal attention to either of the two types of dead-end cases, although Israel and Greece have been surveyed from the standpoint of their cultural developments. I have tried to emphasize the *failure* of adaptive development in a number of societal cases. However, an adequate treatment of the *balance* of successes and failures and the factors determining them would require a different study.[3]

---

3. The problem of failures is treated more fully in E. N. Eisenstadt, *The Political Systems of Empires* (New York: Free Press of Glencoe, 1963) and in a number of Eisenstadt's papers, some of which are included in his *Essays in Comparative Institutions* (New York: Wiley, 1965).

One difference between socio-cultural evolution and organic evolution is that cultural patterns and content can be *diffused,* not only from generation to generation within a society, but also from society to society, as cases like Israel and Greece show. A parallel between organic and socio-cultural evolution is that *structural* analysis must take priority over the analysis of process and change. One need not develop a general analysis of the main *processes* of social change in order to make claims about the *structural patterning* of evolutionary development. This conclusion is established in biology, where morphology, including comparative anatomy, is the backbone of evolutionary theory. Although Darwin advanced ideas about *process* in the principle of natural selection, he stated explicitly that he could not prove in a single case that it has changed one species into another, but only that "it groups and explains well a host of facts . . ." , the majority of which concerned structure.[4] Darwin did not present a developed theory of evolutionary *process* in regard to the genesis of variations. But this did not impugn the scientific status of the theory of organic evolution, as Darwin developed it.

Some sociologists insist that only dynamic analysis has scientific standing. I am not saying that contributions to the analysis of process would not improve evolutionary theory. I *am* saying that the use of available sociological, anthropological, archaeological, and historical evidence to order structural types and relate them sequentially is a *first* order of business. Furthermore, the task is as much theoretical as empirical. If such advanced structural knowledge is to be developed and utilized, social science must do theoretical work as well as continuing empirical research. Max Weber's system of ideal types surpassed, some half century ago, earlier structural analysis. Furthermore, Weber's formulations were associated with vast ranges of historical and comparative material. Notwithstanding Weber's concern with religion and cultural movements, much of his structural theory concerned economic and political organization.[5] The present generation of sociologists is making advances on Weber's work in these fields. In the area of theory, there has been sufficient advance so that most of the difficulties of Weber's "type atomism" can be avoided. To a greater degree, variability can be analyzed as a function of different combinations of the same analytically defined components.[6]

4. Charles Darwin, quoted in the "Preface" to Talcott Parsons, Edward A. Shils, Kasper D. Naegele, and Jesse R. Pitts (eds.), *Theories of Society* (New York: Free Press of Glencoe, 1961).

5. Cf. Talcott Parsons, "Value Objectivity in Social Science: an Interpretation of Max Weber's Contribution," Max Weber Centennial article in *International Social Science Journal* (1965) 27:No. 1.

6. Failure to do this at *each* stage is a shortcoming of Marxian theories of social evolution.

Discussion of the advanced intermediate societies must rely on the humanistic traditions of historical, archaeological, and anthropological research. Their methods have improved in the last two generations. For example, my account of Egyptian society would not have been possible had I based it on the Egyptology of Breasted's era (the early decades of this century). The advances in quantitative social science research are more relevant in dealing wtih the subject of *modern* societies. However, in one historical context advances in quantitative social science techniques are relevant for further study of earlier types of society. Among contemporaneous societies, we can find approximations of earlier societal types involved in the evolutional sequence. The development of the comparative method is being extended to include a variety of underdeveloped societies as well as advanced modern types. Although it was tempting to mobilize such material for these purposes, the difficulties of interrelating it with the historical data concerned with the flourishing of intermediate societies would have been empirically and theoretically formidable. Since a choice was necessary, it seemed logical for an evolutionary study to follow a temporally ordered framework with the exception of contemporary primitive societies, for which no direct historical data exist.

Comparative study is also stimulating interdisciplinary research. Two shifts have emerged. First, anthropology, with its predilection for studying small-scale societies has become less prominent. Considerable comparative work, especially on development, has been done primarily by economists, political scientists, and sociologists. This change has advanced the integration of comparative studies into the larger corpus of social science, a factor affecting both. Second, inter-disciplinary collaboration in the social sciences, which during and after World War II concentrated on area studies of particular national societies and regional complexes, is now emphasizing a comparative perspective. Concomitantly, there has been growing concern with generalization, both theoretical and empirical. Only against this background is the present essay understandable. It attempts general structural analysis and a limited processual one. But, in formulating and validating its propositions, it has also attempted to use the best available empirical materials.

The *structural* ordering of social data should never be dissociated from the analysis of *process* and *change*. For example, *any* processual outcome results from the operation of plural structural factors, all of which are mutually interdependent, even if there is scientific reason to distinguish among them. The factors of production in economic analysis are logical prototypes.[7] In *this* sense, *no* claim that social change is determined by economic interests, ideas, personalities of particular individ-

7. Cf. Neil J. Smelser, *The Sociology of Economic Life* (Englewood Cliffs, New Jersey: Prentice-Hall, 1963).

uals, or geographical conditions is tenable. *All* such single-factor theories belong to the kindergarten stage of social science's development. *Any* factor is interdependent with several others. This truth does not preclude the hierarchical ordering of the factors. I have distinguished two interrelated hierarchies—those of *necessary* conditions and of *cybernetic* control. The former runs from the physical, through the biological and psychological, to the social and cultural elements of action. The various subsystems of these elements are similarly ordered. For example, within the social system, I have called attention to the negative effects of diminutions in mobile economic resources, both goods and manpower, upon the empires' maintenance of differentiated governmental structures. Such maintenance—as well as the prior development of such structures—depends in the conditional sense on the availability of adequate mobile economic resources; if the latter dry up enough, feudalization occurs. However, the presence of such resources in a society does not automatically create the more differentiated type of government any more than atmospheric oxygen, although necessary for the emergence and maintenance of life, alone created human life.

The more important hierarchy for my purposes is the hierarchy of cybernetic control. Basic innovation in the evolution of living systems, both organic and socio-cultural, does not occur automatically with increases of factors or resources at lower (conditional) levels of the cybernetic hierarchies but depends on analytically independent developments at higher levels.[8] Essential as a large population may be for advanced social organization, the pressure of increasing numbers cannot create such organization—rather, it will lead to Malthusian checks. This argument also applies to economic productivity and political power. In the sense of emphasizing the role of the cybernetically highest elements in *patterning* action system, I am a cultural determinist rather than a social determinist. Similarly, within the social system, the normative elements are more *directive* for social change than the material interests of constitutive units. The longer the time perspective and the broader the system involved, the greater is the relative importance of higher, rather than lower, factors in the control hierarchy, regardless of whether it is pattern maintenance or pattern change that requires explanation. The present analysis has been couched on the level of the longest time-perspective and broadest comparative scope. Therefore, in *this* study, the emphasis in accounting for the main patterns of change has been placed at the highest cybernetic level. This level is cultural rather than social and, within the cultural category, religious rather than secular. Within the social category, values and norms, especially legal norms, stand higher than political and economic interests. However, the consequence of following these

8. The reader may wish to refer to chap. 1 for a fuller discussion of these concepts.

priorities involves determining the *broadest* patterns of change rather than explaining *detailed* structures and processes.

High-level innovations do not determine the subsequent development of the relevant systems so automatically that we may neglect all other factors. Quite the contrary; every developmental step depends on a series of conditional factors. I formulate this dependence by maintaining that higher-order factors (within the social system, normative factors) must meet the conditions of becoming institutionalized in order to determine stable patterns of concrete action.[9] This means that they must *gain control* over the relevant conditional factors. This is not to say that the latter factors have only negligible importance. It merely claims that to be controlled, conditional factors must be present in proper combinations, both in terms of one another and in terms of the normative factors and that conditional factors cannot create a new order without independent innovation at a higher normative level.

Differences in non-cultural and non-normative conditions and the ways in which they are combined with the cultural and normative factors account for much of the variation that makes any linear theory of societal evolution untenable. But a feature of the evolutionary process is that greater differentiation increasingly frees the cybernetically higher factors from the specifics of the lower-order conditioning factors, thus enabling the patterns of the cultural system to become more generalized, objectified, and stabilized. These developments enhance the cultural system's potential to control wider ranges of factors at the conditional levels. Thus, a primitive society is not only limited in territory and population, but its culture is relatively specific to its conditions and does not readily integrate with those of other societies. An intermediate society is, in a sense, equivalent to the integration of a number of primitive societies into one societal system. This presupposes an integration at the cultural level between the cultural patterns and the normative system of the society.

A theme in my discussion of the advanced intermediate empires has been that such integrations of particularistic, less generalized structural elements have typically been incomplete. In China, the local elements and the peasant cultures were only partially permeated by Confucian culture. In India, the integrative shortcomings involved both localism (sometimes tribalism) and the segmental rather than differentiated aspects of caste diversity. In Rome and the Islamic empires, ethnic and local particularities failed to be fully integrated into the political and legal structure of the empires either as effectively dominated or, still more, as autonomously

<hr>

9. Cf. Leon H. Mayhew, *Law and Equal Opportunity: A Study of the Massachusetts Commission against Discrimination* (Cambridge, Mass.: Harvard University Press, 1968).

differentiated units. The independence that components gain through differentiation and its relation to variation also has a time aspect. A differentiated component need not be bound to one concrete territory-and-population nor to any particular period. Culture, through documents and other artifacts, can become relatively independent of particular bearers or members of a given society. Thus, a cultural system's consequences for subsequent societies cannot be inferred directly from its mode of involvement in the societal structures of its origin but must be analyzed in a more complex framework. The cases of Israel and Greece are examples of this cultural-temporal independence. A difficult problem for the naive, Marxist-type sociological analysis is to demonstrate how Hebrew and Greek influence on later societies was really based on the economic interests of either the originators or the adopters of these cultural patterns.

Confusion over issues such as these has arisen from the dogma, often implicit, that evolutionary theory must be historical in the sense of historicism. Whether following Hegel, Marx, or later Germans such as Dilthey, historicism denied the relevance of generalized analytical theory (which systematically treats the interdependence of independently variable factors) in explaining temporally sequential socio-cultural phenomena. In challenging this idea, Durkheim and Weber introduced a new era in sociology. Once the problem of causal imputation is formulated analytically, the old chicken and egg problems about the priorities of ideal and material factors lose significance. I hope that the present treatment of the problems of societal evolution will help lay to rest this ghost of our nineteeth-century intellectual past.

THE SYSTEM OF MODERN SOCIETIES

The longer the time span and the wider the comparative range within which an analytical scheme is put to empirical test, the likelier it is that the developmental trends that emerge are both empirically valid and theoretically significant. This perspecive is in the spirit of Weber's views of the nature of sociocultural evolution and of the nature of modern society. The reader familiar with Weber's work will be aware that this book is not an attempt to bring Weber up to date but involves substantial differences in emphasis. How far Weber would have adhered to these differences, had he lived to experience the intervening half-century of social events and scientific development, I cannot know. I agree with Weber, however, in his judgment that the development of Western society in the modern era is of universal significance in human history and in the corollary of that judgment: that the development has not been random but directional. This directionality is one aspect of a threefold conception of the ways in which modern societies constitute a single system. A second is that the modern type has had a single origin, a hypothesis suggested by Weber. The third aspect, the sense in which the modern system has been a differentiated system of several societies, requires elucidation.

Chapter 6 stressed that in feudal times the European system was already differentiated internally along functional lines. This differentiation advanced by the seventeenth century and, along with the extension of the system beyond its original geographical boundaries, persisted into the contemporary world. Later developments in this direction—the division between predominantly Roman Catholic and Protestant areas and among ethnically and linguistically distinctive nations and politically independent states—involved disintegration of the medieval unity of Western Christendom under the Church and the Holy Roman Empire. But the process was not simply one of disintegration; it had positive significance for the system as a whole. Differentiation contributed to the capacity of the system to initiate the conditions for institutionalization of evolutionary change. Despite fragmentation, the West was an area with a common culture based on the Christian religious tradition and its heritage from the Israel and Greece of classical antiquity; this heritage assumed independent significance through both the Roman institutional tradition and its reemergence in the Renaissance. Because of my conviction of the importance of this common heritage, I devoted so such space to it in Chapter 6.

Within this common framework, which included a precariously institutionalized political order, innovations resonated in parts of the system other than those in which they occurred. English common law thus could be linked with the revived traditions of Roman law in England's own heritage and on the Continent and with the traditions of Protestantism—after all, Calvin was a Frenchman and Luther a German. The British gentry could be linked with general patterns of aristocracy, and the economic development of England and Holland was continuous with that of northern Italy and the free-city belt along the Rhine. Culturally, Italian science represented by Galileo was linked to English science represented by Newton; there were also links in philosophy between the French Descartes, the English Hobbes and Locke, and the German Leibniz. The previous chapter spoke of the Americanization of Western Europe in the present century, another example of this interplay. The American heritage is basically European, although in selective form. But the United States has remained part of the same system as Europe and has influenced it.

There has been conflict, frontier primitivism, and lag in some of the older parts of the system relative to the more progressive parts. Some aspects of the Counter-Reformation illustrate such lag, as do some aspects of British and French backwardness in industrial organization relative to the United States. Conversely, until the present generation many cultivated Europeans regarded the United States as a culturally-crude frontier society.[10] These strains are apparent within particular societies and in intersocietal relations, particularly the latter. There are good reasons why manifestations of strains are more salient in intergroup than in intragroup relations. Solidarity is stronger within a group—including a national societal community—than between it and others of its type; therefore there is a tendency to displace conflict into the field of intergroup relations. Second, intergroup order is less firmly institutionalized than is intragroup order; therefore defenses against the cycles of escalating conflict are weaker. In the international sphere, the tendency is for this escalation to culminate in wars because control of organized force is weak at the international level and organized force is the ultimate coercive instrument. The history of modern societal systems is one of frequent warfare. Although the system of modern societies includes built-in mitigating factors with respect to conflict, wars have been highly destructive, notably the wars of religion of the sixteenth and seventeenth centuries, the wars of the French Revolution and the Napoleonic period, and the two world wars of the twentieth century; the present period is under the even greater threat of *nuclear* war. The same system of societies within which the evolutionary process has occurred has been subject to a high incidence of violence, conspicuously in war but also internally, including revolutions.

These facts may nevertheless be compatible with a trend toward reduction of violence both internally and internationally.[11] Current fears of imminent nuclear holocaust raise questions that cannot be answered objectively. I am hopeful that there is sufficient motivation on the side of societal responsibility to make retreat from total conflict, as in the Cuban missile crisis of 1962, probable. One more indication of the importance of the *system* of societies is that the most serious conflicts occur between units that have widely differing roles and values within the system. The Reformation and its aftermath introduced a fissure in the European system—extending to a disturbance of Franco-British relations over the status of the Stuart dynasty. At the same time, both the Roman Catholic and Protestant camps were part of Western Christendom. The

10. When I was a student in Germany more than forty years ago, I was asked by a young woman at a dance why I had chosen to study in Germany. On replying that I was concerned to learn something about German academic culture, she replied that she understood that "Bei Ihnen gibt es wohl keine Wissenschaft," ["America doesn't have any scholarship."] a view that even then I resented but that could hardly be defended today.

11. See Talcott Parsons, "Order as a Sociological Problem," in Paul G. Kuntz (ed.), *The Concept of Order* (Seattle: University of Washington Press, 1968); and Parsons, "Some Reflections on the Place of Force in Social Process," in Harry Eckstein (ed.), *Internal War: Basic Problems and Approaches* (New York: Free Press, 1964), reprinted in Parsons, *Sociological Theory and Modern Society.*

disturbances following the French Revolution were family quarrels as are those of the anti-Communist–Communist cleavage. Marxism—even as it operates in China—is as much a part of the Western cultural heritage as was Protestantism in an earlier period. This conflict is not evidence against the existence of a modern system in my sense.[12] Pessimism over the survival of modern society rests on doubts, especially among intellectuals, about the viability of modern societies and about their moral right to survive without radical change. Some allege that modern society is totally corrupt, can be cleansed only by revolution, and is ripe for it.

My skepticism about this position has been stated at the end of Chapter 9. The substantial increment of value institutionalization that has occurred in the last century is difficult to reconcile with the diagnosis of total corruption; though alienation is intense in important groups, the structural prerequisites for revolution are difficult to discern. For example, structural injustices are not nearly as great as those proclaimed as justification for the coming proletarian revolution by Marx and Engels over a century ago in the *Communist Manifesto*. Yet, with the wisdom of hindsight, we note that the revolution in this classic sense has not occurred in a single industrially advanced country but has been confined to relatively underdeveloped societies—of which the Russia of 1917 was an example—and those under the military domination of such societies, as were Poland and Czechosolvakia after 1945.

The explanation of the prevalence of ideological pessimism about modern societies presents problems beyond the scope of this book.[13] My immediate concern is to establish sufficient doubt of the validity of such views so that the reader will not jump to the conclusion that the trend of modern development over the past several centuries has come to an end and that therefore the evolutionary perspective is not relevant to assessment of the coming phases. Though changes are in process, the sociologist of the twenty-first century will discern probably as many factors

12. The conflicts involved in "imperialism" are associated with the emergence of enhanced adaptive political capacity in some sectors of a system, which leads to political control over less advanced units in areas of a power vacuum. This political control is generally incompletely institutionalized, and a shift of balance can present opportunities for "liberation" movements.

13. Such pessimism is, of course, not new. Christians were pessimistic about the society of the early Roman Empire, which was not totally corrupt, and a similar pessimism became prevalent in the Reformation. A suggestive comparison is with Colonial New England, where, as Perry Miller describes it, under the stress of misfortune, a jeremiad often took place, a kind of orgy of guilty self-accusation by colonists, who insisted that *they* had failed to live up to their obligations on their "errand" into the wilderness. A highly activist, this-wordly value pattern makes people sensitive to the gaps between expectation and performance; at the extreme they attribute *all* such gaps to the shortcomings of the current generation. See Perry Miller, *Nature's Nation* (Cambridge, Mass.: Harvard University Press, 1968).

of continuity with the past as we can discern with the nineteenth century and those previous to it.

CONCLUSION

To repeat the conclusion of Chapter 9, the present crisis centers in the societal community, not in the economy, the polity, or the value system. Compared even to the nineteenth century, there have been major changes in modern societal communities, especially in mutual adjustment to the impact of the industrial and the democratic revolutions. More recently the impact of the educational revolution has increased. The coming phase will center on integrating the consequences of these changes, both mutually and with the exigencies of the societal community. One problem will be in the development of the cultural system in relation to the society; it will be focused on what Weber called the "process of rationalization." Another problem will be the motivational bases of social solidarity within a large-scale society that is highly pluralistic. Neither set of problems will be solved without conflict.

There is one further aspect of processes of evolutionary development. In discussing the generalized media of interchange among units of a social system, namely influence, political power, money, and value commitments, I have stressed their function of facilitating routine interchange among the differentiated units of societies. They may also facilitate creative increases in the extent of operations within societies. Modern economists have shown that money, through the process of lending and investment, can be an instrument for increasing the level of economic production as well as for facilitating exchange in a system of division of labor. This property of money, i.e., its capacity for expanding economic productivity through the credit mechanism, has analogues in the operations of the other generalized media, e.g., power and influence.[14] Thus, the power mechanism can operate to increase the long-run effectiveness of the polity and influence can be used to enhance the capacity for solidarity of the societal community.

Anchorage in a higher-order subsystem of action is the basic condition of the upgrading effects of a generalized medium of interchange. Therefore, cultural development is essential for the evolutionary advance of societies. For example, religious developments underlie major processes of value generalization, and the increase of empirical knowledge underlies the institutionalization of new technologies. Sufficient levels of value generalization, implemented through the legal system, are prerequisite to

---

14. Cf. "On the Concept of Political Power" and "On the Concept of Influence," *Politics and Social Structure.*

major steps of inclusion in the structure of a societal community. A consensual base that promotes adequately extensive operation of the influence mechanism is necessary for major developments in the system of political power. Certain degrees of heightened political integration are prerequisite to the expansion of money economies beyond relatively simple levels.[15]

Anything like a culminating phase of modern development is a long way off—a century or more. Talk of postmodern society is premature.[16] Despite the possibility of overwhelming destruction, my expectation is that the trend of the next century will be toward completion of the type of society that this book has called modern.

15. See S. N. Eisenstadt (ed.), *Max Weber on Charisma* (Chicago: University of Chicago Press, 1968), esp. his "Introduction."

16. See John Porter, "The Future of Upward Mobility," *American Sociological Review*, 33, No. 1 (February 1968), 5–19.

SELECTED REFERENCES

In line with the continued concern with the framework of societal evolution, I should like to suggest standard works on the status of biological evolution: George Gaylord Simpson, *The Meaning of Evolution* (New Haven: Yale University Press, 1950); Ernst Mayr, *Animal Species and Evolution* (Cambridge, Mass.: Harvard University Press, 1963); and articles by Curt Stern, "The Continuity of Genetics," Gunther Stent, "DNA," Robert Olby, "Francis Crick, DNA, and the Central Dogma," and Linus Pauling, "Fifty Years of Progress in Structural Chemistry and Molecular Biology," from *Daedalus* (Fall, 1970).

Sociological concern with social evolution and the analytical comparison of societies stem largely from the classical studies of Max Weber, especially *The Theory of Social and Economic Organization* (Glencoe, Ill.: Free Press, 1947); *The Sociology of Religion* (Boston: Beacon Press, 1963); and the other sections of *Wirtschaft und Gesellschaft*. As Robert Bellah has shown in his essay "Durkheim and History" (*American Sociological Review*, August 1959), Durkheim—for example, in *The Division of Labor in Society* (New York: Macmillan, 1933); and *Professional Ethics and Civic Morals* (London: Routledge and Kegan Paul, 1957)—developed similar perspectives. *Theories of Society* (New York: Free Press of Glencoe, 1961), T. Parsons, E. Shils, K. Naegele, and J. Pitts, eds., contains readings on social theory, along with introductory essays by Parsons and the other editors that interrelate analytical and evolutionary perspectives. "Religious Evolution" by Robert Bellah and "Evolutionary Universals in

Society" by Talcott Parsons (both in the *American Sociological Review*, June 1964), present more recent developments in evolutionary theory. The distinction is made between general and special evolution in M. Sahlins and E. Service, *Evolution and Culture* (Ann Arbor: University of Michigan Press, 1960).

Durkheim's *The Elementary Forms of the Religious Life* (London: Allen & Unwin, 1915), remains basic for understanding primitive societies in an evolutionary perspective. *Structural Anthropology* (New York: Basic Books, 1963); and *Primitive Thought* by Claude Levi-Strauss, present a theoretical position influential in contemporary anthropology. The best introduction to modern kinship analysis is Rodney Needham's brief *Structure and Sentiment* (Chicago: University of Chicago Press, 1962). Lloyd Warner's *A Black Civilization* (New York: Harper Torchbooks, 1964) is an interesting general account of an Australian aboriginal society; W. E. H. Stanner's *On Aboriginal Religion* (Sydney: Oceania Monographs, 1963) is more recent and specialized. *African Political Systems* (London: Oxford University Press, 1940), M. Fortes and E. E. Evans-Pritchard, eds.; *African Systems of Kinship and Marriage* (London: Oxford University Press, 1950), A. R. Radcliffe-Brown and D. Forde, eds., and *African Worlds* (London: Oxford University Press, 1954), D. Forde, ed., contain useful essays on various aspects of selected African tribes. R. Firth's *Primitive Polynesian Economy* (London: Routledge, 1939) is a good analysis of economic processes in a primitive society.

The Face of the Ancient Orient (Garden City, N.Y.: Anchor, 1962), by S. Moscati, is an introduction to the archaic societies of the ancient Near East. Henri Frankfort's *Kingship and the Gods* (Chicago: University of Chicago Press, 1948) is masterful in treating the relations between the political and religious aspects of archaic societies and in comparing the Egyptian and Mesopotamian civilizations. J. Wilson's *The Culture of Ancient Egypt* (Chicago: Phoenix Books, 1951) is more concerned with economic and community organization, as is H. W. F. Sagg's *The Greatness That Was Babylon* (New York: Hawthorn, 1962).

Max Weber's "The Social Psychology of the World Religions" and "Religious Rejections of the World and Their Directions," in *From Max Weber* (New York: Galaxy Books, 1958), H. H. Gerth and C. W. Mills, eds.; and S. N. Eisenstadt's *The Political Systems of Empires* (New York: Free Press of Glencoe, 1963) are general comparative treatments of intermediate societies.

Max Weber's *The Religion of China* (Glencoe, Ill.: Free Press, 1951) remains the best general sociological analysis of traditional China. J. K.

Fairbank's *The United States and China* (Cambridge, Mass.: Harvard University Press, 1959) contains a good brief outline of Chinese social history. Fung Yu-Lan's *A Short History of Chinese Philosophy* (New York: Macmillian, 1962) is an introduction to Chinese culture. Chang Chung-Li, *The Chinese Gentry* (Seattle: University of Washington Press, 1955); and Marion Levy, *The Family Revolution in Modern China* (Cambridge, Mass.: Harvard University Press, 1949) analyze key aspects of Chinese society.

The Wonder That Was India (New York: Evergreen, 1959), by A. L. Basham and *Philosophies of India* (Cleveland: Meridian, 1956) by Heinrich Zimmer, are general treatments of Indian civilization.

The work of H. A. R. Gibb is an excellent introduction to Islam, particularly his *Mohammedanism* (New York: Galaxy Books, 1962); and his study with H. Bowen, *Islamic Society and the West* (London: Oxford University Press, 1957). G. E. von Grunebaum's *Medieval Islam* (Chicago: Phoenix Books, 1961) is also reliable and interesting.

An introduction to Roman history is *Rome* (New York: Galaxy Books, 1960) by M. Rostovtzeff. R. Syme's *The Roman Revolution* (London: Clarendon Press, 1939) is a detailed analysis of the processes by which the Empire emerged at the end of the Republic. *The Legacy of Rome* (Oxford: Clarendon Press, 1923), C. Bailey, ed., contains several fine essays on specific aspects of Roman society.

Though somewhat dated, Weber's *Ancient Judaism* (Glencoe, Ill.: Free Press, 1952) remains unmatched for sociological insight among treatments of early Israel. Martin Buber's *Moses* (New York: Harper Torchbooks, 1958); and *The Prophetic Faith* (New York: Harper Torchbooks, 1960) are fine studies of the religious tradition; W. F. Albright's *From Stone Age to Christianity* (Garden City, N.Y.: Anchor Books, 1957) adds archaeological to documentary evidence in tracing the development of Hebrew society. Werner Jaeger's *Paideia,* vol. 1 (New York: Oxford University Press, 1945) is the foremost modern discussion of Greek culture. *A History of Greek Religion* (New York: Norton, 1964), by M. P. Nilsson, is a sound treatment of its complicated subject. V. Ehrenberg surveys Greek political organization in *The Greek State* (New York: Norton, 1964).

For interpretation of modern society see the work of Max Weber, especially his introduction to the series of studies in the sociology of religion, an English translation of which is reprinted in my edition of *The Protestant Ethic and the Spirit of Capitalism* (New York: Scribner's, 1930).

In the background of Weber's thinking lay that of Marx, most massively developed in *Das Kapital,* 3 vols., F. Engels, ed. (International Publishing Co.), and of Hegel, in his *Philosophy of History* (New York: Dover, 1956).

The theoretical orientation is the author's own. Among items that might be mentioned, let me first cite the *Theories of Society* (New York: Free Press, 1961), of which I was senior editor—including both the selections and the introductory materials, especially my own part in the general introduction, "An Outline of the Social System," Talcott Parsons (pp. 30–79), and my Introduction to part four (pp. 963–93). An essay, "Evolutionary Universals in Society," included in the collection *Sociological Theory and Modern Society* (New York: Free Press, 1967), is important, as is the article under the title "Christianity," in the *Encyclopedia of the Social Sciences,* 8 vols., E. R. Seligman, ed., (New York: Macmillan). Another collection of essays under the title *Politics and Social Structure* (New York: Free Press, 1969), overlaps substantially with *Sociological Theory and Modern Society* but has some additional materials. Finally, an essay, "Equality and Inequality in Modern Society, or Social Stratification Revisited" for *Sociological Inquiry* is pertinent to my general theoretical perspective. [This issue of *Sociological Inquiry* was published by Bobbs-Merrill, under the title of *Social Stratification: Theory and Research* (Indianapolis: 1970).]

Among contemporaries and near contemporaries to whom I am indebted, let me mention Robert Merton, *Social Theory and Social Structure,* 3rd ed. (New York: Free Press); Neil Smelser, *Social Change and the Industrial Revolution* (Chicago: Chicago University Press, 1959) and *Sociology of Economic Life* (Englewood Cliffs, N.J.: Prentice-Hall, 1963); Robert Bellah, *Beyond Belief* (New York: Harper, 1970); Max Weber, *Sociology of Law, Sociology of Religion* (Boston: Beacon, 1964), and other parts of *Economy and Society,* 3 vols., Gunther Roth and Claus Wittich, eds. (Totowa, N.J.: Bedminster); Lon L. Fuller, *The Morality of Law* (New Haven: Yale University Press, 1964) and *Anatomy of the Law* (New York: Mentor, paperback, 1969); S. M. Lipset and Stein Rokkan, eds., *Party Systems and Voter Alignments* (New York: Free Press, 1967) and Lipset's, *First New Nation* (New York: Basic Books, 1963).

On the historical background, three writings of A. D. Nock, *Conversion: the Old and the New in Religion from Alexander the Great to Augustine of Hippo* (New York: Oxford University Press, 1933), *St. Paul* (New York: Harper, 1968), and *Early Gentile Christianity* (New York: Harper, 1964) are particularly relevant. Also, Adolph von Harnack, *Mission and Expansion* (New York: Harper, 1961); Werner Jaeger, *Early Christianity* (New York: Oxford University Press, 1969); Ernst Troeltsch's

Social Teachings in the Christian Churches (New York: Harper, 1960); and Hans Lietzman, *A History of the Early Church* (New York: Meridian; World, 1961) are relevant. On the classical institutional heritage, Ernst Troeltsch, Lot, Henri Pirenne, C. H. McIlwain, Gierke, and Max Weber's *City* (New York: Free Press) are important.

On the medieval society, the source is Marc Bloch, *Feudal Society* (Chicago: Chicago University Press, 1968). However, Troeltsch is also relevant, as are Richard William Southern, *The Making of the Middle Ages* (New Haven: Yale University Press, paperback, 1953), and H. C. Lea, *History of Sacerdotal Celebacy* (New York: University Books, 1966). Literature on the Renaissance and Reformation is enormous. I should like to suggest J. H. Plumb, *The Renaissance* (New York: Harper, paperback); Joseph Ben-David, *Sociology of Science* (Englewood Cliffs, N.J.: Prentice-Hall, 1971); and Paul O. Kristeller, *Renaissance Thought* (New York: Harper, paperback). On certain aspects of the Reformation, besides Weber, *The Protestant Ethic and the Spirit of Capitalism* (New York: Scribner, 1930), and the volume on the topic with a valuable introduction by S. N. Eisenstadt, *Max Weber: On Charisma and Institution Building* (Chicago: University of Chicago Press, 1968), I would like to mention Erik H. Erikson's *Young Man Luther* (New York: Norton, 1958), and David Little's *Religion, Order and Law* (New York: Harper, 1970). Of equal significance is Benjamin Nelson, *The Idea of Usury*, 2nd ed. (Chicago: University of Chicago Press, 1969) .

For the general setting a valuable source is Lord Bryce's *The Holy Roman Empire* (New York: Schocken Books, 1961), and on the religious side, Troeltsch's *Social Teachings* (op. cit.). A monumental survey of the religious problem in England is given by W. K. Jordan in *The Development of Religious Toleration in England,* 5 vols. (Cambridge, Mass.: Harvard University Press, 1932–1940). On the political side, see Max Beloff, *The Age of Absolutism* (New York: Harper, paperback, and Barrington Moore, *Social Origins of Dictatorship and Democracy* (Boston: Beacon Press, 1966). On the earlier origins of parliament, C. H. McIlwain, *The High Court of Parliament* (New Haven: Yale University Press, 1910) are valuable. Also T. M. Marshall, *Class, Citizenship and Social Development* (New York: Doubleday, Anchor, paperback, 1964); Robert K. Merton's classical essay on *Science, Technology and Society in Seventeenth Century England* (New York: Harper, 1970); and Richard Henry Tawney, *Religion and the Rise of Capitalism* (New York: Mentor, paperback) should also be consulted.

For somewhat later developments, on the political side, a comprehensive source is R. R. Palmer's *The Age of the Democratic Revolution*

(Princeton, N.J.: Princeton University Press, 1969). Michael Polanyi's *The Great Transformation* (Boston: Beacon Press, 1944) is also illuminating. And with respect to the sweep of the Industrial Revolution, see not only Clapham's *The Economic Development of France and Germany*, 4th ed. (New York: Cambridge University Press, paperback, 1935), but also David S. Landes, *Unbound Prometheus* (New York: Cambridge University Press, 1969, paperback). On the background of political thought, J. W. Allen, *A History of Political Thought in the 16th Century* (New York: Barnes & Noble, 1960) should be consulted. For the social psychology of the development of the Democratic Revolution, see F. Weinstein and G. M. Platt, *Wish to Be Free: Society, Psyche, and Value Change* (Berkeley and Los Angeles: University of California Press, 1969).

For the American case, Alexis de Toqueville's *Democracy in America* (New York: Vintage, paperback) continues to be a major reference. Various works of Perry Miller are important for the cultural background, notably *Errand into the Wilderness* (New York: Harper, 1956, paperback) and for the transition into the nineteenth century, *Life of the Mind in America* (New York: Harcourt Brace Jovanovich 1965). S. M. Lipset's *First New Nation* (op. cit.) is also valuable. On specifically religious development, J. J. Loubser's *Development of Religious Freedom* (Cambridge, Mass.: Harvard University Press, 1964, Ph.D. dissertation). Beyond this, the literature becomes almost unmanageably diverse: Oscar Handlin, *The Uprooted* (Boston: Little, Brown, 1951); Clinton Rossiter, *Seedtime of the Republic* (New World, 1953); Louis Hartz, *The Liberal Tradition in America, an Interpretation of American Political Thought since the Revolution* (New York: Harcourt Brace Jovanovich, 1955), various works of V. O. Key and Richard Hofstadter, A. A. Berle and Gardiner Means, *The Modern Corporation and Private Property*, rev. ed. (New York: Harcourt Brace Jovanovich); Frederick Lewis Allen, *The Big Change, America Transforms Itself* (New York: Harper, paperback, 1969); Andre Siegfried's *America Comes of Age* (New York: Harcourt Brace Jovanovich, 1927); and Gunnar Myrdal's *An American Dilemma* (New York: Harper, 1944).

For the latter phase of modernization one might suggest Cyril Black, ed., *Transformation of Russian Society: Aspects of Social Change since 1861* (Cambridge, Mass.: Harvard University Press, 1960); Alex Inkeles and Raymond A. Bauer, *The Soviet Citizen* (Cambridge, Mass.: Harvard University Press, 1959); Gregory Grossman, *Economic Systems* (Englewood Cliffs, N.J.: Prentice-Hall, 1967); Merle Fainsod, *How Russia is Ruled*, rev. ed. (Cambridge, Mass.: Harvard University Press, 1963); Harold Berman, *Justice in USSR: an Interpretation of Soviet Law* (Cambridge, Mass.: Harvard University Press, 1963); Robert Bellah, *Tokugawa Re-*

ligion (Boston: Beacon Press, 1970); Masao Maruyama, *Thought and Behavior in Modern Japanese Politics* (New York: Oxford University Press, 1963); Stephen R. Graubard, ed., *New Europe* (Boston: Beacon); S. H. Hoffmann et al., eds., *In Search of France* (Boston: Harvard University Press); and Alex Inkeles and David H. Smith, *Becoming Modern,* (Cambridge, Mass.: Harvard University Press, 1974).

GLOSSARY

action the structures and processes by which human beings form meaningful intentions and implement them in concrete situations.

activism a philosophy of mastery over physical or social obstacles as opposed to passive acceptance or mystical escape.

adaptive upgrading the process by which a wider range of resources is made available to social units so that their functioning is freed from some of the ascriptive restrictions imposed on less evolved units. For example, modern factories can produce a greater variety of goods more economically than could peasant households because factories have available to them more generalized commitments to render service from those who work in them.

ascription assignment to roles because of biological or relational *qualities* (age, sex, community of residence) rather than *performance* or performance capacity.

authority a socially recognized right to make a binding decision on behalf of an interactive system.

behavioral organism the adaptive subsystem of the individual: the locus of the human facilities that underlie the other systems. It embodies conditions to which action must adapt and comprises the mechanism of interrelation with the physical environment, especially through the input and processing of information in the central nervous system and through motor activity in coping with exigencies of the physical environment.

collectivity a social system having (1) definite statuses of membership and nonmembership and (2) a differentiation of statuses among members so that some categories of members are expected to function in ways not expected of other members.

cultural system a complex of symbolic meaning—the code in terms of which it is structured, the particular clusters of symbols it employs, and the conditions of its utilization, maintenance, and change as part of action systems.

differentiation the process by which a unit or subsystem having a well-

249

defined place in the society divides into units that differ in *both* structure and functional significance for the wider system. If differentiation is to give rise to a more evolved system, each newly differentiated substructure must have enhanced adaptive capacity for performing its primary function as compared to the performance of that function in the previous, less specialized structure.

economy   the aspect of the societal system that functions to order technological procedures socially and to control them in the interests of social units, whether individual or collective.

facilities   possessions significant as the means to some ultimate goal rather than rewarding in themselves.

fiduciary subsystem   relates the society to the cultural system and, through it, to ultimate reality. The term, "fiduciary," refers to trusteeship roles that bearers and transmitters of the cultural tradition play vis-à-vis the rest of society.

ideology   the belief system, true or untrue, shared by members of a society or of a collectivity within a society. The sharing is not a coincidence because subscribing to the belief system is an obligation of membership.

individualism   the belief that an individual possesses some fundamental rights that arise from his inherent worth and are not derived from his membership in kinship or other social groups. This belief is supported by a form of social organization in which individuals participate as individuals rather than as representatives of groups.

influence   generalized capacity to shape attitudes or opinions by implicit or explicit appeals to common group membership.

integration   the coordination of two or more structural units such that (1) specialized contributions complement one another and (2) role players in the differentiated units commit themselves psychologically to the system as a whole.

interpenetration   a zone of shared structural components on the boundaries of two or more action systems, e.g., the internalization of social objects and cultural norms within the personality system or the institutionalization of normative components of cultural systems as constitutive structures of social systems.

money   a generalized material inducement as well as a medium of economic exchange.

particularism   a relationship defined in terms of common group membership, for example, kinship, rather than in terms of common qualities.

personality system   the *agency* of action processes; hence it implements cultural requirements. On the level of reward in the motivational sense, the optimization of gratification to personalities is the goal of action.

polity   a complex of decision-making roles that relate the society to the goals of its individual members through collective decisions.

power   generalized symbolic capacity to make and make stick binding decisions on behalf of a collectivity.

segmentation   a process by which units proliferate that are not structurally differentiated from one another. For example, the family system of the United States consists of millions of structurally similar nuclear families. Sometimes a large social system is segmented rather than differentiated.

social system   constituted by processes of mutual orientation of actors toward one another such that each actor is both actor and object of orientation for other actors as well as for himself. This mutual orientation gives rise to mutual responses of a plurality of goal-directed actors in a symbolically defined environment.

social values conceptions of desirable types of social systems that regulate the making of commitments by social actors. (Keep in mind that there are other kinds of values also—such as personality values, which are conceptions of desirable personality characteristics. But social values are more important for an understanding of societies.)

societal community the integrative subsystem of a society constituted (1) by a normative order and (2) by criteria of membership-defining rights, obligations, and differential influence.

society the type of social system characterized by the highest level of self-sufficiency relative to its environments, including other social systems. Being politically organized, it has a sense of community as well as loyalty to some corporate agency of a governmental kind.

strain psychological distress arising (1) from expectations of significant others that the individual does not feel he can fulfill or (2) from the failure of significant others to live up to what the individual feels are legitimate expectations.

stratification the differentiation of the population on a prestige scale of kinship units in such a way that the distinctions among such units, or classes of them, become hereditary to an important degree.

technology the primarily physical reference of the complex that includes the *economy* as its social system reference.

universalism a relationship defined by the possession of an attribute—for example, all students in a class who get high grades—rather than one defined in terms of common group membership.

value a conception of the desirable; a criterion of choice between alternative principles of personal or social organization.

value generalization the couching of a value pattern at a higher level of generality than in a less evolved situation in order to make it relevant to a broader range of exigencies. For example, premarital chastity was a specific version of sexual morality, but conceivably the legitimation of premarital sexuality requires a more complicated (generalized) notion of sexual ethics than the legitimation of sexual exploitation.

INDEX

Citizenship (cont.)
French Revolution and concept of, 169, 171–72
membership in societal community and, 176–78
naturalization and, 188
in Soviet Union, 217, 219
in United States, 188, 189
City-states
in Christianity, 117–18
in Mesopotamia, 64–65
in Palestine, 101
in Rome, 86
See also Polis organization
Clan organization in advanced primitive society, 38–39
Clapham, J. H., 164n
Clark, Kenneth, 184n, 209n, 222n
Class, social
in archaic society, 52
in China, 76–77, 78–79
in Egypt, 55
in England, 149, 151–52
in feudal Europe, 122–23, 149–50
in Greece, 109, 110
in India, 81
in Islamic empires, 87
in Mesopotamia, 65
in Prussia, 163
in New Europe, 224–25
in Roman Empire, 43
two-class system, 73, 87, 167, 225
in United States, 186
Class consciousness, 186
Clement (Christian theologian), 117
Cluniac order, 119
Cochrane, Charles N., 97n, 117n, 119n
Coercion, 14
as aspect of power, 15–16
Coke, Edward, 152–53
Collegial pattern of organization, 199–200
Common law, 153–54, 158, 177
Common Market, 223, 224
Communist Manifesto (Marx and Engels), 239
Communist party, 196
in Soviet Union, 216, 217, 219
Community, alleged deterioration of, 210
Confucius and Confucianism, 74, 80, 83
ancestral cult and, 79
archaic character of, 73
familial relationships and, 77
institutionalization of, 74–75, 83
rationalism of, 80–81
Constantine (Roman emperor), 118
Constituency, of government, 196–97

Constitution, in modern legal systems, 174–75
Cooley, C. H., 2
Corporate organization
associated structures and, 181
authority in, 168
bureaucracy in, 198
professionalization of higher management and, 198
Corwin, Edwin S., 188n
Coulborn, R., 54n
Counter-Reformation, 141–42, 169, 237
differentiation frozen in, 161
Cranach, Lucas, 131
Creel, H. G., 74n, 80n
Cromwell, Oliver, 151n
Crozier, Michael, 194n, 223n
Cuban missile crisis, 238
Cultural legitimation, 136
Chinese system of, 25
in Egypt, 56
for ethnic-territorial societal community, 42
explicit, as breakthrough, 11–12
literacy and, 69–70
by literate priesthood, 51–52
in Mesopotamia, 64, 65
morality and, 113–14
religion and, 40–41, 46, 52–53
in Roman Empire, 97
value commitments and, 137–38
Cultural relativism, 230–31
Culture (shared symbolic systems)
distinguished from society, 99, 115
in Parsons' theory of action, 4–5, 6
as pivotal concept for Parsons, 2
social evolution and, 115–16
Cumont, Franz, 97n
Cybernetic control, hierarchy of, 8–9, 234–235
Czechoslovakia, 239

D

Dahl, Robert, 223n
Darwin, Charles, 25, 232
Darwinism, 194
David (Israeli king), 101
De Bary, W. T., 82n
Decentralization of power and authority, 209
De Gaulle, Charles, 223
Democratic polity
elective office in, 197
as evolutionary breakthrough, 15–18
leadership base in, 197